Welcoming
Wildlife

TO THE GARDEN

Welcoming Wildlife

TO THE GARDEN

Creating Backyard & Balcony
Habitats for Wildlife

Catherine J. Johnson
Susan McDiarmid

Projects & Illustrations by
Edward R. Turner

Hartley
&Marks
PUBLISHERS

Published by

HARTLEY & MARKS PUBLISHERS INC.

3661 West Broadway   P.O. Box 147
Vancouver, B.C.   Point Roberts, WA
V6R 2B8   98281

Printed in China

Quotations from *Circle of the Seasons,* by Edwin Way Teale,
published 1953, used with permission of the University of Connecticut.

LIBRARY OF CONGRESS CATALOGING-IN-PUBLICATION DATA

Johnson, Catherine J., 1958–
    Welcoming wildlife to the garden : creating backyard and balcony habitats for wildlife /
Catherine J. Johnson, Susan McDiarmid ; projects & illustrations by Edward R. Turner.
      p. cm.
    Includes bibliographical references and index.
    ISBN 0-88179-201-2 (pbk.)
    1. Gardening to attract wildlife. 2. Wildlife attracting. I. McDiarmid, Susan, 1969–
II. Turner, Edward R., 1940– III. Title.

QL59.J62 2004
639.9'2—dc22   2003059501

639.92

CONTENTS

PROJECTS

Our Connection with the Natural World

PEOPLE EVERYWHERE are discovering the joys of inviting the natural world back into their surroundings. Wild creatures can be enticed to spaces as small as balconies and ledges, so that anyone, anywhere, from the busiest of cities to the quietest of acreages, can watch wildlife through their windows. In nature, people regain a sense of awe, and a feeling of interconnectedness with the creatures who share our world. We marvel at a pair of nesting robins that dive-bomb passersby to protect their young, and are amazed by the coordinated efforts of an ant colony transporting food particles larger than themselves. Observing nature enables us to see beyond our own lives.

For most people, providing food, water, and shelter for wildlife is satisfying. To ease lives and help restore habitat, and in doing so, perhaps aid in the increase of declining species, gives us a feeling of worth. Even animals we may not often see, such as towhees scuffling beneath low shrubs or the owl whose pellet we find in the morning, add to our sense of purpose. Being close to wildlife is a thrill. It's a personal experience each of us can discover.

With careful planning it is possible to transform entire neighborhoods, one yard at a time, into swaths of inviting pathways for wild creatures, and the welcome can extend into existing areas such as parks and wildlife sanctuaries. Our commitment to wildlife can even grow to influence the way we exercise our political will and economic activity. It all stems from the plants we choose and the insects, birds, and mammals we attract to our own small at-home habitats. The increased understanding that people gain from creating a garden or planter for butterflies, or from landscaping a yard to at-

Downy woodpecker and chestnut-backed chickadee feed on suet.

tract and feed migrating birds, is part of the hope we have for a world in which all creatures, including humans, can live and thrive together. We can remain a part of the natural world and help renew the earth, and can do it in our own backyards, making them into places where wild things flourish.

Backyard Ecology: A Balancing Act

W<small>HEN YOU EMBARK</small> on the journey to welcome wildlife to your backyard or balcony, you will become a steward of the wildlife and something of an ecologist. You will learn which plants are native to your ecosystem and suitable for your lot, balcony, or window ledge, and encourage them in order to attract wildlife. To sum up the principles of ecological gardening: Should it be here? How does it connect with other life forms in the garden?

Your adventures in backyard ecology will lead you to approach gardening and landscaping quite differently than you would traditional gardening. In learning about native plants and wild habitats you will discover that some of the underpinnings of traditional gardening are in direct opposition to the teachings of ecology. Of course, you don't have to abandon the flower beds you worked so hard to develop. Nor do you have to completely get rid of your lawn. How "wild" your yard becomes is a matter of taste. Just be prepared to find out that the adventure of creating your own wildlife habitat in the backyard, or on your balcony or rooftop, may change the way you think about many things. Even if the area you have to work with is only a patch of lawn in the suburbs, or a windowsill in a downtown core, you are likely to find an endlessly intriguing universe in that modest area. And becoming a wildlife steward need not be expensive. One package of seeds planted in a window box with homemade, composted soil can feed butterflies or birds, and bring a season of enjoyment to the viewer.

Becoming familiar with the flora and fauna around you is the beginning of becoming an accomplished wildlife steward. From a distance, almost any bird or flower looks natural and therefore "good." This is not quite correct. The

Basic birdbath weighted with stone.

Harvestman on trillium.

shrub with a profusion of scentless blossoms in your garden may be lovely to look at, but if closer examination reveals it to be an import from the Amazon you will have to rethink its benefits. Does it provide food or shelter for wild creatures? Because the natural habitat of the shrub may be quite different from the one in which it is growing, considerable maintenence may be required to keep it thriving. You may need to alter its soil, give it much more water than your area can provide naturally, and treat it with chemical pesticides to keep away insects it was never intended to encounter. How beautiful is the shrub in light of this new information?

And what about those unidentified birds in your yard, flitting and squabbling by the dozens? Surely they are an indication that we are on the right path to attracting wildlife. Actually, if those birds turn out to be, for example, house sparrows and European starlings, you may have some planning ahead of you. Introduced birds endanger native birds mainly by evicting them from nesting cavities, and you may wish to discourage them from taking up residence in your wildlife haven. So what is a wildlife steward to do?

Woodland garden using existing native plants.

Dense thicket makes excellent wildlife shelter.

Good intentions are clearly not enough. What is needed is information about where you live and what creatures, without human interference, would be living there now. Each region of North America contains plants and soil types which make up habitat suitable for particular wild species. Your first task is to look carefully at the area you want to revitalize. Make a list of the plants that grow in your yard, assess the composition of your soil, and observe the animals and insects there (Chapter 11). Now take a visit to any wild places you might have nearby, such as parks and bird sanctuaries. What grows and lives in these natural settings? Use plant identification guides for your area and ask local plant nurseries specializing in native plants what they would suggest for a yard like yours. All this will be preparation for restoring the natural ecology of your backyard.

Introducing native plant species to your yard will entail some changes in the way you look at gardening. As an ecological gardener you will be coming at those plantings from a perspective that many traditional gardeners would find backwards. For instance, some of the plants in your window boxes will be there solely for caterpillars to munch on.

Traditional gardening often attempts to force order on the natural world. As Sara Stein writes in *Noah's Garden,* "Gardening strives to defeat chance, or at least to rig the odds." The wildlife steward, on the other hand, may choose to allow each seemingly disparate element to thrive. Rather than forcing nature, we can facilitate nature's processes while recognizing, contending with, and hopefully compensating for the inevitable "human factor."

As wildlife stewards, we will get the opportunity to choose which natural processes to encourage in our yards, and which ones to avoid, while creating our wildlife habitats. We can stall our backyard's inevitable return to complete

Collision

This morning something happened in the backyard that I have never seen occur there before. It was a collision. I had tossed some peanuts from the back door onto the frozen ground. A gray squirrel ran down the trunk of a maple tree and headed for one of the nuts. At the same time, a bluejay, that had been hopping about among the limbs of a cedar tree, flew toward the same nut. Neither seemed to see the other until it was too late. They arrived at the nut at the same time and collided. The jay flew up with a shriek. The squirrel rushed away in a panic. It was minutes before they came down from their respective trees. This time they went to separate peanuts.

Edwin Way Teale – Circle of the Seasons 1953

4

wilderness at many stages. Wildlife gardeners strike a balance between the needs of the human occupants and the needs of the wild creatures we hope to attract, between our neighbor's ideas of order and our wild guests' need for sustenance and shelter.

Working With Others

Wildlife gardening is contagious. Once your neighbors see the results of your backyard habitat they will likely be intrigued, and hopefully inspired, to try to attract creatures to their own yards. A glimpse of a backyard filled with butterflies and birds often makes tidy traditional gardens feel sterile and lifeless. If people show interest in your backyard habitat, try to encourage them and give as much information as you can. The more people in your area who practice gardening for wildlife, the better your chances of giving wild things safe passage through your neighborhood with a selection of suitable homes and habitats.

Sharing tips and experiences will enrich your role as a wildlife steward. You may find that joining others in the pursuit of enticing wildlife into the backyard will help to develop a sense of community on your block, and possibly even further. Some cities, such as Vancouver, BC, offer programs such as "Green Streets" whereby residents collaborate with the city to plant and maintain traffic circles and corner bulges. The idea is primarily to beautify neighborhoods and provide gardening opportunities, but small plantings, city-wide, create corridors for wildlife as well, especially when native plants are used.

One way you can begin to communicate with others about your stewardship program is to post a sign on your property describing wildlife gardening. Your sign can be simple or it can go into detail about using native plants to attract wildlife. It could also describe other wildlife gardening principles such as the basic components of a garden (food, shelter, and water) and the avoidance of pesticides (see page 6 for sample of sign).

Wildlife Gardening Clubs

For your own interest and education, consider starting a wildlife gardening club or join an existing club. You can also join research programs sponsored by universities, community groups, clubs, and the government. If you want to start a club in your area, post notices in community centers, community service newsletters, and stores that sell bird feeders and bird food. In the United States you can join the National Wildlife Federation's Backyard Wildlife Project, and in Canada you can contact Environment Canada for information. Various state and provincial gov-

Western meadowlark.

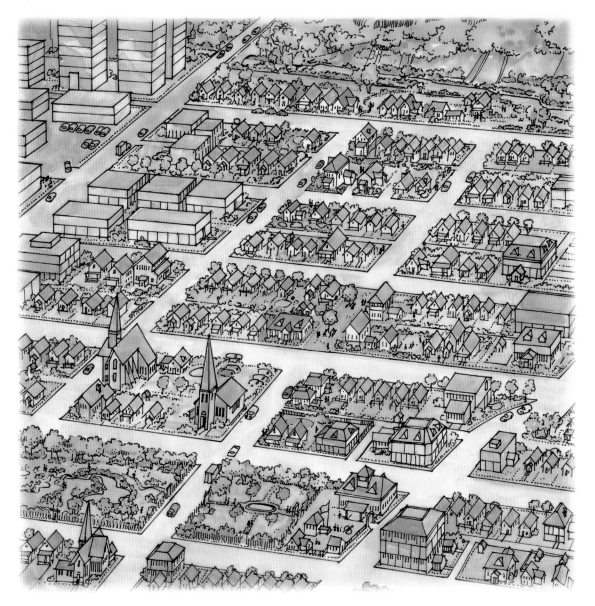

A network of greenways connect safe habitats for wildlife throughout a community.

ernments have their own habitat programs, and these groups will be very helpful in providing information about native plants and animals in your area. Anyone with a backyard or a windowsill can join and you will generally receive a registration certificate and a newsletter. You can also join clubs devoted specifi-cally to a particular type of wildlife. Clubs devoted to birds are common all over North America, and butterflies also have a great number of enthusiasts. The Internet is a good source for wildlife gardening groups with whom you can trade information and stories for a worldwide perspective.

Butterfly garden.

The end result of increased numbers of wildlife gardeners will be large networks of *greenways*, or safe places like backyard habitats that provide sus-tenance and shelter to wild creatures. Ideally, greenways will run through neighborhoods, connect with parks, and carry on into undeveloped and agricultural lands, giving migratory birds, butterflies, and other creatures a safe path to travel. Greenways can wend their way through completely urban areas, provided people make the effort to practice wildlife gardening at every opportunity, from balconies to rooftops. And the result of many individuals working together to turn their small patches of space into wildlife habitats will be healthier neighborhoods as well as a healthier planet.

Wildlife Garden in Progress

This is a garden for wildlife. It has been planted with native plants that provide wild creatures with food and shelter. In the far right corner is a butterfly garden. It contains plants used for butterflies in their larval and adult stages. The rocks scattered throughout the wildflower patch are used by butterflies to bask on in the sun.

The pond to the left is home to various aquatic plants and insects, minnows and frogs. On the far left of the garden is a bird food patch; it contains oats, soybeans, two types of millet, and above it, hanging feeders.

Along the side, you will notice a mix of flowering shrubs and raspberry canes, and in the tree above you is a nest box, currently occupied by a pair of chickadees.

The feeders and bird food patch help to sustain songbirds on their migratory journeys each year. There have been up to fourteen different species feeding in a season. The small house on the pole to your left is a bat house—bats are only active after dusk and are very beneficial in keeping insects down. To help increase natural diversity, no pesticides are used in this garden.

Sample sign for your yard: just alter to fit your own habitat.

CHAPTER

1

The Basics

CREATING A WILDLIFE habitat garden depends upon the provision of food, shelter, water, and a safe place for wildlife to rear their young. This applies from balconies to larger properties. If all you have room for is a container garden, the number and range of wild guests you will be able to attract will be limited yet still worthwhile. If you are lucky enough to have a piece of land with room for a pond, a corner for a bog, and space for a wildflower meadow surrounded by grasses and shrubs, then you will be able to attract a far more diverse clientele than a gardener with a single type of habitat.

Diversity

Diversity is the key to attracting wild creatures. In the habitat garden, diversity means having a variety of beneficial plants that provide various habitat values. A landscape with good diversity has the potential to attract a wider variety of birds, insects, amphibians, and mammals than could otherwise be expected in an unenhanced area of the same size. By creating diversity through planning, the wildlife steward takes an active role in attracting numbers of wildlife visitors to the garden. For instance, an acre of lawn will attract very little life, whereas the same acre diversified with a small dust

Meadow that has replaced lawn.

Native plants in a seaside garden.

Seed heads in snow are valuable to birds.

patch, a mudhole, a wildflower meadow, some tall grasses, a weed patch, several flowering shrubs, and a couple of large trees will attract many times the number of wild occupants.

Why Native Plants?

Human creations such as bird-houses, bat houses, and various feeders will account for only a tiny proportion of your backyard habitat. Plants provide most of the needs of wild creatures; they give shelter for nesting and roosting in their foliage, their bark, and their cavities, and food in the form of nuts, seeds, fruit, berries, and sometimes leaves. Foliage also provides water from dew and raindrops. The best habitat plants are those that have evolved naturally in an ecological region. Native plants need little maintenance in order to flourish. Because they have developed alongside the creatures they house and feed, they often have symbiotic relationships (parasitic and otherwise). A good example of this is the monarch butterfly which is dependent on certain species of milkweed for both food and protection. Monarchs can feed on all milkweeds as larvae and adults, but they need the milkweeds that contain poisons to render *them* poisonous to would-be enemies. Non-poisonous milkweed variations are becoming more common, with the result that monarchs have lost part of their protective mechanism. These new milkweeds are being spread by human land use and are not native to the areas in which they are spreading. The increased incidence of non-poisonous monarchs

Steller's jay on adapted feeder.

8

Overstory

Trees

Shrubs

Herbaceous

Successional layers.

could have serious long-term conse-quences for the health of the species.

Layering, Succession, and Disturbance

Like human habitat that ranges from basement apartments to highrises, wild-life habitat exists on different levels as well; these are the layers into which plants can be divided. The four layers of plant life are herbaceous (such as perennials, annuals, grasses, and sedges), shrubs, midstory, and overstory. Each layer pro-vides habitat for different types of crea-tures.

Layers follow one another in a vegeta-tion developmental process called suc-cession. The first layer of vegetation, the herbaceous, is dominated by plants called first stage colonizers. These spread rap-idly, creating humus, and enhancing soil fertility, preparing it to receive the next in line—grasses and perennial plants that make up the wildflower meadow and complete the herbaceous layer, preparing it to receive the next layer of shrubby growth. Shrubs create shade, setting the stage for the next layer—trees. The first trees are usually prolific, but short-lived, deciduous species that make up the mid-story and create the right conditions for a next generation of trees—the overstory. The overstory is the highest layer and these shade-providing trees eventually take over from the midstory trees to cre-ate a mature forest.

Mule deer in an edge zone.

Depending on the geography of a particular area, succession ends with what is called a climax community. In the previous illustration of the successional layers, the fully mature forest would be the climax community. It is a combination of plants and animals that remains stable unless disturbed, usually by fire or human interference.

There are two types of succession: primary and secondary. Primary succession occurs when an area starts as bare rock and proceeds to a climax community. Secondary succession occurs when a climax community is disturbed and then regains its foothold. An untended lawn provides an excellent illustration of secondary succession. The lawn, composed of non-native grasses that need to be mowed, weeded, and watered, constitutes a disturbance. If the lawn is left untended it will be invaded by weeds. These weeds will be followed by native grasses and wildflowers. The eventual climax community that emerges on that untended lawn may be a prairie or a forest, depending on the ecosystem in which the lawn is located.

Edges

One thing to keep in mind is that unless you are the proud owner of a great forested tract, most of the habitat you can provide will be something called an "edge," which is where one type of ecosystem meets another. Most of the creatures you will attract will be edge creatures: those that can live in a transition zone where herbaceous plants and shrubs blend into a mature forest or prairie.

Edges are ecological zones with the highest diversity of plant species and therefore, the highest diversity of wildlife. Edges are created by openings: lawns, paths, vegetable and flower beds all create edges as they nestle up against shrubs and trees. Edges provide sun, flowers, fruit, and access to the various layers, making them habitat for a variety of insects, birds, and animals. So edges are a good thing, right? Well, not completely. Unfortunately, edges allow a level of predator penetration that would not be possible were the area intact.

Our understanding of edges should extend beyond our backyards to an appreciation of places that are not edges and hopefully never will be. Species that tend to thrive in edges are the most adaptable. The destruction and fragmentation of forests creates a lot of edge, which is good for creatures such as jays, deer, coyotes, and butterflies. This fragmentation, though, takes a devastating toll on less adaptable creatures who require a great deal of space, such as owls, bears, cougars, and many species of songbirds. So if you have a woodlot that adjoins a forest, or are able to influence potential development of a forest or park, lend your support to keeping the forested areas as intact as possible. Partnerships with woodlot owners to maintain large

Pathways through native shrubs create edges on a small scale.

blocks of continuous forest can be very successful and may mean the difference between survival and extinction for many non-edge species.

Managing Succession and Layers

Wildlife gardeners are not at the strict mercy of succession. For instance, it isn't necessary to stand back and watch your property be swallowed up by forest. You can manage the succession that occurs in your backyard "wilderness" through

Bare · Herbaceous Plants · Grasses and Perennials · Shrubs · Woodlot or Forest

A bit of layering in a rooftop habitat.

A birdbath next to shelter is an excellent attractant.

choice of plants and the way you cultivate those plants. And aesthetics need not be ignored. A native garden can still be a beautiful garden, it will just look a bit wilder than a traditional garden that has been neatly manicured and trimmed. Wildlife stewards are, like traditional gardeners, trying to "rig the odds." But we are trying to rig them in favor of nature.

Water Worlds

The element most often lacking in backyard and balcony habitats is water. Birdbaths, ponds, bogs, and puddles all play an important role in providing for wildlife needs. Fresh, clean water is difficult to come by for animals in urban and suburban areas. A successful water attraction has the potential to lure many wildlife visitors, and few garden activities are more entertaining than birds preening and playing in a birdbath. Your avian visitors will be joined by a variety of insects, mammals, and amphibians, giving you a good sense of the importance of water for wildlife. In Chapter 13 you will learn how to create several types of birdbaths, ponds, drip systems (for their alluring noise and visual invitation), and a bog. These projects will be as rewarding as any that you undertake in your wildlife stewardship.

For the Birds

THE LABORATORY of Ornithology at Cornell University estimates that there are around 70 million birdwatchers in North America. That makes birding second only to gardening in popularity. And a hobby that combines gardening with birdwatching is an irresistible pull for countless people. It is the fascination with birds that is largely responsible for bringing many people around to the idea of creating habitat gardens. Over 8500 bird species have been counted around the globe, and birdwatching is an interest with people in almost every part of the world.

And really, what's not to like? Birds are entertaining, beautiful, and useful. Flight of course is one of their primary charms. We also have the music of birdsong in spring, and in winter their calls tell us that life still stirs. The antics of birds are always fascinating, and they consume insects that may be a problem for our crops.

People who want to entice birds into their surroundings generally start with a basic feeder. It can be as simple as seed sprinkled on the ground. That approach, if you've been bitten by the birding bug, will soon give way to more specialized "built" feeders aimed at favorite birds. Before you know it, you may also have a backyard or balcony filled with native

Providing a selection of seed types.

Spacious rooftops can sport a variety of features.

Cedar Waxwings

Early in spring, a family hung pieces of burlap and cotton batting over their clothesline for the cedar waxwings they'd seen in the fir trees. A pair of the birds landed on the line, pulling the material off, piece after piece. Nearly a month later the mom noticed waxwings flittering around the fir branches and spotted a sloppily constructed nest made entirely of burlap and cotton. It had no real sides and construction material dangled over the branch; a small indentation in the middle showed where the young birds had been raised. Tidy-looking birds with messy nests—a surprise for this family of birders.

plants that provide food and shelter, nest boxes placed where birds and nestlings will be safe from predators, and a desire to attract as many species as possible. Or perhaps you will be content with just a suet feeder. Regardless of how far down the birding path your hobby takes you, there are a few points to consider before you embark on any feeding program or sheltering project.

Water

A really successful wildlife habitat will offer a place for birds to bathe and drink as well as to feed, nest, and roost. Birdbaths and drips may prove even more popular than feeders or nest boxes (see Chapter 13 for a selection of water projects for the wildlife habitat).

Types of Feeders and Feed

Birds, like any dinner guests, have preferences for location and cuisine. Careful landscaping can provide much of the birds' natural food requirements, while feeders have the advantage of being easy to place so you can watch the action. In Chapter 12 you will learn which shrubs, flowers, and trees provide the best fodder and shelter for birds, and how to plant them for maximum benefit. Your feeders and their locations should likewise be planned to best meet the needs of the birds you hope to attract and placed so that they are easily visible from a window you frequent. If you have to climb onto a counter in order to view your feeder, it won't be much fun. Ideally, your

Western tanager.

feeders should be visible from the kitchen or main areas so you can enjoy the birds' antics while you relax with a coffee, or work at your desk or counter.

Your feeder should also be easily accessible for filling and cleaning. If the feeder has to be hung high, you can rig a rope system for getting it down. Feeders are best placed at least five feet above the ground unless you are specifically targeting ground-feeding species.

Feeder varieties run the gamut from very simple to very complex. You can make feeders yourself or buy commercial varieties. You may want to begin with a basic feeder and become more specialized as you get to know your visitors.

The most basic feeder and the one that is said to work best for getting birds' attention is the open, or table, feeder. Any table will work or you can build a tray and suspend it from a post to keep predators away (see Project 1, page 23 for predator-proofing your feeder and nest box poles).

The ground itself can serve as a feeder but be careful where you sprinkle the food. There should be shelter nearby and you should be able to clean up the area regularly to avoid wet and moldy seed, and rodents. Don't let debris accumulate as birds can be made sick by unhygienic conditions. Doves, cardinals, jays, juncos, quail, starlings, thrashers, and towhees are just a few of the birds that prefer ground feeding. You can often provide for their needs with the feed that falls from your hanging feeders. Make sure the food in your feeder is protected from rain because damp seeds and nuts spoil quickly. You can also place the food in a tray feeder, with or without a roof, directly on the ground, and refill according to conditions. If you find that the larger birds, such as jays and crows, are eating most of the food, try adding a tube feeder to your habitat. These birds are not generally able to use perches on a tube feeder, thus freeing it up for less aggressive birds.

Preventing Window Collisions

Some people use their window ledge as a feeder to get a close-up view of the birds. One of the major drawbacks to this approach is the

Red-shafted flicker on suet cage.

Building a Brush Pile

Top left: *Preparing to build a brush pile.*

Top right: *Laying foundation sticks.*

Right: *Intertwining the sticks.*

Bottom left: *Weaving sticks into a "songbird sculpture."*

Bottom right: *Completed brush pile is used for shelter by various wildlife such as birds, small mammals, reptiles, and amphibians.*

Seed pods provide bird food in winter.

risk of birds flying into the window if startled or chased. You can minimize the risk by putting up sheer curtains in front of the window, or even better, a very fine mesh screen between the window glass and the feeder. One possible advantage of sheer curtains is that you will be able to see through them but the birds will not, so they will be less shy about feeding just inches from you. Hanging strips of surveyor's tape or other fluttering material works well and some people stick commercial hawk decals on windows. These methods can also be used on deck glass. Feeding birds from a window ledge will entail some cleaning, but the intimate view of your feathered friends will be worth it. For an up-close and personal feeder see Project 8.

Shelter

Birds are most likely to use a feeder located close to some form of shelter such as trees, shrubs, tall grasses, or brush piles that can be used for perching, hiding, and getting out of the elements. Remember though, that a feeder nestled right amongst cover will be an easy target for a lurking cat. Feeders should also not be placed too close to trees or other objects that might be used as launching pads by hungry squirrels. Place feeders eight to ten feet from the nearest limb to maintain a safe distance. Evergreen trees are particularly popular shelter.

If a Bird Hits the Window

If a bird does hit your window and you find it lying stunned on the porch or ground below, you can aid in its recovery. Take the bird in your cupped hands and hold it, or set it on your leg with your hands cupped loosely over top—the heat generated from your body will often bring the bird around. (This is not good practice for children or people not entirely focused on the task.) This can take anywhere from a few minutes to an hour

17

The Guardian Birds

About four o'clock this afternoon, I discovered a running attack going on in a maple tree. A gray squirrel was leaping from limb to limb, seeking to escape from a diving bluejay. Whichever way it turned, the bird was close behind. It finally found sanctuary near the trunk, secreting itself where two limbs projected out, one close above the other.

This bluejay, for the past day or so, has been on the aggressive, diving at cats, chasing squirrels, driving away other birds. The explanation? Its fledglings are almost ready to leave the nest. I discovered this nest by chance in the thickest part of a spruce tree. For bluejays, unlike robins and most other birds that reveal the presence of their nest by mounting excitement when you draw near, remain perfectly silent no matter how close you come. If you discover their secret, you do it without any help from them.

Newspapers, during the latter days of May and early June, are likely to carry stories about mystery birds diving on pedestrians in unprovoked attacks. Almost always, these bird bombers are screech owls or bluejays. And, invariably, their attacks begin just about the time that their young, in some near-by nest, are approaching the time of their first flight. The brave parent birds are simply trying to protect their young by driving away everything that represents danger to them. Too often, the conclusion of the story has been that the police have been called in and the "vicious birds" have been shot. A little understanding of what really is happening would prevent such needless tragedies.

Edwin Way Teale – Circle of the Seasons, 1953

or more depending on how hard the bird hit the glass. A small box with folded fabric in the bottom can substitute if you don't have time to sit, but punch a few holes in the lid. When you hear the bird scrabbling inside the box, it is generally ready to take flight. If night has fallen, though, keep the bird in the box, safe and away from cats, until morning. Unfortunately, some birds are killed on impact by a broken neck or severe concussion, so any precautions you can take are worthwhile.

Cleaning Feeders

Dirty bird feeders spread disease. You can minimize the threat of disease by following these guidelines:

- Make sure the birds have enough space at your feeder. If your feeder is overcrowded get another one, preferably with a different type of food.
- Feed birds only high-quality food, and immediately dispose of moldy or rotten food.
- Make sure your feeder has no sharp edges on which birds might cut or scrape themselves. Birds have very high metabolisms and as a result, infections spread quickly.
- Clean and disinfect your feeder regularly. Scrape the droppings off any perch areas and wash out the feeder using vinegar and/or hydrogen peroxide with hot water.
- Suspend a tray below each hanging feeder and dump it once a day.
- If you see a sick bird, notify other peo-

ple who feed birds to be extra careful to keep their feeders clean.

· Keep rodents out of your feed sources as they may carry disease.

Food for All

Along with the type of feeder you choose, the food you use will determine the birds you attract. Feeding different foods in a variety of feeders can prevent any one bird, or group of birds, from monopolizing your generosity. Too many birds competing for not enough food can cause stress and injury.

Birdseed Mixes

Birdseed mixes can be successful or a waste of money. The standard mixes available in grocery stores contain a lot of seeds of little interest to most birds. These seeds are thrown to the ground where they feed rodents and less fussy diners. Stores that specialize in bird products will carry mixes aimed at particular types of birds. You are likely to have more success with these varieties. A third option is to buy seed in bulk and mix it yourself. One very popular mix is 50 percent sunflower seeds, 35 percent white proso millet, and 15 percent cracked corn. Figure out what your favorite bird guests prefer and then tailor your seed mixes to their needs (see Bird Guide, Chapter 3).

A few of the most popular types of seeds for birds are the black oil sunflower seeds, regular striped sunflower seeds, niger thistle, cracked corn, and white and red proso millet. Unsalted peanuts and other nutmeats are favorites, as are raisins and suet, and some fruits and berries. Suet is an animal fat that doesn't freeze solid, making it an ideal energy source for birds in the winter. It can be purchased in chunks and put out whole, or melted down with other ingredients and formed (see Projects 6 and 7). There are also ready-made suet cakes available wherever seed is sold. Suet will go rancid in warm weather, so is best as a winter bird food.

Getting Their Attention

Birds are attracted to white food. In their order of sight, white is the first color they see. When you begin feeding, you may want to put out some safflower seed on a table or ledge to initially draw the birds. Besides being white, safflower seed is unpopular with squirrels. As soon as you have built up a bit of a clientele, switch the food to appropriate types of seed and nuts, then branch out into more specialized feeders. Make sure to

Black-capped chickadee.

Leaf mulch and litter for ground-dwelling species.

Merry-Go-Round

Hardly had Nellie thrown some crusts of bread into the backyard this morning, before the starlings and English sparrows came flying. One sparrow grasped a part of a crust and tried to take wing. The bread was too heavy. As it clung to the fragment, a starling walked up and grabbed the other end. The sparrow clung to its prize. The starling jerked. The sparrow hung on. In the end, the starling swung the bread, with the sparrow hanging to it, around almost in a half circle. It suggested a hammer thrower at a track meet. This was too much for the smaller bird. It flew away and the starling ate the bread.

*Edwin Way Teale –
Circle of the Seasons, 1953*

keep your feeders filled once the birds discover them. If you only fill them after they've been emptied, the birds will find food elsewhere.

Storing Seeds

Store your seeds in a cool dry place. If you are storing a lot of seeds, particularly outside, keep them in a rodent-proof container, such as a metal garbage can. Seed exposed to moisture can harbor mold and bacteria, and too hot tem-peratures will dry out the seed inside the shell.

Eggshells and Grit

Birds benefit from a bit of grit to help them digest their food, particularly in the winter and spring. The grit sits in their crop and helps grind up their food. You

Douglas squirrel.

20

Bendire's thrasher.

can add grit to your feeder year round. Crushed eggshell, oyster shells, or sand works well. With eggshells, it is recommended that you rinse the shells then bake in a 300°F oven for approximately 10 to 15 minutes to eliminate chances of salmonella bacterial growth. You can buy oyster shells at some farm feed stores.

Sapsuckers Drumming

Like most people, the first time you hear a sapsucker drumming on metal you'll probably think he has a problem – or will have if he doesn't stop the head-banging. How can a woodpecker confuse metal with wood? They'll drum on tin roofs, power pole tin, aluminum sailboat masts, or metal mailboxes. The sound echoes up and down a street like a carpenter hammering nails at high speed.

The male sapsuckers are doing this for a reason. They're trying to attract a mate, and he who drums loudest usually wins. Male sapsuckers used to compete by drumming on old, hollow trees – that sound is still very effective – a deep rat-a-tat and a different tone from every tree. But some bird discovered the unsurpassed loudness of metal and the idea caught on.

Spring mornings are a favorite time for drumming. You may be awakened early by a courting sapsucker, but watching the red-hooded head, intent on attracting a female, holds a primitive charm.

21

PROJECT

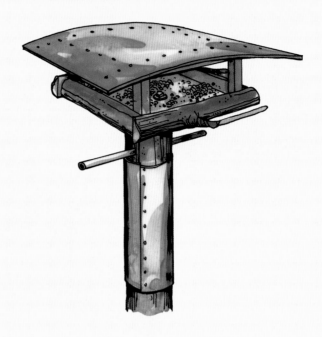

TOOLS & MATERIALS

- Table saw and jigsaw or band saw
- Hammer
- Socket wrench
- Tray – 16" square of ¾" plywood
- Sills (4) – large branches split or sawn in half
- Posts (4) – 1" square × 8" long
- Rafters (2) – ½" × 2" × 22" (cut in a curve at the top)
- Cross-pieces (2) – 1" square × 14" long
- Roof – 20" × 24" (¼" plywood, ⅛" Plexiglas or sheet metal)
- Water-resistant glue
- Common nails – 1" and 2"
- Lag screws (2) – 4" long with two large washers

FIGURE 1

FIGURE 2

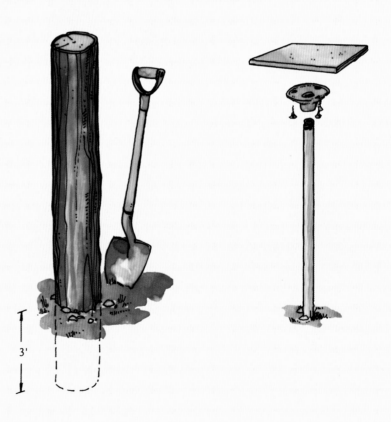

3'

A simple tray feeder can be made by fastening a square of plywood to the top of a wooden or metal post. The post should be set at least 3' in the ground (Figure 1) to ensure stability. If possible, it is also a good idea to set it in concrete. The tray should sit high enough and far enough away from branches and other objects that it cannot be reached by predators. A metal pipe is an effective mount for a tray feeder because it cannot be climbed. To mount a tray on a metal pipe, thread a standard flange onto the pipe and screw the plywood tray section to it from underneath (Figure 2). Make sure to mount the tray only as high as you can reach to fill it.

Wooden posts have the disadvantage of being easily climbed by predators with claws. A metal or plastic sheath (Figure 3) or a cone guard (Figure 4) will keep these animals away. One advantage of a wooden post is that you can drill a 1" hole through it to insert a galvanized metal pipe (which will protrude through either side) to support a ladder. This will allow you to make the tray quite high and still be able to reach it for filling.

FIGURE 3

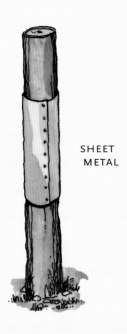

SHEET METAL

FIGURE 4

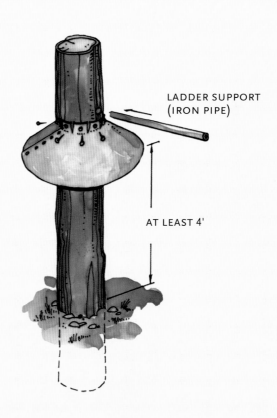

LADDER SUPPORT
(IRON PIPE)

AT LEAST 4'

1 To make a feeder tray, attach a 16"
square of ¾" plywood to the top of an
iron post using a metal flange as described above or a couple of lag screws
with large washers if it is a wood post
(Figure 5). To reduce spillage, make a
sill for the plywood. A large split

branch will give the tray a rustic appearance (Figure 6). If the feeder is not
sheltered in an enclosed area it's a
good idea to cover it with a roof to
shield the feed from the rain.

2 To make a roof, cut four 8" lengths of
fir or cedar two-by-two.

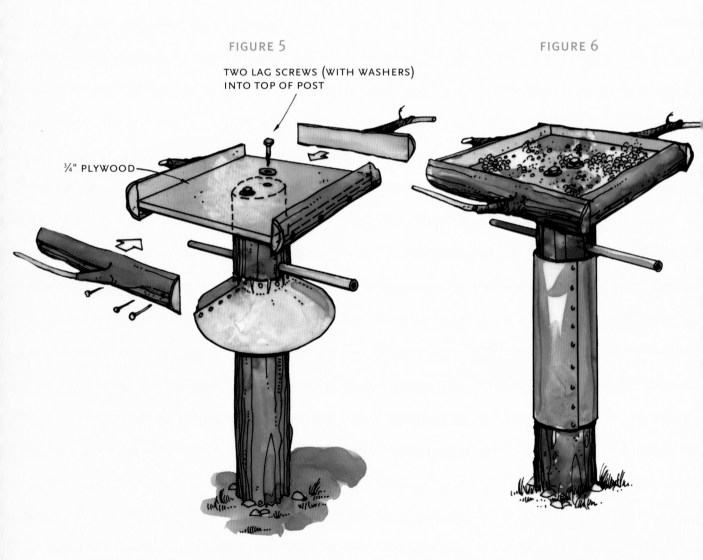

FIGURE 5

TWO LAG SCREWS (WITH WASHERS)
INTO TOP OF POST

¾" PLYWOOD

FIGURE 6

3 Cut a ½" × 1" notch in the top of each post as shown in Figure 7 to provide a recess for two ½" × 2' × 22" plywood roof rafters. Glue and nail these in place. To make the roof stronger, glue and nail two ½" cross-pieces between the rafters opposite each post.

4 The roof (Figure 8) is made of a 20" × 24" sheet material flexible enough to follow the curves of the rafters. This material can be ¼" plywood painted with two coats of exterior enamel, ⅛" clear Plexiglas or medium weight galvanized metal. (If Plexiglas is used, it is best to screw it in place through pre-drilled holes to avoid cracking the material.) The roof should overhang the rafters by 1" at either end and by 2" at the sides.

FIGURE 7   FIGURE 8

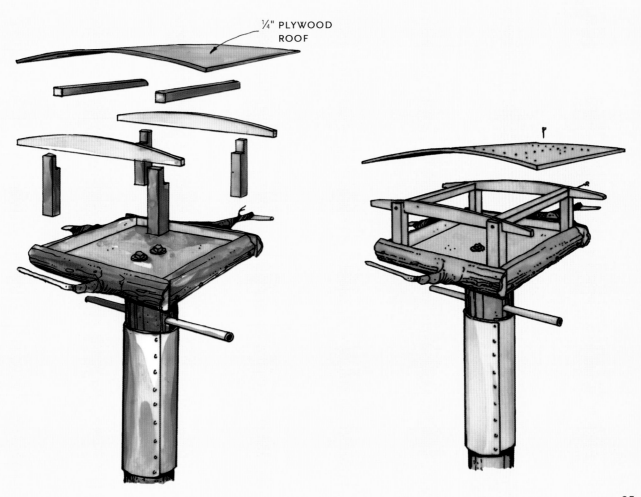

¼" PLYWOOD ROOF

FANCY CORN COB FEEDER

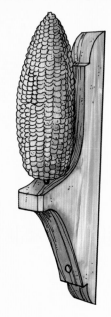

TOOLS & MATERIALS

- Band saw or scroll saw
- Drill with ⅛" diameter bit
- Hammer
- Fir or cedar two-by-six × 14" long

This wooden bracket can be nailed to a post, a tree, or the side of a building to attract birds and/or squirrels.

1. Enlarge side view (below) on photocopier until sized to match dimensions. Use as a pattern to cut out feeder bracket from two-by-six fir or cedar.

2. Drill ⅛" holes through the back for mounting.

3. Drill a ⅛" pilot hole for a 6" common nail to reduce the chance of splitting the wood when you drive the nail.

4. Cut off head of nail to allow corncob to be impaled as shown.

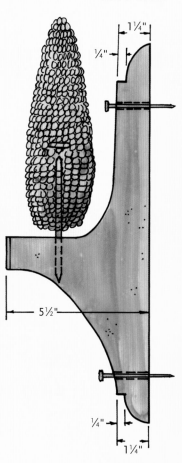

FRONT VIEW   **SIDE VIEW**

14"   1½"   7"   4½"   ¾"   1½"

1¼"   ¼"   5½"   ¼"   1¼"

26

SCALE INCHES

PEANUT HEART FEEDER

This simple feeder is easily made from readily available materials. Hang the finished feeder so that predators cannot reach it and it is sheltered from rain.

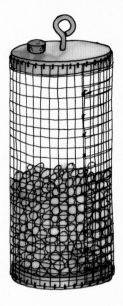

TOOLS & MATERIALS
- Band saw
- Stapler
- Hammer
- Electric drill
- ⅛" and ¾" diameter drill bits
- One 10" square of hardware cloth
- Two ½" thick wooden disks, 3" diameter
- One 1" screw-eye
- One cork

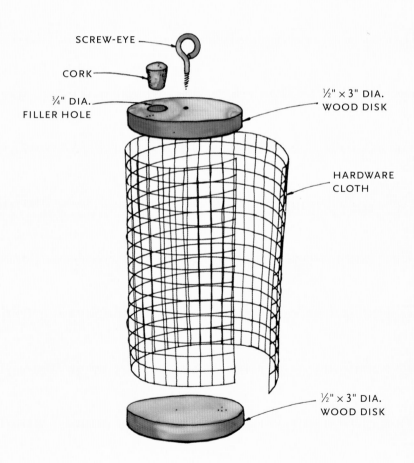

SCREW-EYE

CORK

¾" DIA. FILLER HOLE

½" × 3" DIA. WOOD DISK

HARDWARE CLOTH

½" × 3" DIA. WOOD DISK

1. Carefully trim a 10" square of hardware cloth to remove any sharp edges.

2. Cut out two ½" thick wooden disks 3" diameter.

3. In the center of one of the disks drill a ⅛" diameter pilot hole and install a screw-eye on which to hang the feeder. Off center on the same disk drill a ¾" diameter filler hole. Use a cork as a stopper for the filler hole.

4. Tack or staple the hardware cloth around the disks at the top and bottom to form an overlapping cylinder. Use only stainless steel staples to prevent rusting and breakage. Tie the hardware cloth in several places with string where it overlaps.

THISTLE FEEDER

- Table saw
- Electric drill with ⅜", 1½", and 2" diameter bits
- Hammer
- Staple gun
- Log (with bark on) – 5" or 6" diameter × 12" long
- Top block – ¾" plywood, 2" × 2¾"
- Bottom block – ¾" plywood, 2" × 3"
- Sides – two pieces ⅛" Plexiglas 2½" × 10½"
- Wire mesh – four pieces, 2½" square
- Roof – cedar slab (with bark on) 5" × 7" long
- Perches – four ⅜" diameter hardwood dowels, each at least 3" long
- Screw-eyes (2) – 1" long
- Heavy cord – minimum 2' long
- Glue

This rustic thistle feeder is made from two halves of a small log with Plexiglas for sides. It can be hung from a tree branch or under the eaves of a building. The feeder has its own roof held loosely in place by cords, which allows access to the inside through the top for filling. This type of feeder is the most economical way to provide expensive thistle, or "niger," seed for finches and siskins.

1 To make this feeder, split a 12" long cedar log about 5" or 6" in diameter and plane the inside faces flat. Cut two ⅛" × ¼" slots parallel to each other and 3" apart (outside dimension) on each face as shown opposite.

2 On the center line of the outside faces (through the bark), drill two 2" diameter access holes and two ⅜" diameter holes for the perches, referring to the dimensions shown opposite. Staple a 2½" square of wire mesh over each of the access holes on the inside and glue four ⅜" diameter dowel perches in place, allowing them to protrude about 2½".

3 Using ¾" plywood, make a bottom block 2" × 3" and a top block 2" × 2¾". Drill a 1½"

diameter filler hole in the top block only. Glue and nail the two halves of the log to these blocks where shown. Install a large screw-eye in each half about 1" down from the top to hold the cords by which the feeder is suspended.

4 Cut or buy two ⅛" thick sheets of Plexiglas 2½" × 10½" and slide them down into the slots on the inside faces until they hit the bottom block.

5 Cut a third cedar slab (with bark on) 7" long by approximately 5" wide for the roof. Drill two ⅜" holes through the roof as shown. Make a large knot at one end of a 2' length of cord, then thread the other end up through the one screw-eye and through the underside of the hole in

the roof. Thread the cord down through the other hole in the roof and down through the other screw-eye. Make another large knot at this end of the cord and the feeder is done.

6 To fill the thistle feeder, simply slide the roof up the cord and fill through the hole in the top block.

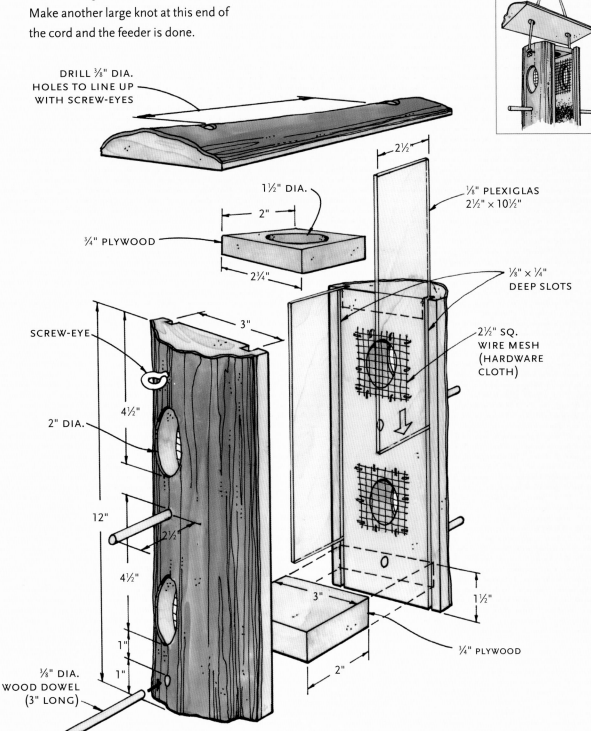

DRILL ⅜" DIA. HOLES TO LINE UP WITH SCREW-EYES

1½" DIA.

2"

¾" PLYWOOD

2¾"

2½"

⅛" PLEXIGLAS 2½" × 10½"

⅛" × ¼" DEEP SLOTS

2½" SQ. WIRE MESH (HARDWARE CLOTH)

SCREW-EYE

3"

2" DIA.

4½"

12"

2½"

4½"

1"

1"

3"

⅜" DIA. WOOD DOWEL (3" LONG)

2"

¾" PLYWOOD

1½"

CLEAR FEEDER

TOOLS & MATERIALS

- Hand saw
- Drill with 1½" diameter speed-bore bit
- Tin shears
- Hammer
- Staple gun
- Two large screw-eyes
- Two pieces of 3' long one-by-eight (nom.) western red cedar
- Two pieces of 10" long one-by-two (nom.) western red cedar
- Two pieces ⅛" thick Plexiglas, 9" × 9"
- One piece of tin or thin plywood (for flap) 2" × 3"
- 1¼" galvanized nails
- Stainless steel staples
- Caulking

1. Cut one 3' cedar board in half to make the two sides of the roof 18" long each. Cut the other 3' cedar board in three pieces: one piece 8½" long for the bottom, and two pieces 13¾" long for the sides.

2. To make a peak, draw a line down the center of each board, then measure 3¾" down each side from the top. Join these points with a pencil line to the center of the top edge to guide you in cutting the peaks (Figure 1).

FIGURE 1
SIDE LAYOUT

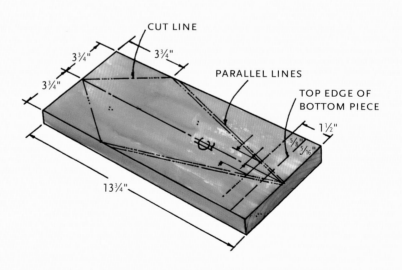

3 On the inside face of each side, cut ¼" deep slots with a hand saw to hold the sheets of Plexiglas. These slots must be at least ⅛" wide so they will have to be made with two saw cuts each. To mark these out, locate the center line of each board and mark the line 5⁵⁄₁₆" on either side of the center line. This will locate the inside edge of the Plexiglas which will form an opening ⅝" wide and ¾" above the bottom for the seeds to spill out. Draw a line from each of these marks to the corresponding shoulder (Figure 2). Then draw lines parallel to these ⅛" apart. With the sides of the feeder clamped to a work surface, saw along each line to a depth of ¼", then chip out the wood

between the lines with a knife (except below the line you drew parallel to the bottom – the glass must rest on wood ¾" above the bottom of the feeder. If necessary, glue strips of wood into the slots to support the glass).

4 On one side only measure 3¾" down the center line from the peak to locate the center of a 1½" diameter seed filler hole.

5 You can attach simple suet holders to either side of the feeder using two of the triangular off-cuts left from forming the peaks. They should be nailed in place from the inside face of each side; the top of each triangular shelf should be 3¼" above the bottom of each side.

FIGURE 2

MAKE TWO SIDES

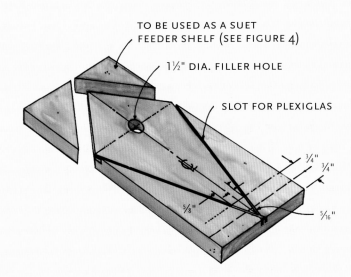

TO BE USED AS A SUET
FEEDER SHELF (SEE FIGURE 4)

1½" DIA. FILLER HOLE

SLOT FOR PLEXIGLAS

¾"

¾"

⅝"

5⁄16"

6 Now the feeder is ready to be assembled. Nail each side to the bottom. Nail a 10" long one-by-two rail on either side of the feeder at the bottom (Figure 3). This should stiffen up the feeder so the sides are perfectly parallel and vertical. Slide the glass into position in the slots (Figure 3). Nail the two 18" long roof pieces to the sides and to each other with a 4" overhang at either end. *Note:* Caulking should be applied in the joint where the two pieces of the roof meet (Figure 4) so rain won't find its way inside.

FIGURE 3

ASSEMBLY

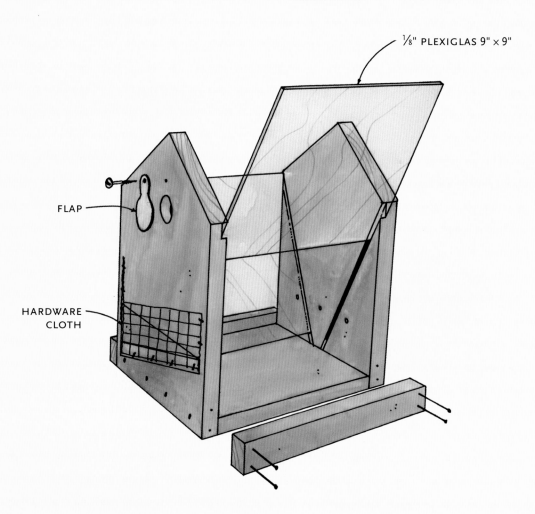

⅛" PLEXIGLAS 9" × 9"

FLAP

HARDWARE
CLOTH

7. A flap to cover the seed filler hole can be cut from tin or thin plywood using the pattern (Figure 4) enlarged on a photocopier. It is screwed in place so that it can be pivoted out of the way in order to fill the feeder with a funnel.

8. Hardware cloth can be stapled onto the triangular shelves to hold suet (Figure 3).

9. To suspend the feeder, install a 1½" screw-eye 4½" from each end of the ridge of the roof as shown.

10. As an option, if the feeder is to be placed on a railing, two strips of two-by-two cedar nailed to the bottom as shown below will keep it from slipping off.

FIGURE 4
SECTION THROUGH FEEDER

FIGURE 5
**PATTERN FOR TIN
OR PLYWOOD FLAP
(ENLARGE ON PHOTOCOPIER)**

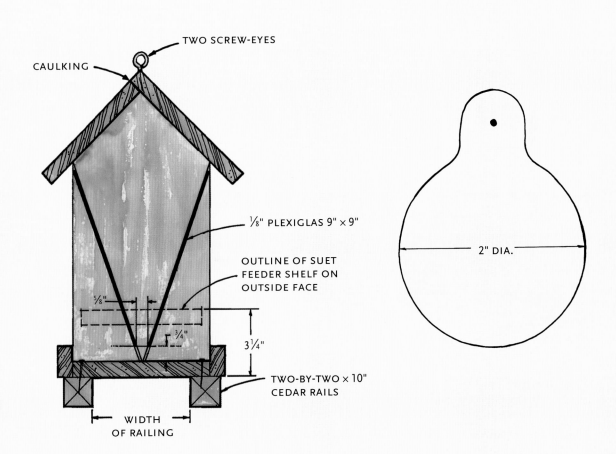

TWO SCREW-EYES

CAULKING

⅛" PLEXIGLAS 9" × 9"

OUTLINE OF SUET
FEEDER SHELF ON
OUTSIDE FACE

⅝"

¾"

3¼"

TWO-BY-TWO × 10"
CEDAR RAILS

WIDTH
OF RAILING

2" DIA.

6
PROJECT

SUET FEEDERS & RECIPES

TOOLS & MATERIALS

- Drill with ³⁄₁₆" diameter bit
- Scissors
- Hardwood veneer 1" × 48" (Birch or maple veneer can be purchased at most hardwood supply stores. A 4' long strip 1" wide coiled three times around will make a medallion about 4" diameter.)
- Wire mesh
- Small eye-bolt with ³⁄₁₆" shaft and two nuts
- Water-resistant glue

Plastic mesh bags make ideal suet feeders. Nuts and produce are often sold in these small bags, but you can make your own by cutting a circle of any size from a large onion or carrot sack of the same material; draw closed with string (Figure 1). This type of feeder is suited to pieces of solid suet sold at meat markets. Use thread spools or plastic pipe to keep squirrels from reaching the suet.

Pine cones (Figure 2) can be stuffed with one of the suet recipes and hung from tree branches for feeders that blend into their surroundings (even if you hang them in trees of a different species!).

Try drilling holes in a small diameter log, about 12"–18" in length, then fill them up with Nutty Suet Mix (Figure 3). Screw an eyehook into the top of the log and hang the feeder in a tree. Even larger birds such as flickers enjoy a treat like this and will swing crazily back and forth as they peck at the suet.

Coconut halves make sturdy feeders. Just saw the husk in half, drill three holes evenly spaced along the edge, and hang with wire (Figure 4). Pour the suet mix in while still liquid then hang when it has cooled and hardened.

FIGURE 1

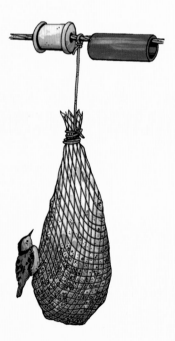

FIGURE 2

FIGURE 3

FIGURE 4

This unique suet feeder is easily made from wood veneer called "edge banding" which is available at most lumber/hardware stores.

1. Apply water-resistant glue to the veneer as you coil it. Drill a hole just large enough for a small eye-bolt to fit through the layers where the ends overlap. The eye-bolt will need two nuts: one on the outside of the veneer and one on the inside (Figure 5).

2. Cut a circular piece of wire mesh ½" larger in diameter than the inside of the coiled veneer. Bend the edges 90° to form a circle just large enough to fit firmly in-side the medallion (Figure 6). This should be tight enough to hold itself in place.

3. Fill the medallion with suet on either side of the wire mesh (Figure 7) and hang it from a tree branch, under the eaves of your house or shed, or against a tree trunk. You may need to experiment with location if squirrels start to chew it. Hanging the suet under branches is useful if there is a problem with starlings or house sparrows, as only birds that feed upside down (woodpeckers, nuthatches, chickadees, etc.) can then get at it.

Basic Suet Seed Cakes

- Coarsely ground suet from the butcher shop
- 1 Tbsp water (or as needed)
- Mixed seeds

Melt the suet in a pan on medium heat, adding a bit of water as necessary to replace the water lost to evaporation. Add the seeds, pour into muffin tins lined with cupcake papers, and cool until hardened. *Note:* If you cannot obtain suet, you can substitute a mixture containing 1 part vegetable shortening, 1 part peanut butter, 1 part cracked corn, 1 part flour, and 3 parts cornmeal.

Nutty Suet Mix

- 3 cups suet
- 3 cups cornmeal
- 1 cup chunk peanut butter
- Assorted nutmeats (unsalted), dehydrated egg, finely chopped apples, honey or brown sugar, raisins

Melt the suet in a pan, then add the cornmeal, peanut butter, and whatever ingredients you think the birds may enjoy. Do not add any ingredients that are spicy.

FIGURE 5

FIGURE 6

FIGURE 7

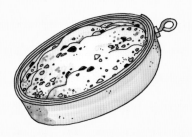

FEEDER STATION
MASON JAR & SUET HOLDER

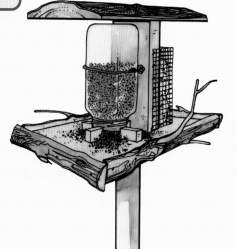

TOOLS & MATERIALS

- Hand saw
- Hammer
- Screwdriver
- Staple gun
- Platform – ¾" plywood, 8" × 11"
- Divider – 1" × 5" × 7¼" red cedar
- Roof – 8" × 11" slab of fir or cedar
- Crossed battens (2) – ½" × ¾" × 3½" long
- Suet holder – 5" × 10" wire mesh
- Stainless steel staples
- Mounting post – 2½" to 3" diameter galvanized iron 6'
- Mounting flange – galvanized iron to match mounting post
- Screws (2) – 2½" galvanized flat-head
- Nails (2) – 3" galvanized common
- Screw eyes (2) – 1¼" galvanized
- Bungee cord (with a hook attached to each end) long enough to wrap around jar snugly
- Split branches

This feeder station provides different kinds of feed separately. Seeds and grains can be dispensed from the jar on one side and suet offered on the other side. The slab roof provides shelter from the rain.

1 To make the feeder you will need a ¾" thick platform and an upright divider (preferably 1" thick western red cedar) screwed to it from the underside (Figure 1).

FIGURE 1
SECTIONAL (END) VIEW

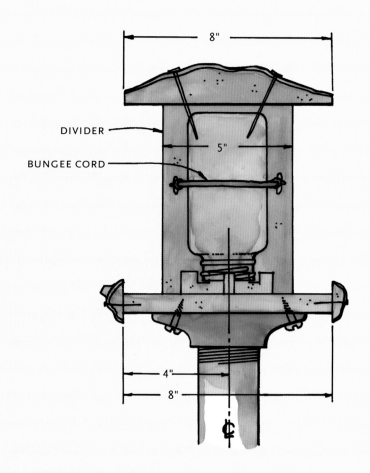

DIVIDER

BUNGEE CORD

8"

5"

4"

8"

2 Nail a shallow slab of wood (with the bark still on) to the top of the divider to create a roof.

3 To allow the jar to dispense seed, it must sit on a pair of crossed battens, notched to receive the edges of the mouth (Figures 3 and 4). Make the crossed battens from ¾" fir using the dimensions shown and nail it in place next to the upright divider on the platform. Screw two screw-eyes into the divider as shown. You can hook the bungee cords to these eyes to secure the jar in place.

4 Carefully trim the edges of a 5" x 10" rectangle of wire mesh and staple it to the edges of the divider as shown (Figure 2).

5 The perimeter of the platform should be trimmed with wood to form a raised lip. This will give the birds something to perch on and help keep the seeds from spilling to the ground. To com-

FIGURE 3

MOUTH OF JAR

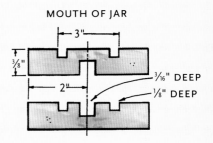

├─ 3" ─┤
³⁄₈"
├── 2" ──┤
³⁄₁₆" DEEP
⅛" DEEP

FIGURE 2
SECTIONAL (SIDE) VIEW

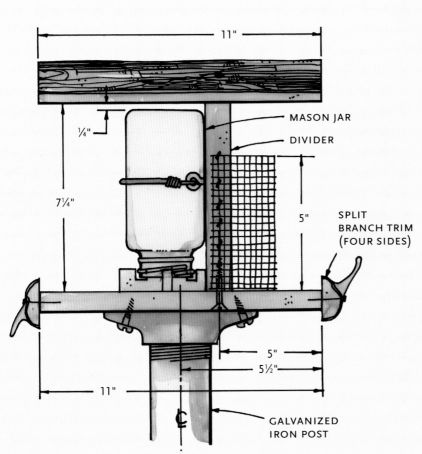

11"
¼"
7¼"
MASON JAR
DIVIDER
5"
SPLIT
BRANCH TRIM
(FOUR SIDES)
5"
5½"
11"
GALVANIZED
IRON POST

FIGURE 4

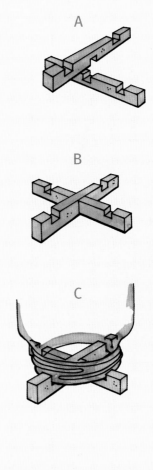

A

B

C

plete the rustic appearance of the feeder, split some straight branches and nail them in place to all four sides of the platform (Figure 2).

6. Finally, bury an iron pipe (threaded at one end to take a wide flange) at least 2' into the ground. This will serve as a predator guard. Screw the metal flange to the underside of the platform as shown. *Note:* As an option if you make the platform larger, it can easily accommodate a feeder station with two jars. Mount one on either side of the

divider and fill each with a different type of seed (Figure 5).

7. To secure the jar in place, fill it with seeds and holding a piece of cardboard over the mouth to keep the seeds inside, turn it upside down. Keeping the cardboard over the mouth of the upside-down jar, center it over notches in the crossed battens. Pull the cardboard away with the jar in place allowing the seeds to spill out (Figure 6). This sounds trickier than it is!

FIGURE 5

SECTIONAL (SIDE) VIEW

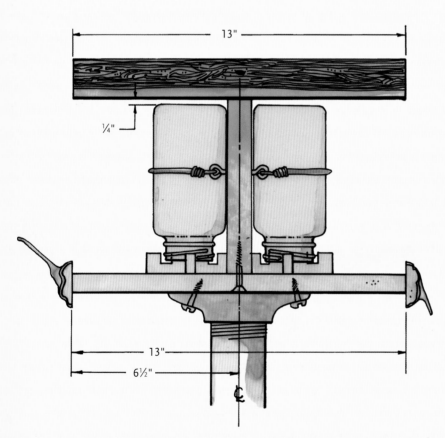

13"

¼"

13"

6½"

FIGURE 6

A

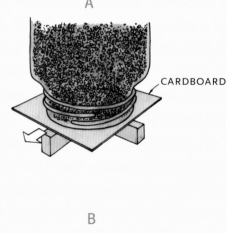

CARDBOARD

B

A windowsill is an ideal location for a bird feeder. It keeps the birds close for observation, is generally safe from predators, and provides easy access for filling. This windowsill feeder goes a step further and brings the birds right inside the house. The feeder is designed to rest on the sill of a wooden window without being screwed on or nailed in place. The window comes down on top of the feeder to provide a weather seal which allows the feeder to be used year-round. There are a variety of locks available for use on wooden sashing.

TOOLS & MATERIALS

- Table saw, band saw and jigsaw
- Router with ⅛" bit
- Drill with ⅛", 3⁄16", and ¼" bits
- Hammer
- Screwdriver
- Top – ¾" fir plywood with an oak or mahogany veneer
- Bottom – ¾" fir plywood
- Interior bracket – 2" × 12" oak or mahogany
- Sides – 2" and 6" pieces, ¾" × 16" oak or mahogany
- Interior viewing "window" – ⅛" Plexiglas 16½" × (to suit width of opening)
- Exterior sill stop – two-by-four × 6"
- Draught stops (2) – 1½" × 1½" × width of window opening
- Filler lid – 6" and 8" diameter disks of oak or mahogany
- Common nails – 1½" long
- Brass screws – 1½" long

1 Cut the top and the bottom of the feeder from ¾" plywood. Make the top 2" larger than the bottom at the outside edge to provide an overhang. Using the top view shown (Figure 1) and the bar scale as a guide, cut out the top and bottom with a band saw and jigsaw. The width of the feeder should match the inside dimensions of the window to be used. *Note:* If you wish to make the feeder more attractive, you can use oak-faced plywood for the top. You may also wish to cover the edges of the plywood with veneer wherever they can be seen inside the house.

FIGURE 1
TOP VIEW

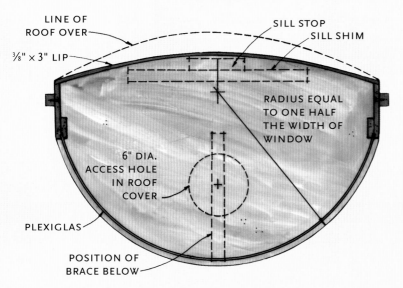

LINE OF ROOF OVER

SILL STOP
SILL SHIM

⅜" × 3" LIP

RADIUS EQUAL TO ONE HALF THE WIDTH OF WINDOW

6" DIA. ACCESS HOLE IN ROOF COVER

PLEXIGLAS

POSITION OF BRACE BELOW

2. Use a router to cut a ⅛" to ¼" deep channel ¾" in from the edge of the top and bottom to receive a curved sheet of Plexiglas.

3. Cut a 6" diameter hole in the top to give access to the feeder from inside the house.

4. Make the sides of the feeder from two two-by-six pieces of oak or mahogany, 16" long (to match the plywood top). These pieces should be glued together as shown (Figure 1), keeping the ⅛" × 14" deep groove between them for the Plexiglas.

5. Assemble the top, bottom, and sides, slipping the curved Plexiglas into place at the same time. The Plexiglas does not need to be glued or otherwise fastened in place. Glue and screw the bottom and the top to the sides.

6. Trim the exterior edge of the bottom with a ⅜" × 3" sill (fir or red cedar nailed in place will work well) to reduce the amount of seed spillage.

7. Make a cover for the access hole by gluing a 6" and an 8" diameter disk together to form a plug. These disks can be cut out with a band saw or a jigsaw. To finish the plug, drill a ¼" diameter hole in the center of the lid and glue a small wood knob onto it. Knobs are available at fine woodworking and finishing stores.

FIGURE 2
SECTIONAL (SIDE) VIEW

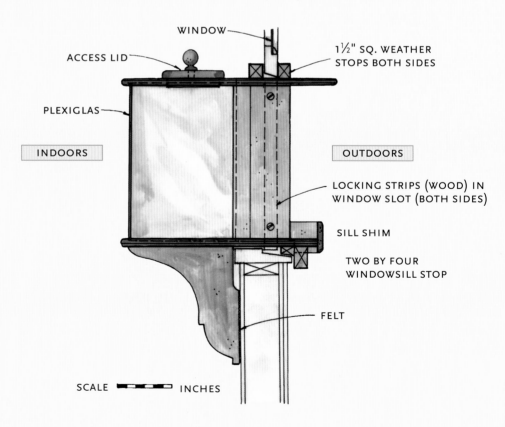

WINDOW

ACCESS LID

1½" SQ. WEATHER STOPS BOTH SIDES

PLEXIGLAS

INDOORS

OUTDOORS

LOCKING STRIPS (WOOD) IN WINDOW SLOT (BOTH SIDES)

SILL SHIM

TWO BY FOUR WINDOWSILL STOP

FELT

SCALE ▬▬▬ INCHES

8. Although the feeder rests on the windowsill, it must be held in place so it doesn't fall in or out of the window. An angle bracket of oak or mahogany 1½" thick, screwed in place inside the house will hold the feeder level and secure. Use a band saw to cut the 12" high × 11" deep bracket from a two-by-twelve board.

9. Glue and nail a 6" long two by four to the outside edge of the windowsill.

10. As shown in Figure 3 place a wood shim on the sloping surface of the sill to keep the feeder level.

11. Once the feeder is in place on the sill, lower the window to rest on top of it. To prevent drafts, glue a 1½" square piece of oak or mahogany the length of the window on the top inside of the house. Glue and nail another one (this can be fir or cedar) on the exterior portion of the top so the window will fit between them.

12. Finally, to make the feeder even more secure, screw a strip of wood to the outside of each side. These should fit into the window slots of the window frame and will have to be screwed in (without glue) from the inside of the feeder. They will lock the feeder in place and will have to be taken out in order to move the feeder.

13. You can oil or varnish the wood surfaces of the feeder and the exterior can be painted to match the house. Do not put any finish on the inside bottom surface of the feeder as it may poison the birds.

FIGURE 3
FRONT VIEW (INDOORS)

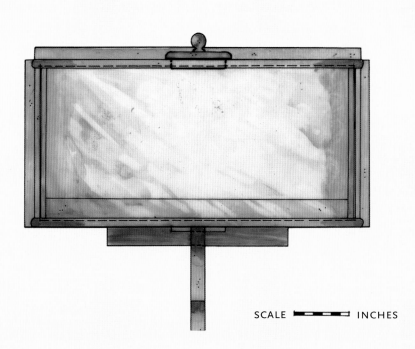

SCALE ▬▬▬ INCHES

Nest Boxes for Birds

Good nesting spots are hard to come by for urban and suburban birds. Approximately fifty species of birds will use nest boxes. If you can go the whole way and give birds food, shelter, and water, you will be doing a great service. The more carefully you design and place your bird houses for particular species, the bigger your contribution to helping sustain the wild bird population.

Before you put up a nest box, review the following information, as well as Chapter 9, on discouraging predators. Nesting birds and their young are very vulnerable and need all the protection you can give them. Next, try to find out which birds in your area are most likely to be attracted to a nest box then provide that species with a box that suits its needs. The box should be placed so that it faces away from wind and rain and is not in di-

rect sunlight all afternoon. When to put up your bird boxes varies significantly over North America. Contact your local natural history society or birdwatchers' group for the best month to have them ready.

Make sure the house you build or buy is chosen from a bird's perspective. Often the most charming nest boxes are those least likely to be chosen by a nesting pair. Complicated bird houses in bright colors are unique decorator items, but not great homes for birds. In general, birds prefer plain finishes and natural colors. Purple martins will accept white houses, but gray and brown are a safer bet for exteriors with most birds. Interiors should be left natural. Make sure the material you use to build the house will not act like an oven in warm weather. Metal, aside from aluminum (see Purple Martins sidebar, this chapter), and plastic are notorious for this. Wood is the safest choice and it should be at least ¾" cedar or exterior grade plywood. Rooves should provide an overhang at the entrance hole, and floors should have a ⅜" drainage hole in each corner or have a recessed floor.

Discouraging House Sparrows, European Starlings, and Predators

House sparrows and European starlings are aggressive imports whose success in adapting to habitats throughout North America has come largely at the expense of native bird species. Many backyard birders take an active role in discouraging them (see individual listings in Nesting and Feeding Preferences on page 54).

These and other birds will peck at nest box openings to make them larger. To avoid this, screw a 3½" square piece of sheet metal (with a hole the same size as the entrance) to the front of the box or to the wood baffle block (page 152). Make sure that no sharp edges from the metal are exposed. Birds can be injured, sometimes fatally, by even mild scratches that become infected. Metal plates and baffle blocks are a common deterrent, but the wood around a hole can be chewed up by squirrels. Other types of baffles are cone baffles and metal baffles on posts (see pages 150 to 152). These, like the deterrents listed above, can be used with feeders or nest boxes.

Blowfly Trap

One of the most serious parasites to plague nest boxes are blowfly larvae. These creatures feed on nestlings at night, attaching themselves to the baby birds' feet and facial areas. During the day the larvae hide at the bottom of the nesting material, thereby protecting themselves from the adult birds. Blowfly larvae can weaken nestlings, and in great numbers, kill them. They are a problem for bluebirds, robins, and many types of swallows, house wrens, and other small birds.

To protect nestlings from blowfly larvae, bend a piece of ⅜" hardware cloth as shown in Figure 1 and place it in the bottom of the nest box. When the larvae retreat to the bottom of the nest box, they will fall through the wire holes and be unable to make their way up again to parasitize the nestlings (Figure 2). This trap was invented by Ira Campbell of Timberville, Virginia. He compared nest boxes

FIGURE 1

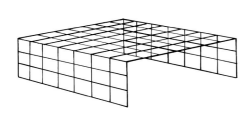

FIGURE 2

GRUBS

Moss hanging basket given over to nesting finches.

with blowfly traps to those without and found that there were no nestling deaths due to blowflies in the 53 boxes with traps, but 12 deaths in the 47 boxes without traps.

Design Variations

1. Hole size – varies with species of bird.
2. Predator access restrictors – adjust hole design to make predator access difficult without limiting it for birds.
3. Hole height above floor – varies with species of bird.
4. Interior dimensions of box – varies with species of bird.
5. Box venting – holes, notches, or gaps at top of sides.
6. Box drainage – holes or gaps in bottom.
7. Box mounting – depends on interior access and/or surface to be mounted on.
8. Roof slope – must quickly shed rain without allowing water to seep inside box. Should shield entry hole from slanting, wind-driven rain.
9. Interior access – front, side, or roof should open for nesting observation and yearly nest clean-out.
10. Material – should be as natural as possible without toxic paint or caulking. No bright colors.

Nest Box Basics

Building a nest box can be as easy or as complicated as you like. The most functional boxes are plain and simple, but many builders enjoy creating showpieces. Nest box building is a very satisfying pursuit that allows you to create homes for one of nature's most attractive creatures.

All nest boxes, plain or elaborate, must include some basic features. Wood is the most appropriate material for building boxes. Western red cedar is best because it's light, durable, and weathers well, but exterior grade plywood can also be used. Red cedar should be ¾" thick but the plywood can be ½" to ⅝" thick depending on the size of the nest box.

The interior dimensions of the box, height from the floor to the bottom of the entrance hole, and the diameter of the hole itself are three features that determine which birds are most likely to use a particular box. The size of the entry hole is a factor of which each species seems to be instinctively aware. The hole should be just large enough to allow access for the intended species. Entrance holes can be further modified to discourage specific predators (see page 152 Baffle Blocks). Never put a perch on a bird house. Cavity nesters do not require a perch, and including one only allows predators easy access to eggs and nestlings.

Other important considerations when designing a nest box are:

- Ventilation: it is important to provide small holes, notches, or gaps high up on the sides.
- Drainage: provide holes or corner gaps in the floor. You can also recess the floor up inside the box to prevent water wicking in from the bottom.
- Roof slope: the roof must shed rain without allowing water to seep inside the box. It should also shield the entry hole from wind-driven rain.
- Mounting: the box can be hung on the side of a wall or post, or it can be nailed or screwed in place. For instance, if the front of the box opens, make sure it is easy to screw through the back wall from the inside.
- Human access to the interior: necessary for cleaning the inside of the box after the fledglings have left. This will also provide a means of observing the growth of the nestlings. Access can be provided by a hinge on the front, on one side, or on the roof.
- Finish: red cedar has its own protective oils and needs no special treatment. Long exposure to sun and rain can eventually de-laminate plywood but you can extend its life with a thick coat of exterior enamel every couple of years. Never paint the inside of a nest box.

Nesting Materials

If you really want to be hospitable, offer the birds a selection of nesting materials. Small piles of twigs, a mound of moss, small pieces of burlap, cotton batting, a container of mud with some clay (kept moist), feathers, dog or horse hair, and pieces of string or twine (no longer than 4" per piece so the birds cannot be inadvertently strangled), help to make the job of building easier for your bird guests.

Bird Guide

Nesting and Feeding Preferences
Regional field guides with distribution maps can be consulted to determine which birds may be expected in which areas. To note as well, nesting and feeding behavior for individual species may vary considerably between regions.

Blackbird, Red-winged: nests in thick vegetation of marshes; prefers grains and seeds, as well as cracked corn in ground feeder or hanging tray feeder.

Bluebird, Eastern: nests in tree cavities, nest boxes; suet, raisins, berries (in feeder or on shrubs); may enjoy a birdbath.

Bluebird, Mountain: see Eastern Bluebird.

Bluebird, Western: see Eastern Bluebird.

Bobwhite, Northern: may nest in brushy yards with tall grass; will feed on seeds, grains, and cracked corn sprinkled on the ground.

Bunting, Lazuli: nests in brush and thickets; may visit a feeder during migration; offer mixed seed containing millet.

Bunting, Indigo: found nesting in wood-

Fledgling Foothold

When young birds are ready to leave the nest, a rough surface on the inside of the nest box will help them. You can provide this by making shallow, horizontal cuts below the entrance hole. You can also fasten a piece of hardware cloth below the hole with stainless steel staples, making sure that no rough edges remain that could cut or scratch the birds.

PETERSON STYLE BLUEBIRD BOX

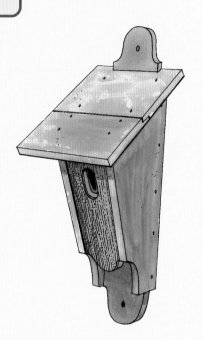

1 Using a compass, draw a 1½" radius circle at each end of a 2' long one-by-four, each centered 1½" from each end. Draw "shoulders" 2" from each end as shown and cut out these decorative designs with a coping saw or band saw. This board will become the back upon which the nest box is built. Drill a ³⁄₁₆" diameter hole through the center of each circle where screws will be placed to mount the box on a wall or post.

2 Again using a compass, draw a 1½" radius half circle centered 1½" from one end of a 13" long one by four. Draw shoulders at 1½" from

FIGURE 1

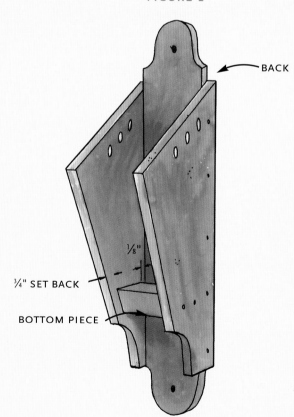

BACK

⅛"

¾" SET BACK

BOTTOM PIECE

the end as shown and cut out. Measure 2¾" from the other end, draw a 1⅜" diameter circle centered on the board and another one centered 1" below it. Drill a 1½" diameter round hole or fashion an elliptical hole or slot of the same proportion for the entrance, making it 6" above the floor. This will become the front of the nest box.

③ Make the sides from two one by ten cedar boards by copying the side view shown to make a pattern. It is important to have one 90° corner. Cut out the shape of each side, then drill three vent holes near the top of each.

④ To assemble the nest box, nail the sides to the back with galvanized finishing nails placed about 4" apart. To position the sides, line up the bottom end of each with the shoulders at one end of the back piece (see front view below).

⑤ Make the bottom from a small piece of two-by-three and locate it 5½" up from the bottom shoulders of the back with a ⅛" gap for drainage behind. Bevel the front edge of the bottom piece to match the angle of the front of the box and set it in at least ¾" to allow space for the front piece of the box. To measure and shape this bottom piece, do a trial fitting using a ⅛" thick piece of cardboard (or thin plywood) as a temporary spacer behind it. Cut the bevel with a saw or chisel it out then glue and nail the bottom in place through the sides. *Note: Don't forget to put the ⅛" thick temporary spacer behind the bottom block before it's nailed in place.*

FRONT VIEW

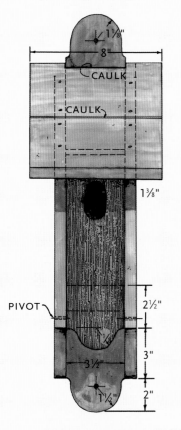

SIDE VIEW

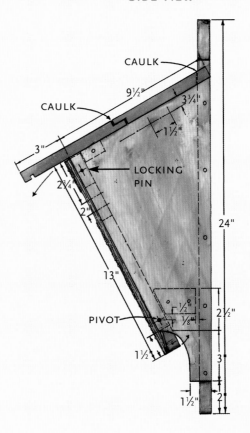

SCALE ▭▭▭▭ INCHES

6 To install the pivoting front, clamp it in place as shown in Figure 2. Note that the front face should be flush with the front edges of the sides and the top edge flush with the top of the sides. Nail the one by two front stop in place as shown. The pivots themselves are two galvanized common nails through ⅛" diameter holes drilled in the sides. To locate these holes, measure ½" down and ⅜" in from the front edge. Drill the holes (one on either side as shown) through the sides only, then drive a common nail through each hole and into the edge of the front.

7 Remove the clamps. The front of the nest box will fall forward with the "tail" coming to rest under the bottom. This will allow you easy access to the inside for inspection and cleaning. To hold the front in a closed position, drill a ⅛" diameter hole at the top of the box through either side and into the edges of the front. Use two common nails or two bent pieces of heavy wire as "locking pins" as shown in the side view.

8 Finally, to make the roof, nail two pieces of shiplap in place. The rear piece should be notched out with saw and chisel as shown in Figure 2 to fit around the back of the box which protrudes up above it. This joint must be well caulked to keep it watertight. The lap joint shown in the side view must be caulked as well. The "drip stop" under the front edge of the roof (usually cut on a table saw) is optional.

FIGURE 2

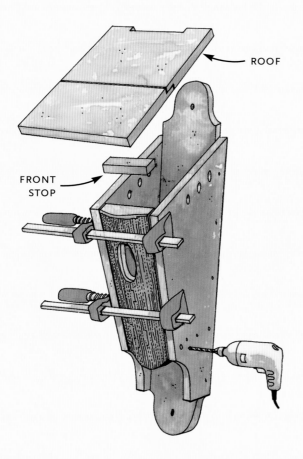

ROOF

FRONT
STOP

TURNER STYLE BLUEBIRD BOX

This simplified and improved version of the Peterson style nest box for bluebirds is made up of six pieces, one of which serves as the mounting post itself. The wood used is western red cedar which is ideal for its rot-resistant qualities.

1. Cut off the top of the post at an angle. The block should be 4" long on the front face and 2" long at the back (Figure 1).

2. Measure down 12" on the front of the post and use two 1" deep saw cuts and a chisel to make a 3¾" wide notch (Figure 1). Fit the square end of the top block into the notch and screw it in place from behind (Figure 2). Use water-resistant glue as well if you feel it's necessary.

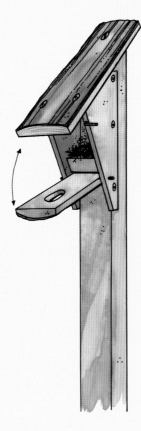

TOOLS & MATERIALS

- Skill saw and table saw
- Hammer
- Screwdriver
- Drill with ⅛" and 1⅜" diameter bits
- ¾" chisel
- Post – four by four red cedar (the post, a nominal four-byfour, actually measures 3½" square. Select one that is knot-free and 10' to 12' long.)
- Sides – ¾" red cedar 10" × 20"
- Front – cedar slab 3½" × 15"
- Roof – cedar slab 8" × 20"
- Large screw – 3" galvanized r.h.
- Regular screws (9) – 1¼" galv. f.h.
- Common nails – 1½" galvanized
- Locking pins (2) – large cup hooks

FIGURE 1   FIGURE 2

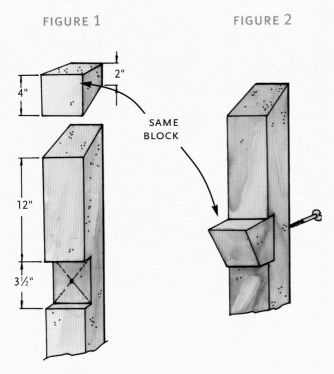

SAME BLOCK

2"
4"
12"
3½"

3 Cut two side pieces 10" × 20" as shown in the side pattern A. The angle of the front face must match that of the small block screwed into the post. Note that a "notch" is left at the top for ventilation.

4 Using a shallow red cedar slab with the bark still on, cut a front piece 3½" wide × 15" long (Figure 6). Drill two 1½" diameter round holes (one above the other) to fashion an elliptical hole for the entrance, making the bottom of it 6" above the floor.

5 To assemble the nest box, screw or nail the sides to the post (Figures 3 and 5). The sides lap the post by 1½" and the top edge of the sides must be flush with the angle at the top of the post so the roof will sit flat (Figure 5).

6 Now position the pivots so the front of the nest box will open flat for cleaning (Figure 5). Drill a ⅛" diameter pilot hole through each side, ¾" from the front edge and ¼" below the bottom corner of the small angled block (Figure 5). Now put the front piece in place

FIGURE 3

FIGURE 4

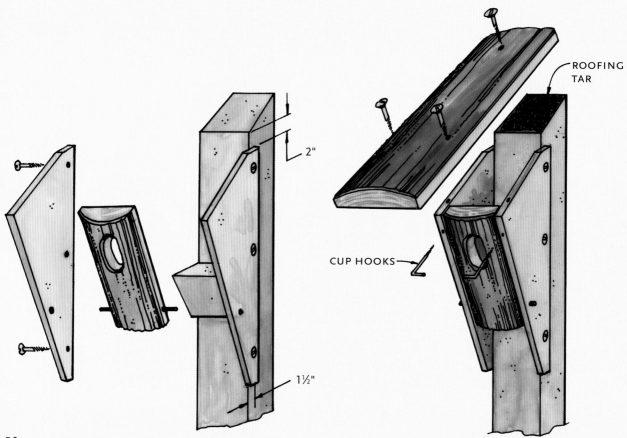

2"

1½"

ROOFING TAR

CUP HOOKS

and with the top ⅛" below the top edge of the sides, drill through the pilot holes into the edges of the front piece. Now drive metal pivot pins through these holes into the front piece. The pivot pins can be common or finishing nails or simply short pieces of heavy wire. The bottom end of the front piece should now swing under the small angled block when the box is opened (Figure 5). To hold the front piece upright (in the closed position) screw a pair of cup hooks into the edges of the sides near the top (Figure 4).

7 Finally, cut a shallow cedar slab 8" wide by 20" long for the roof. Nail it in place over the end of the post and the sides of the nest box. It's a good idea to liberally coat the end of the post with roofing tar (Figure 4).

8 In your selected garden location, dig a hole in the ground to sink the end of the four-by-four post at least 3' deep. Pack gravel and earth (or better, pour concrete) around the post until it is solid.

FIGURE 5
**PATTERN A
(SIDE — MAKE TWO)**

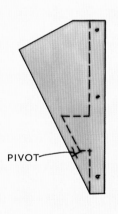

PIVOT

FIGURE 6
**PATTERN B
(FRONT)**

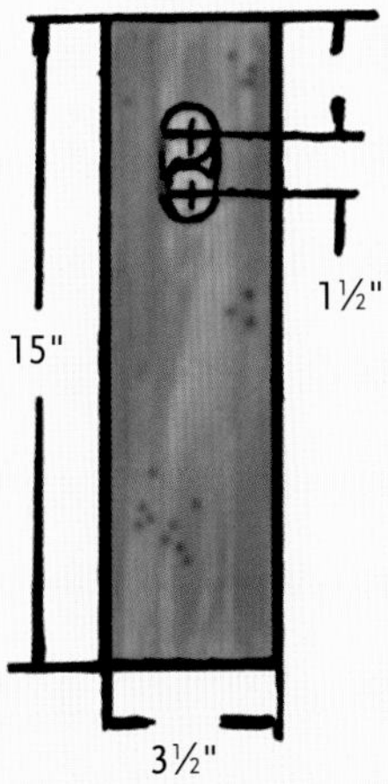

15"

1½"

3½"

FIGURE 7
**SECTIONAL VIEW
(SIDE VIEW)**

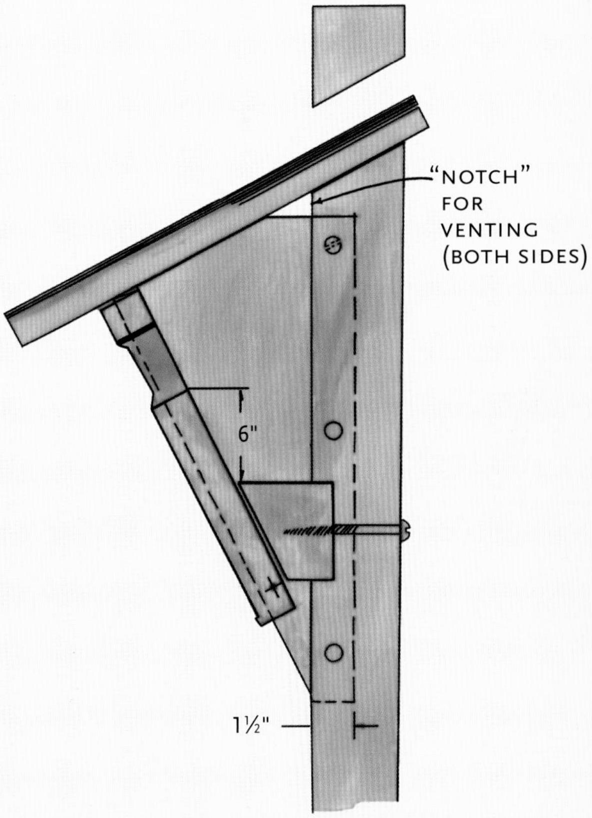

"NOTCH"
FOR
VENTING
(BOTH SIDES)

6"

1½"

PROJECT 11

— BASIC SWALLOW NEST BOX —

One of the easiest birds to attract to most yards is the swallow. There are several species common to most parts of North America, with the violet green swallow and the tree swallow being the two species that will use a nest box. Once an adult pair establishes themselves, it is common for them to return to the same box the following year. It's great fun to watch each swallow pair fly back and forth with nesting material to set up house, then to observe them as they rear their young.

Swallows need clear, open space around their nest boxes, and because they feed on insects during flight, they also like proximity to water such as a creek, wetland, or pond. You can mount the nest box on a post, bare tree trunk, or on the wall of a building up under the eaves, placing it at least six feet off the ground.

Building a nest box for swallows is easy: just cut out six pieces of ⅜" or ½" thick red cedar to the dimensions shown, then nail them together in the sequence described below. The front of the box is pivoted at the top so you can open the box to clean it at the end of each season.

1. Cut out the six pieces of the nest box to the sizes shown in the materials list.
2. Cut the four corners of the bottom piece off at 45 degree angles.
3. Measure two inches down from the top of one edge of each side piece, draw a line from that point to the top back corner and cut the angle that the top will rest upon.
4. Drill a row of three ¼" diameter vent holes about 1" down from the top of each side.
5. Measure 5" up from the bottom of the back piece, draw a line across, then nail the bottom piece on at that line.
6. Drill three or four ⅛" diameter pilot holes through the back piece below the bottom as shown for mounting on a post or wall.
7. Nail the sides to the back and bottom.
8. Hold the front in place, measure 4" to 6" up from the bottom on the inside of the front to locate the bottom of the entry hole. Drill an ⅛" diameter hole 1" down from the top front corner of both sides; through the sides, into the edges of the front for the pivot nails.
9. Drill the entry hole through the front piece.

10 Hold the front in place again, and hammer the pivot nails through each side into the edges of the front piece.

11 Nail the roof to the back and sides (be sure the roof is flush with the back and that it overhangs equally on either side).

SECTION

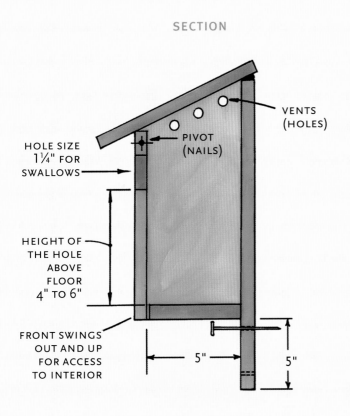

VENTS (HOLES)

PIVOT (NAILS)

HOLE SIZE 1¼" FOR SWALLOWS

HEIGHT OF THE HOLE ABOVE FLOOR 4" TO 6"

FRONT SWINGS OUT AND UP FOR ACCESS TO INTERIOR

5"

5"

FRONT

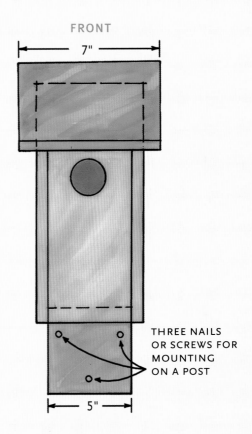

7"

THREE NAILS OR SCREWS FOR MOUNTING ON A POST

5"

BOTTOM

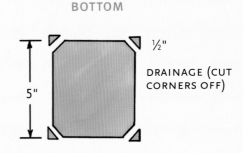

½"

DRAINAGE (CUT CORNERS OFF)

5"

Bird Nests

In these days of spring, materials, infinitely varied, are being employed in the construction of birds' nests. The time-honored twigs and hairs and rootlets, mosses and feathers, are being supplemented with a surprising number of modern odds and ends.

Not far from here, a wood thrush incorporated an empty Camel cigarette package in the side of her nest. Another wood thrush made use of torn-up bus tickets and a third, nesting near a refreshment stand in an Indiana park, collected discarded pop bottle straws. At Darby, Pennsylvania, a starling added a one dollar bill to its nest and, in a number of instances, English sparrows have made use of cigarette stubs. Small nails, carried from a building project to a birdhouse, formed the steel nest of a house wren.

Edwin Way Teale – Circle of the Seasons, 1953

land clearings, hedgerows, and brushy pasture; may visit a feeder during migration; offer millet, chopped nutmeats, and canary seed.

Bushtit: elaborate hanging nests found in open oak and pinyon-junipers, shrubby borders, and mixed woodlands; flocks seen in heavily planted yards; feeds on insects, suet, suet mixes, peanut butter, sunflower seeds, nutmeats.

Cardinal, Northern: will nest in shrubs and small trees; prefers yards with fruit trees and seed-bearing trees and shrubs, as well as open areas; will take sunflower seeds, nutmeats, and suet from tray or platform feeders and from the ground.

Catbird, Gray: nests in thickets close to the ground; attracted to birdbaths; will eat steamed raisins and cooked breakfast cereal; may eat moistened grains and seeds.

Chickadee, Black-capped: will nest in bird houses and snags; particularly enjoys suet and suet mixes, sunflower seeds, and nutmeats from a variety of feeders; may visit year-round.

Chickadee, Carolina: will nest in bird houses and snags; particularly enjoys suet and suet mixes, sunflower seeds, and nutmeats from a variety of feeders; may visit year-round.

Chickadee, Chestnut-backed: see Black-capped Chickadee.

Chickadee, Mountain: see Black-capped Chickadee.

Cowbird, Brown-headed: lays eggs in nests of other birds; will feed on nearly anything from any type of feeder. *Note:* Because cowbirds are parasitic nesters they are considered "undesirable" by many people. They lay their eggs in other birds' nests and allow these foster parents to raise their voracious young. Nestlings of the parasitized birds may be smothered or killed by the cowbird nestlings. These birds are not generally encouraged at feeders but most bird lovers do not discourage cowbirds as actively as they do house sparrows and starlings.

Creeper, Brown: will use artificial nests or loose bark low on a tree; needs mature trees in your yard to be induced to visit; will eat suet smeared on trees.

Crow, American: generally nests in the tops of evergreen trees; will

Western bluebird with prey.

eat almost anything, particularly cracked corn, mixed seed, and sunflower seeds from a platform feeder or from the ground. May deter small songbirds. Consider neighbors if you enjoy crows, as these birds can be noisy and messy, especially in numbers.

Dickcissel: nests in open weedy meadows and grain fields; will eat seeds and grain from feeders.

Dove, Ground: will nest on fence posts, branches, in brush, and on ground; prefers seeds, grains, and berries.

Dove, Mourning: will nest on ledges or conifer branches; prefers ground feeding on seeds and grains; will use birdbaths for drinking and preening.

Dove, Rock: nests on ledges around bridges and buildings; will take seed, grain, peanuts, bakery goods, and various other tidbits. *Note:* Rock doves are imports. They may begin to overwhelm your feeders or endanger native birds. Refrain from table feeding until they move on unless you enjoy this species which is easily enticed to urban balconies; be considerate of neighbors as Rock doves are messy!

Finch, House: very flexible nesting habits; will nest in hanging baskets, in nooks, on ledges; offer seed mixes, particularly sunflower and niger thistle; will drink from nectar feeders; will use birdbaths.

Finch, Purple: nests in conifers or mixed woods; attracted to trees and shrubs that offer seeds; hanging feeders stocked with sunflower seeds, mixed seed, niger thistle, and nutmeats.

Flicker, Northern: will nest in bird houses and snags; attracted to bird feeders; will forage for ants on lawns; will also eat suet, cracked corn, and nutmeats.

Goldfinch, American: nests mainly in brushy fields, forest openings; seen at hanging feeders stocked with sunflower seeds, niger thistle; also attracted to seed heads of flowers in the garden as well as to grasses, trees, and shrubs that offer seeds; easily drawn to baths and drips.

Grackle, Common: prefers to nest in evergreens; likes

Mountain bluebird.

Friend of the Killdeer

A pair of killdeer nested this spring in a coal yard a mile or so from here. One of the workmen took a special interest in the welfare of the birds. He protected the nest. He kept everyone away as the time of hatching drew near. Once the baby birds appeared, he devoted himself to keeping the little family together. He was unaware that young killdeer can run almost the moment they step from the egg and that they normally scatter and hide for safety. He thought the little birds were getting lost and tried to put them all back in the nest again. Around and around the coal yard he ran in pursuit of the fleet-footed chicks. They hid behind pieces of coal. They scuttled this way, darted that. At the end of the day, their benefactor was worn out and thoroughly convinced that the family was irretrievably scattered and lost.

Edwin Way Teale – Circle of the Seasons, 1953

12

— WREN HOUSE —

TOOLS & MATERIALS

- Band saw
- Drill with ⅛" and 1" diameter bits
- Hammer
- Two strap clamps
- Small hardwood log – 6" to 8" diameter minimum
- Two pieces of ½" red cedar – to suit the size of the log
- ½" or ¾" square fir – length to suit the inside of the hollowed log
- Galvanized common nails – 1½" long
- Picture or baling wire

This unique nest box for wrens is designed to blend in with the natural surroundings when it is hung from a branch or a roof overhang. This project requires a band saw, but if you don't have access to one, perhaps a woodworking friend would make the cuts for you.

1 Find a small, preferably hardwood log, 6" to 8" in diameter and at least 8" to 9" long. Select a section with interesting burls or branch stubs and saw the widest end flat.

2 Make two saw cuts as shown in Figure 1 to form a peak about 6" high.

3 Use a band saw to cut out the center of the log, leaving a minimum of ¾" thick walls.

FIGURE 1

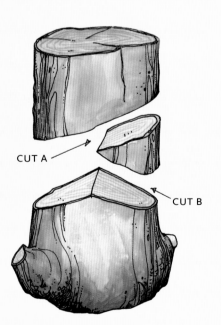

CUT A

CUT B

FIGURE 2

TOP VIEW

START BANDSAW CUT HERE

FIGURE 3

SCRAP (REMOVE)

BOTTOM

Remove the wood from the center and cut off a ¾" thick slice to form the bottom of the wren house (Figure 3).

4. For house wrens drill a 1" diameter entry hole (1¼" for Bewick's wrens) centered 6" up from the bottom of the log.

5. Glue the sides and the bottom back together with the help of strap clamps, available at most hardware stores (Figure 4).

6. Suspend the wren house with two wires attached to a ridgepole nailed inside the hollowed log right at the peak. Cut a piece of ½" or ¾" square fir just long enough to fit snugly inside the opening (Figure 6). Drill two ⅛" diameter holes through the ridgepole 4" apart through which the wires will be threaded (Figure 5). Nail this ridgepole in place as shown in Figure 5.

7. Cut two pieces of ½" thick western red cedar for the roof. These should be just large enough to overhang the log by 1" in all directions.

8. Bevel one edge of each to match the angle at the top so the roof will lie flat. Glue and nail these roof pieces together as shown in Figure 6. Do not attach them to the log.

9. Drill two holes through the peak of the roof 4" apart and thread a wire down through one hole in the roof, through the ridgepole, and back up through the pole and roof again.

10. Suspend the wren house from the wires and slide the roof up and down the wires when you need to clean or check the inside.

FIGURE 4

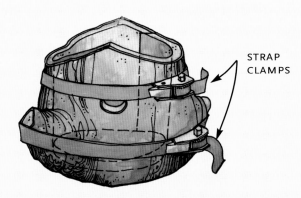

STRAP CLAMPS

FIGURE 5

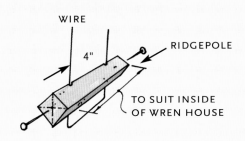

WIRE

4"

RIDGEPOLE

TO SUIT INSIDE OF WREN HOUSE

FIGURE 6

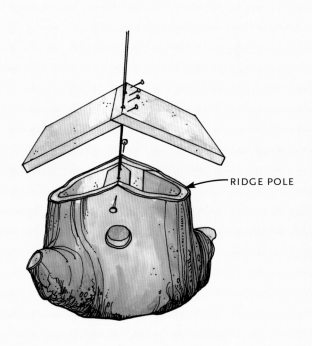

RIDGE POLE

BARN OWL NEST BOX

This nest box is large and spacious inside, and has a relatively large entrance hole (6" × 6"). It can be made with ½" plywood glued and nailed together with a removable front.

TOOLS & MATERIALS

- Table saw or skill saw and jigsaw
- Electric drill with 2" diameter hole saw and ½" diameter bit
- Hammer
- ½" exterior grade fir plywood
- Bottom – 21" × 22"
- Roof – 22" × 23"
- Back – 15½" × 21"
- Sides (2) – 22" × 15½" (at the back) and 18½" (at the front)
- Front – 18" × 22"
- ¾" × 1½" fir
- Two vertical battens, 18"
- One horizontal batten, 19½" long

1 To make the box, cut out six pieces of plywood to the dimensions shown. Note that the two side pieces are higher at the front by three inches so the roof will slope back to shed rain.

2 Drill at least six to eight ½" diameter drain holes along each side of the bottom, at least 1" from the edge. Drill another six to eight drain holes randomly spaced over the rest of the bottom piece. Nail the back to the bottom, then add the sides, then the roof.

3 Glue and nail a vertical ¾" × ½" batten on the flat at either side of the opening, then another across the top (shown below).

4 Nail two hooks (to latch the front in place) on either side of the opening

on the outside of the box as shown below.

5 Mark out a 6" square, centered in the front (or a circle 6" in diameter), 5" from the bottom edge, with a 2" diameter hole.

6 Saw a hole at each corner, then cut out the opening with a jigsaw. Fit this piece over the front of the box and drive four common nails into the edges to line up with the hooks.

7 You can paint the outside of the box with dark enamel to prolong the life of the plywood. Also, to help the box blend in with natural surroundings, nail strips or slabs of bark to the outside. Make sure the nails don't penetrate to the inside of the box and keep the hooks outside of the bark.

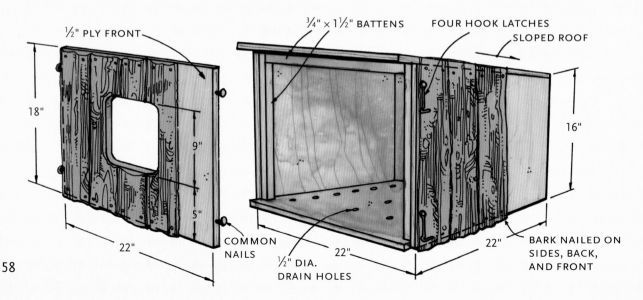

½" PLY FRONT

18"

9"

5"

22"

COMMON NAILS

½" DIA. DRAIN HOLES

¾" × 1½" BATTENS   FOUR HOOK LATCHES

SLOPED ROOF

16"

22"

BARK NAILED ON SIDES, BACK, AND FRONT

22"

Hairy woodpecker eating suet.

ground feeders; offer seeds, crackers; will wash food in a birdbath.

Grosbeak, Black-headed: nests in trees or shrubs; eats sunflower seeds and pieces of fruit from feeders.

Grosbeak, Evening: will nest in forks of trees; attracted to well-planted yards with lots of fruit and seed trees; offer sunflower seeds in a hanging feeder.

Grosbeak, Rose-breasted: fondness for nesting in densely planted gardens; offer food year-round, especially sunflower seeds, mixed seeds, melon seeds and suet; attracted to water.

Jay, Blue: will nest in evergreen shrubs and short trees in yards; a lively presence at feeders preferring sunflower seeds, nutmeats, acorns, and suet from ground feeders; may eat nestlings of other birds.

Jay, Scrub: see Blue Jay.

Jay, Steller's: prefers to nest in conifers; will take seed, fruit, berries, peanuts, and suet from nearly any type of feeder; favors acorns and hazelnuts right from the tree; may eat nestlings of other birds.

Junco, Dark-eyed: nests on, or near, ground at edges, preferably close to water; brush piles for shelter; ground feeders who prefer seeds and nutmeats.

Kestrel, American: will nest in cavities in trees (should be at least 15 feet from ground), on buildings, and in nest boxes; feeds on small birds, reptiles and mammals, and insects.

Killdeer: will nest on the ground or a flat rooftop covered in gravel; feeds on insects, worms, and grubs.

Kinglet, Golden-crowned: nests in shrubs and trees but not often near human habitation; is an insect eater; may take suet, peanut butter.

Kinglet, Ruby-crowned: nests in shrubs and trees but not often near human habitation; insectivorous but may visit suet feeders with chopped nutmeats or fruit.

Martin, Purple: in the East, compartment nest boxes need open landscape with trees in the vicinity, while in the West, the birds nest in

Nests in November

Falling leaves have revealed secrets hidden behind the summer foliage. Now I know where the crows nested in the tupelos across the swamp. Now I know from which upper branch the oriole's nest was slung in one of the garden maples. These nests, appearing one by one, have set my mind running back over some of the unusual places I recall where birds have nested and raised their broods.

There was an Eastern phoebe that brought grass and hair and moss and formed her nest on the top of an electric light socket. And some time ago, when a bell at a Catholic church, in Troy, New York, began tolling steadily, it was discovered that a bird's nest had been built across the relay points in the control box, closing the circuit and starting the bell ringing.

Edwin Way Teale – Circle of the Seasons, 1953

— PURPLE MARTIN HOUSE —

TOOLS & MATERIALS

- Table saw or skill saw and jigsaw
- Hammer
- Screwdriver
- Pliers
- Front – ½" plywood (16" × 20")
- Back – ½" plywood (16" × 23")
- Sides (2) – ½" plywood (each 7" × 23")
- Bottoms (3) – ⅝" plywood, each 6" square
- Roof – fir or cedar slab with bark attached 8" × 8"
- Mounting blocks (2) – 1½" × 7" × 7" fir
- Perches – coat hanger wire
- Pivots (common nails) – 2½" long (galvanized)
- Finishing nails – 1½" long (galvanized)
- Water-resistant glue

Because the purple martin is known to be a gregarious species in eastern North America, building a house for one family can mean building a house for dozens of birds (see Note on page 63). The following design is made up of four three-family units fastened together. It should be mounted high on a pole using a system of pulleys which will allow the whole community of nest boxes to be raised and lowered for cleaning.

1. To make each of the three-family units, cut out backs, sides, fronts, and three bottoms to the dimensions shown (Figure 1).

2. Cut back the very top corner of the sides as shown to provide ventilation. Cut back the four corners of each of the bottoms as shown to provide drainage and ventilation from below.

3. The interior height of the three nesting areas should be 6" clear. Mark out the locations of the three bottoms on the back piece, then nail them in place from behind.

4. Glue and nail the sides in place.

5. Mark out the location (thickness) of each "bottom" on the front piece and, measuring 1" up from the top surface of each, mark the lowest point of the entry holes. These holes are 2" to 2½" in diameter (Figure 2).

6. On either side of the holes and 1" below the lowest point of each, drill two ¹⁄₁₆" diameter holes 4" apart. These will hold the ends of the wire perch.

7. To make each perch, bend a 9" long piece of coat hanger wire 2½" from each end and hammer it into the ¹⁄₁₆" diameter holes in the plywood until the ends are flush with the inside face. Be very sure the ends of the wire don't protrude into the box!

8. Lay the front piece in place between the sides, flush with the bottom. Drill a ⅛" diameter hole through each side and into the edges of the front piece ¾" down from the top.

9. Drive a galvanized common nail into each side to form a pivot (Figure 1).

10. Drill another hole ⅛" in diameter, 1¼" up from the bottom of each side and ¼" from the front edge to allow you to push in a bent piece of heavy wire to hold the front shut (Figure 1).

11. To finish the nest box, make a roof by nailing a thin slab of cedar or fir to the top edges of the back and sides only. This slab should overlap the sides by ½" and the front by at least 1".

12. Make three more of these boxes.

FIGURE 1

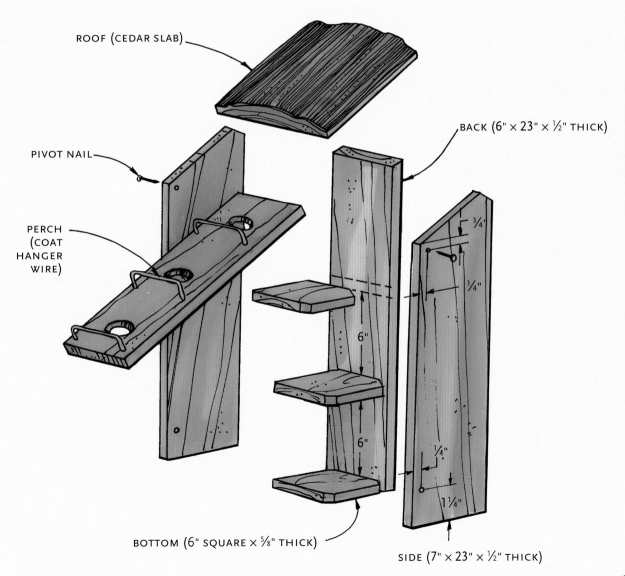

ROOF (CEDAR SLAB)

BACK (6" × 23" × ½" THICK)

PIVOT NAIL

PERCH (COAT HANGER WIRE)

¾"

¼"

6"

6"

¼"

1¼"

BOTTOM (6" SQUARE × ⅝" THICK)

SIDE (7" × 23" × ½" THICK)

13 Using a two by eight plank, cut two pieces, 7" square. Using a jigsaw, cut a 3⅜" diameter hole in the center of each (Figure 3).

14 Drill two 1" diameter holes opposite each other on the edge of the large hole (Figure 3).

15 Working from inside each nest box, drill and screw through the back into each block (two screws in each), spacing them 13" apart vertically (Figure 4).

Repeat this until all four boxes are clustered together.

16 Note that a 45 degree corner will have to be trimmed from the inside corners of each roof to get them to fit (Figure 4).

17 The ideal pole for mounting this collection of nest boxes is a 3" diameter galvanized pipe set at least 3' into the ground, preferably in concrete.

FIGURE 2

FIGURE 3

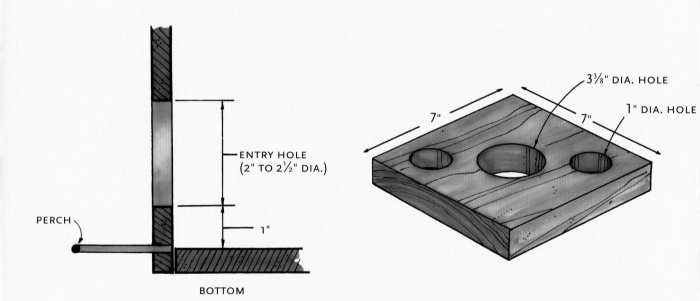

ENTRY HOLE
(2" TO 2½" DIA.)

1"

PERCH

BOTTOM

3⅜" DIA. HOLE

1" DIA. HOLE

7"

7"

18 A heavy metal strap welded to the top of the pole (as shown on page 60) will allow you to attach two pulleys with shackles.

19 Put two screw-eyes into the top block between the nesting units (Figure 5) and tie a ½" diameter rope to each. Thread the ropes through the pulleys and down through both 7" square mounting blocks to the ground.

20 Weld or bolt cleats near the base of the pole (Figure 6) to provide a place to tie the ropes off when the purple martin nest boxes are raised.

Note: On the west coast of Canada and the U.S., purple martins have not shown any inclination to apartment dwell. They have successfully nested in individual boxes though, placed 5 to a piling along the waterfront with approximately 25 boxes per site.

FIGURE 4

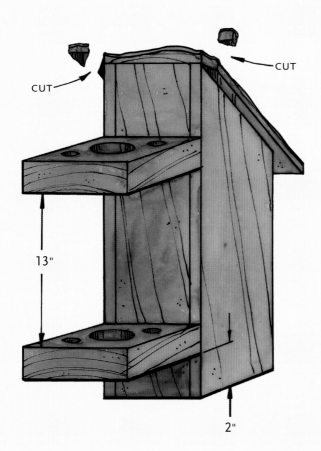

CUT

CUT

13"

2"

FIGURE 5

FIGURE 6

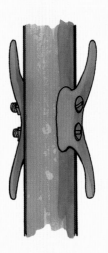

Purple Martins

Too many insects in town? That was the case in Griggsville, Illinois in the early Sixties. The town of 1200, situated between the Mississippi and Illinois rivers, implemented an insect-abatement program using birds, rather than pesticides, to beat the bugs. When a conservationist named J.L. Wade suggested they attempt to entice purple martins—whose diet is strictly flying insects—in large numbers, a local service club took on the challenge.

As the species had also shown an inclination to nest in man-made apartment boxes in and around towns, consultation with ornithologists and naturalists arrived at a unique two-storey, twelve-compartment bird box engineered of aluminum. Ten degrees cooler than wooden nest boxes, and safer than the gourds used in southern states, the aluminum houses were maintenance-free, did not harbor parasites, and repelled starlings with their shine. Starting with twelve boxes mounted on telescopic poles along the main street (a.k.a. Purple Martin Boulevard), the town now sports forty on the same street, plus another forty at Purple Martin Junction; there is also a tower with six hundred nesting compartments at the town center and several individual colonies throughout the area.

In any given spring, the majority of these boxes are occupied; the rivers, ponds, and sloughs all supply food for adults and young. Griggsville is commonly referred to as the "Purple Martin Capital of the Nation" and has sparked martin societies and landlordship across the United States and Canada.

groups of single boxes near water; may accept crushed eggshells below a house they are inhabiting; insectivorous.

Mockingbird, Northern: nests in shrubs; male needs a territory of one to two acres; prefers trees and shrubs with berries, as well as feeders stocked with berries; will take soaked raisins, sliced apples and oranges, suet, and peanut butter; may become territorial over fruit or berry-producing shrubs and keep other birds from the entire area.

Nuthatch, Red-breasted: nests in tree cavities, will use nest boxes; usually visits in winter; eats at feeders that provide suet (best against tree trunks), nutmeats, sunflower seeds.

Red-breasted nuthatch.

Nuthatch, White-breasted: nests in tree cavities, will use nest boxes; eats at feeders with nuts, suet, sunflower seeds; likes oaks and other deciduous trees.

Oriole, Hooded: nests in tall deciduous trees often in residential areas; visits nectar flowers and nectar feeders; offer fresh fruit in feeders.

Oriole, Northern: may nest in backyard trees; visits feeders offering most standard bird food, especially soaked raisins, apple and orange halves, millet, suet, and sugar solution from nectar feeders.

Oriole, Orchard: found in suburban shade trees, in orchards and in creekside groves; sugar solution in hummingbird feeders, fruit in feeders.

Owl, Common Barn: will nest in building cavities and in nest boxes; feeds mainly on rodents.

Owl, Eastern Screech: will nest in cavities, including nest boxes; feeds on rodents.

Pheasant, Ring-necked: will take grains, seed, and cracked corn sprinkled on the ground.

Phoebe, Black: will use nesting shelves or sides of buildings; likes water; insectivorous.

Phoebe, Eastern: will use nesting shelves; may occasionally visit feeders for tidbits.

Quail, California: will feed from the ground on all kinds of grain, grasses, berries, grapes, acorns; enjoys ground-level birdbaths.

Redpoll, Common: nests only in subarctic and tundra; winter feeds from hang-

Tree swallow young.

ing or ground feeders; prefers sunflower seeds and niger thistle as well as suet and nutmeats.

Robin, American: nests in trees, nest boxes, or shelves; forages in lawns for earthworms; feeds from wild and cultivated plants that bear fruit and berries; uses feeders only in dire circumstances for soaked raisins, suet, and bread crumbs; birdbaths for bathing and drinking.

Sapsucker, Red-breasted: nests in tree cavities; feeds on sap and insects; may take pieces of apple, or cut-up cherries and strawberries at a feeder, as well as mixed seed, suet, and nutmeats; feeds at trees and shrubs that produce fruits and berries.

Sapsucker, Yellow-bellied: see Red-breasted Sapsucker.

Siskin, Pine: builds nest in low-hanging conifer branches; feeds from both hanging and ground feeders stocked with sunflower seeds and niger thistle, suet, nutmeats and finely cracked corn; feeds on seed from tall weeds, and seeds of trees.

Sparrow, American Tree: nests in the Arctic; ground or tray feeders; forages for weed seeds; will eat millets, finely

ROOSTING BOX

TOOLS & MATERIALS

- Table saw, skill saw, or jigsaw
- Hammer
- Screwdriver
- Electric drill with $\frac{1}{8}$", $\frac{3}{8}$", and $2\frac{1}{2}$" diameter bits
- Bottom – $\frac{3}{4}$" plywood, $7\frac{1}{2}$" × 9"
- Back – $\frac{1}{2}$" plywood, 9" × 13"
- Sides (2) – $\frac{1}{2}$" plywood, 8" × 13" (sloped toward the front to a height of 11")
- Front – $\frac{1}{2}$" plywood, 10" × 13"
- Hinge batten – $\frac{3}{4}$" × $1\frac{1}{2}$" × 9" long piece of fir or other wood
- Roof – cedar slab, 12" × 12"
- Perch – $\frac{3}{8}$" hardwood dowel, $2\frac{1}{2}$" long
- Roosting dowels (3) – $\frac{3}{8}$" diameter hardwood, 10" long each

1 This box is simple to make using $\frac{1}{2}$" plywood for the back and sides, nailed to a $\frac{3}{4}$" plywood bottom measuring $7\frac{1}{2}$" × 9". Drill $\frac{3}{8}$" diameter holes through the sides at the locations shown in Figure 1 to receive the three roosting dowels (which are glued in place).

FIGURE 1

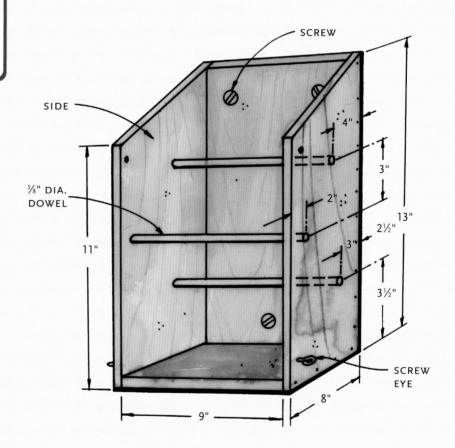

SCREW

SIDE

$\frac{3}{8}$" DIA. DOWEL

11"

4"

3"

2"

13"

$2\frac{1}{2}$"

3"

$3\frac{1}{2}$"

SCREW EYE

9"

8"

2 Attach the box to a tree, post, or the side of a building using screws through the back on the inside.

3 The hinge at the top will allow you to open the box and clean it (Figure 3).

4 Locate the access hole and perch in the front as shown (Figure 2).

5 To form a sloping roof, add a slab of cedar with the bark on. It's a good idea to put a bead of caulking on the back and sides where they meet the roof to prevent rain from penetrating and running down the walls. The roof should overhang the box by several inches at the front and at least an inch over the sides.

FIGURE 2

FIGURE 3

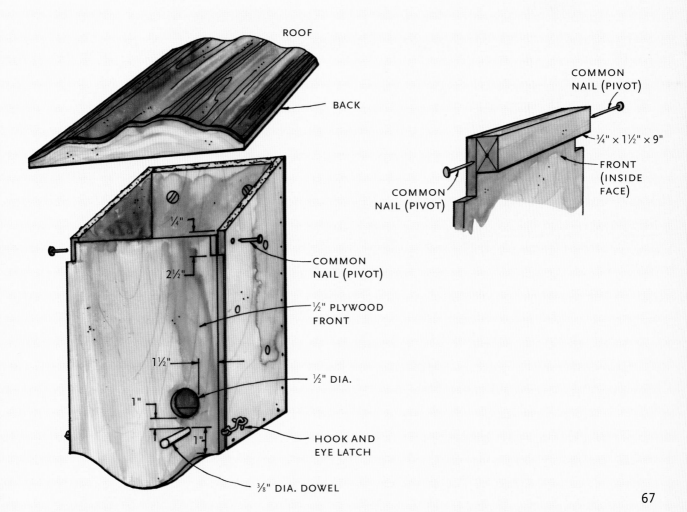

ROOF

BACK

COMMON NAIL (PIVOT)

¾" × 1½" × 9"

FRONT (INSIDE FACE)

COMMON NAIL (PIVOT)

¼"

COMMON NAIL (PIVOT)

2½"

½" PLYWOOD FRONT

1½"

½" DIA.

1"

1"

HOOK AND EYE LATCH

⅜" DIA. DOWEL

NESTING SHELF

TOOLS & MATERIALS

- Table saw or jigsaw
- Hammer
- Screwdriver
- Electric drill with ⅛" diameter pilot bit
- Platform – ½" plywood, 6" to 8" square
- Back – ½" plywood, 6" to 8" × 12"
- Angle bracket – ½" plywood, 4" × 6" triangle
- Side – ½" plywood, 6" × 6" triangle
- Top (roof) – ½" plywood, 6" or 8" × 8"

For those birds that will not nest within a confined space, all that is needed is a small open platform attached high up a wall or under the eave of a building. This platform need only be 6" square for swallows and phoebes or 8" for robins. To allow such a platform to be removed for the winter (for cleaning and to prevent decay), nail it to a backboard as shown, with an angled bracket below.

To protect the nest from prevailing side winds, add a side piece. You can also add a roof if necessary. As long as the platform retains an open feeling, birds will use it for nesting.

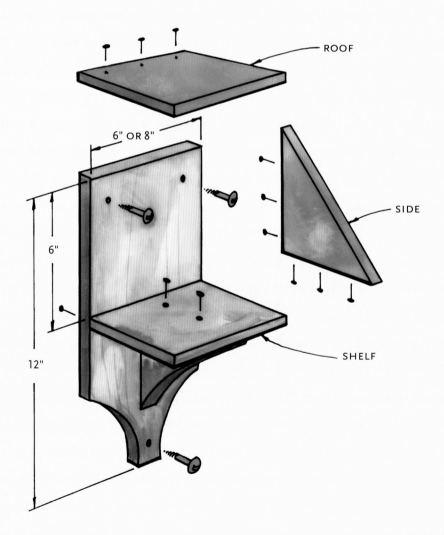

ROOF

6" OR 8"

SIDE

6"

SHELF

12"

17

FIGURE 1

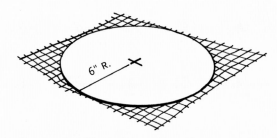

6" R.

TOOLS & MATERIALS
- Drawing compass
- Heavy scissors
- Pliers
- Cardboard – 12" × 12"
- Hardware cloth – 12" × 12"

FIGURE 2

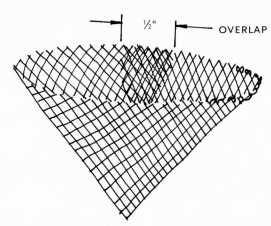

½" ◄── OVERLAP

1. Using a compass, draw a 12" diameter circle on a piece of cardboard.

2. Use the cardboard pattern to cut out a circle from a 12" square of ⅜" hardware cloth (Figure 1).

3. Make a cut from the outside of the circle to the center to allow the hardware cloth to overlap into a cone (Figure 2). Bend the rough wire ends into the mesh to hold the conical shape.

4. Using wire or nails, secure the cone to the branches of a tree, keeping it out of the way of predators (Figure 3).

FIGURE 3

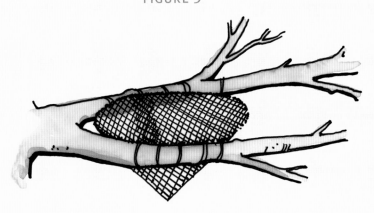

Barn swallow.

cracked corn, canary seed, may eat striped sunflower seeds.

Sparrow, Chipping: prefers conifers for nesting; ground feeder who takes most food that falls from hanging feeders.

Sparrow, Fox: omnivorous ground feeders on a mix of seeds, berries, and insects; will eat millets, finely cracked corn, canary seed from ground or tray feeders.

Sparrow, Golden-crowned: nests near timberline at higher elevations, also streamside thickets and bogs; ground feeder who prefers mixed seeds; may also eat flowers and buds.

Sparrow, House (English): almost any cavity will suffice for nesting, such as tree holes, nest boxes, building crevices, or even tree branches; prefers millet, bakery crumbs, kitchen scraps, sunflower seeds from ground or platform feeders; dislikes hanging feeders. *Note:* House sparrows are not popular at most feeders and nest boxes. They may bully native birds and keep them away, as well as pecking to death or dislodging nestlings. After a positive identification, house sparrow eggs can be removed from nest boxes to prevent the birds from taking up residence. People who have only a balcony or window ledge to offer may wish to encourage house sparrows, but people who can attract a greater variety of birds may not.

Sparrow, Song: may nest in yards with dense shrubbery; ground or tray feeders; will eat millet, canary seed, finely cracked corn.

Sparrow, White-crowned: grassy open

places and shrubby cover are nesting essentials; builds nest on, or near, ground but will occasionally nest in small trees; ground feeders on mixed seed preferring peanut kernels and hulled sunflower seeds.

Sparrow, White-throated: nests on, or near, the ground under dense thickets, along edges; ground feeders on mixed seed preferring finely cracked corn and red millet.

Starling, European: will nest in almost any cavity or on ledges; nearly any feeder they can access that offers suet, millet, nutmeats, or sunflower seeds; voracious eaters of insects; fruit from shrubs and trees. *Note:* Starlings are imports. They are aggressive and adaptable enough to take over feeders and nest boxes intended for other birds. Nest box holes smaller than 1½" in diameter will prevent starlings from taking up residence. If they are monopolizing your feeders, try adding more feeders so other birds have a chance, or stop feeding for a short time. Starlings are discouraged by swinging feeders and shiny objects.

Swallow, Barn: nests on or near buildings; insectivorous.

Swallow, Tree: nests in tree cavities, bird houses (should be more than one in close proximity); may eat the fruit of bayberry shrubs and occasionally other small fruits.

Swallow, Violet-green: uses bird houses; prefers areas with housing, wires for perching; prefers fields or large lawns close to bodies of water for insect hunting.

Swift, Chimney: nests in chimneys; strictly insectivorous.

Tanager, Scarlet: nests on branches, preferably in oak trees; may take fruit from platform feeders; will feed on sugar-water solutions.

Tanager, Summer: nests in dense woodlands; may visit feeders for fresh fruit, raisins, suet, and nutmeats.

Tanager, Western: nests on branches above five feet; eats fresh fruit, raisins, suet from a platform feeder.

Thrasher, Brown: nests in shrubs; uses feeders on or near ground; prefers seeds, grains, nutmeats, and halved oranges; particularly enjoys fruit directly from shrubs and trees.

House sparrow.

Barn Swallows

A coastal family was hired to build a shed on floats and tow it by boat to a logging camp. A week after the walls were up, barn swallows began to build. Making trip after trip with mud in their beaks, they constructed their cup-shaped nest under the eaves. The family never thought to dissuade the birds. When it was time to move the shed, there appeared to be eggs in the nest – one adult bird was usually peaking over the edge of the mud cup and the birds took turns flying in and out. The idea of removing and relocating the nest didn't seem reasonable. As the shed delivery was already late, the family hooked up the towline and left the harbor. From the boat they could see the swallows behind them, flying around the shed, and swooping up under the eaves. After ten hours of travel up the inlet, the family arrived at the logging camp, shed and birds in tow. An unexpected change of scenery for the swallows!

The Flocking Birds

Ten thousand tree swallows, at least, swirl and sweep and drift like clouds of smoke as we follow the Jones Beach parkway to Captree today. Beyond the Tobay sanctuary, two hundred or more black-crowned night herons mill about over the tree tops. Everywhere the flocks are growing. Everywhere the birds are slipping away by day and by night. During these weeks, species after species, flock after flock, fare forth in the great adventure of fall.

The swallow flocks are loosely knit. They have none of the compact, disciplined movement of the shorebirds. The swallows fly wildly, unpredictably, feeding as they go. One flock sweeps low around us. For a moment, we are engulfed by dodging, skimming swallows. Electric in the air is the excitement of the migrants. We watch the birds that will never know a winter, moving away down the island, heading for the Jersey coast and the long Atlantic flyway to the south. We watch them with emotions tinged with envy. How free they seem, how fortunate! Part of the fascination that surrounds the southbound flocks is the ever-recurring illusion that the traveler is leaving his troubles behind.

Edwin Way Teale – Circle of the Seasons, 1953

Thrasher, Curved-bill: nests in cactus; visits feeders and birdbaths; prefers cracked corn, milo, millet, watermelon.

Thrush, Hermit: will nest in small trees or on the ground; prefers heavily planted yards; will visit feeders stocked with pieces of fruit; uses birdbaths.

Thrush, Wood: nests in trees or shrubs; may come to yards or feeders stocked with fruit, berries; attracted to water.

Titmouse, Plain: nests in birdhouses; prefers sunflower seeds, suet.

Titmouse, Tufted: nests in tree cavities and birdhouses; will use almost any feeder with nutmeats, suet, and sunflower seeds.

Towhee, California: nests in brushland and scrub, streamside thickets, and around human habitation; ground feeders offering seeds, grains, especially sunflower seeds, millet, and cracked corn; will use birdbaths.

Towhee, Canyon: see California Towhee.

Towhee, Green-tailed: nests in underbrush and dense shrubbery; will take seeds and nutmeats, cracked corn, sunflower seeds; will take advantage of any berry-producing bushes you have, such as raspberries and blackberries; will use birdbaths.

Towhee, Rufous-sided: will nest on, or near, the ground in yards with dense shrubbery or a brush pile; will feed on the ground below feeders and amongst cover; offer sunflower seeds, mixed seeds, nutmeats.

Rufous-sided towhee.

Black-headed grosbeak pair.

Warbler, Orange-crowned: nests on, or near, the ground; visits feeders in the winter, preferring suet, suet mixes, peanut butter, and nutmeats.

Warbler, Yellow: nests in thickets, along edges, or in streamside trees; attracted to drips, fountains and birdbaths; rarely visits feeding stations.

Warbler, Yellow-rumped: prefers to nest in conifers; attracted to feeders containing suet, suet and peanut butter mixes, millet, raisins; eats wild fruits.

Waxwing, Cedar: nests in trees and shrubs; prefers fruits and berries in heavily planted yards; will eat halved apples, moistened raisins; will use a birdbath.

Woodpecker, Downy: nests in snags, nest boxes; hanging feeders offering sunflower seeds, suet, peanut butter mixes, nutmeats, baked goods, wild berries; insectivorous.

Woodpecker, Hairy: see Downy Woodpecker.

Woodpecker, Red-bellied: see Downy Woodpecker.

Woodpecker, Red-headed: nests in bird houses, snags; platform feeders with nutmeats, cracked corn, sunflower seeds.

Wren, Cactus: nests in cactus and thorny shrubs; bird feeder with suet, nutmeats, watermelon.

Wren, Carolina: will nest in cavities, nest

Crumbs

A migrant brown thrasher has spent the day in our backyard. I see it, about four P.M., under the cedar tree by the kitchen window. A bluejay has carried a crust of bread to a limb of the cedar, about six feet from the ground. Holding the bread on the limb with one foot, it pecks at it. Fragments fall to the ground. There, the brown thrasher, hopping about, dines on these crumbs from the bluejay's table.

Edwin Way Teale – Circle of the Seasons, 1953

73

boxes, hanging baskets; likes shrubs and brush piles; may take suet, nut-meats, peanut butter mixes, corn-bread during winter.

Wren, House: uses natural cavities, nest boxes, and nooks; prefers yards with lots of tangled foliage and woodpiles; suet, cornbread, white bread crumbs may attract them.

4

Hummingbirds

Hummers, as they are affectionately called, deserve a section of their own. The smallest of all birds, hummers alone are able to hover as well as fly backwards, sideways, and forward. They have the fastest heartbeat of any bird and some of the most colorful plumage. Their nests are tiny cups fashioned from plant matter and spiderweb silk, with eggs no bigger than peas. In climates that are warm year-round, they may even raise three broods in a season. Hummingbirds have tremendous nutritional requirements and can be easily enticed to our backyards and balconies if we offer what they need.

You can provide a haven for hummers for the duration of their stay. In cooler climates, spring arrival of hummingbirds coincides with the blooming of wildflowers and blossoming shrubs. This is a good time to put your feeders out. Hummers can benefit by the extra nectar until there is an abundance of flowers, and after that,

feeders are still used with great frequency. Use a combination of feeders and flowers to create the ideal habitat (see the following section on hummingbird gardens). Hummingbirds must feed approximately every 10 to 15 minutes, consuming twice their weight in nectar each day. Most of their food should come from natural sources but they will also benefit from the sugar-water solution in feeders.

The guidelines that apply to all bird feeding are even more important with hummingbirds. Consistency is essential. Once hummers are accustomed to your source of food, you have a responsibility to keep feeding them, especially during winter months. If you go on holiday, arrange for a neighbor to fill your feeder (making sure that the neighbor knows how to make the nectar solution and will be diligent about cleaning the feeder). Make sure the feeder is only filled with a nectar solution of one part sugar to four

Foxgloves attract hummingbirds.

Hummingbird

On a morning after rain, one wildlife steward and her daughter saw a rufous hummingbird dart among the flowers of a photinia shrub. They watched, fascinated, as the hummer stopped feeding, alighted in the middle of a wet, waxy leaf, and began to preen and bathe, tossing water droplets onto its back with its long beak. Again and again, the tiny bird ruffled its feathers, spraying raindrops as it shook.

parts water (instructions follow). Never use honey in your feeder as it ferments quickly and can cause a fungal infection in hummingbirds' tongues. Sugar substitutes should not be used either, as hummingbirds can starve to death if that is all they're eating. Feeders should be kept in the shade to avoid fermentation of the nectar, and cleaned every two days, or even every day in hot weather, to prevent mold from building up. Thoroughly wash the feeder with a solution of diluted vinegar each time you refill it. Use a bottle brush and pipe cleaner to get to the hard-to-reach parts.

Bees, wasps, and other insects can be a problem at hummingbird feeders. You can discourage them by placing a wire mesh bee guard at the entrance to the feeder. If finches are monopolizing your hummingbird feeder, try removing the perch.

Make sure the feeder has a red "lure" on it to attract the hummingbirds, but skip the red dye in the nectar solution; it may not be good for the birds and it isn't necessary. You'll want to keep to the recommended 1:4 proportions of sugar to water in your feeders as this ratio is closest to that found in flowers that hummingbirds frequent, according to most authorities. Too much sugar, according to some sources, can lead to fatal damage of hummingbirds' livers.

Hummingbirds are quite aggressive with one another, becoming territorial over feeders. If your feeder becomes overpopulated, hang another one out of sight of the first.

The hummingbird family, Trochilidae, contains over three hundred species, thirteen or fourteen of which regularly breed in North America with various other species occasionally coming into

18
PROJECT

A simple hummingbird feeder can be made from a plastic pop bottle, some wire, a cork, a straw, and a bit of red plastic. To make one, find a cork or rubber stopper that will fit tightly in the end of a clear plastic pop bottle. Drill a hole in the stopper just large enough to fit a red plastic drinking straw. If you can't find bendable drinking straws, gently heat a regular straw and you should be able to bend it. Cut the pop bottle in half and with a coat hanger or other stiff wire, form a loop in which the inverted bottle top can be held. At the other end of the wire form a hook to hang the feeder to the branch of a tree or shrub. Finally, cut a flower-like design from a piece of bright red plastic material and cut a hole in it the size of the drinking straw. Slip this "flower" over the end of the straw to attract the hummingbirds. Fill the feeder with nectar solution and hang it up.

TOOLS & MATERIALS
- Pliers, scissors, wire cutters
- Drill with bit
- Clear plastic pop bottle
- Cork or rubber stopper
- Plastic drinking straw (preferably the bendable kind)
- Coat hanger wire
- Red plastic

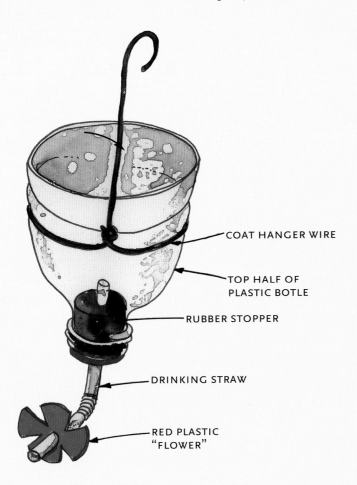

COAT HANGER WIRE

TOP HALF OF
PLASTIC BOTLE

RUBBER STOPPER

DRINKING STRAW

RED PLASTIC
"FLOWER"

Homemade Hummingbird Nectar Solution

- 4 cups water
- 1 cup sugar
- Feeder with red feature(s), such as a red plastic flower to draw the hummers

Boil the water and then stir in the sugar. (Remember: Do not use honey as it ferments too quickly and can harm the hummingbirds, and never use a solution with more than one part sugar to four parts water.) Boil the sugarwater for five minutes then let the solution cool before filling the feeder. The liquid can be stored for up to three weeks if it is kept refrigerated.

Ruby-throat

It is midmorning. The heat is mounting but some of the freshness of the night is still in the air. While I was away, rain relieved the drought of the hillside. I sit in the grass, leaning back against the bark of an apple tree, thinking of nothing in particular, letting my gaze wander about over the hillside. As I sit there a sudden airy swish of a sound reaches my ears. A ruby-throated hummingbird has arrived among the buddleia blooms of the garden. All along the Atlantic coast and inland beyond the Mississippi – two thirds of the way across the continent – there is only one species of hummingbird, the familiar and remarkable ruby-throat.

Edwin Way Teale – Circle of the Seasons, 1953

the United States and Canada. Hummingbirds can be very difficult to tell apart, particularly the females and the young. For more information on which species of hummingbirds you might attract to your backyard or balcony, refer to a North American field guide.

Gardening for Hummingbirds

Bird experts agree that in order to create a first-class hummingbird habitat you should combine both feeders and natural sources of nectar. Hummingbirds benefit greatly from a carefully landscaped garden that produces flowers continuously throughout the growing season.

To attract hummingbirds, combine flowering perennials and annuals with shrubs and trees in your garden. Emphasize red flowers but plant orange, yellow, pink, purple, blue, yellow, and white as well. Opinions vary as to the order of hummers' color preferences, but all agree that red is the favorite. Hummingbirds particularly feed from the so-called "bird flowers," which are red, tubular, and rich in nectar. They are also the flowers most readily pollinated by hummingbirds. Different species of the birds have developed beaks to suit the flowers most frequented. Any brightly colored flower will attract hummers and if they discover that a particular flower is a good source of nectar, they will continue to visit that flower wherever they encounter it. Hummingbirds also feed on small insects, tree sap, and fruit juice. They will use water sources to bathe and drink from as any bird will, but require less of it, so a very

Rufous hummingbird female.

shallow bath could be set up in your habitat. Keep in mind that hummingbirds bathe in water droplets on leaves, so you needn't supply much.

The following is a starter list of hummingbirds' favorite plants. Happily, many of the flowers that draw hummers also attract butterflies; when you look at the plant lists for the butterfly garden you will find some overlap between the two. A colorful garden, lush with blossoms, will attract both hummingbirds and butterflies, and will provide an intriguing outdoor classroom for you and your family.

Flowers

Ajuga (*Ajuga reptans*)
Bee Balm (*Monarda didyma*)
Begonia/Wax Begonias (*Begonias semperflorens*)
Bergamot, Wild (*Monarda fistulosa*)
Bleeding Hearts (*Dicentra formosa & D. spectabilis*)
Bluebells (*Mertensia virginica*)

Canna, *"Assault", "Dazzler", "Lucifer", "Orange Perfection" (Canna* x *generalis)*

Cardinal Flower *(Lobelia cardinalis)*

Century Plant *(Agavaceae americana)*

Cigar Plant *(Cuphea ignea)*

Columbine *(Aquilegia sp.)*

Coral Bells *(Heuchera sanguinea)*

Dahlia *(Dahlia)*

Daylilies *(Hemerocallis hybrid)*

Delphinium *(Delphinium elatum)*

Firecracker Plant *(Russelia equisetiformis)*

Firepink *(Silene virginiana)*

Fireweed *(Epilobium angustifolium)*

Four-O-Clocks *(Mirabilis jalapa)*

Foxglove *(Digitalis purpurea)*

Fuchsia *(Fuchsia sp.)*

Geranium *(Pelargonium sp.)*

Gladiolus *(Gladiolus sp.)*

Hollyhock *(Alcea)*

Impatiens/Touch-Me-Not/Busy Lizzie *(Impatiens sp.)*

Indian Blanket *(Gaillardia pulchella)*

Iris *(Iris sp.)*

Larkspur, Prairie *(Delphinium cardinale)*

Lily, Tiger *(Lillium tigrinum)*

Lupines *(Lupinus sp.)*

Mallow, Rose *(Lavatera trimestris)*

Mexican Sunflower *(Tithonia rotundifolia)*

Milkweed/Butterfly Weed *(Asclepias tuberosa)*

Monkeyflower, Scarlet *(Mimulus cardinalis)*

Nettle, Scarlet Hedge *(Stachys ciliata)*

Nicotiana/Flowering Tobacco *(Nicotiana)*

Obedient Plant *(Physostegia virginiana)*

Paintbrush, Indian *(Castilleja sp.)*

Penstemon, Scarlet *(Penstemon barbatus)*

Pentas *(Pentas lanceolata)*

Petunia *(Petunia sp.)*

Phlox, Summer *(Phlox paniculata)*

Red-hot Poker *(Kniphofia uvaria)*

Sage, Pineapple *(Salvia elegans)*

Sage, Scarlet *(Salvia splendens)*

Shrimp Plant *(Justicia brandegeana)*

Sweet Rocket *(Hesperis matronalis)*

Sweet William *(Dianthus barbatus)*

Yucca, Red *(Hesperaloe parviflora)*

Zinnia *(Zinnia elegans)*

Lush rooftop garden could entice hummers

Hummingbird Folklore

A courtship dive of a hummingbird can be startling. Especially to new birders and anyone who is not expecting it. The loud BZZZttt of a hummingbird ripping past the side of your head has caused many people to mistakenly think that the birds were attacking them, and the myth of, "They'll poke your eyes out" was born. There has never been a recorded incidence of a hummingbird attacking a human, they are merely attempting to scare an intruder away.

Another popular misconception about hummingbirds is that they migrate on the backs of geese, tucked snugly into the feathers. And no wonder this is a popular belief! It sounds practical, but is entirely untrue. Hummingbirds certainly migrate, but under their own wing power, with some species traveling distances of up to 2000 miles.

Xantus's Hummingbird

Gerry and Lloyd Patterson, two birders on the coast of British Columbia, Canada, were host to a Xantus's hummingbird, a non-migratory resident of Southern Baja in Mexico. If not strange enough (a first for Canada!), it was winter when the bird arrived in the Pattersons' yard. The couple's daughter noticed it feeding from a scented pink geranium in the window box, then from the winter jasmine and hardy fuchsia. When the North American field guides didn't reveal any bird that resembled the visitor, several local birders were notified and came for a look. They in turn called bird experts from elsewhere in the province. The ID confirmed, the Rare Bird Alert phone line was contacted, and birders began to "flock" in.

Gerry and Lloyd hung out feeders to entice the bird to stay – and so it did, from mid-December 1999 until April 2000. The exotic, black-cheeked hummer attracted a crowd of nearly 1400 out-of-town birders and several hundred locals. "It's like winning the World Series," and "Absolutely astonishing; how did this happen?" were comments made by excited birders who came from as far away as Nova Scotia and Kentucky. How it happened may never be discovered with any certainty. Speculation includes being blown off course in an El Nino-generated hurricane, illegal importation, escape from a collector, or "hitchhiking" aboard a ship.

The Pattersons spoke to nearly everyone that came through their yard and were impressed by the sharing of binoculars and telescopes between strangers. Lloyd said, "It was a fun winter. Everyone was friendly." Some visitors brought gifts, such as sugar and books, and the couple was pleased that over the four-month period, the only adverse signs of the throngs were one cigarette butt and a candy wrapper. Celebrity status surprised the Pattersons, who did interviews for newspapers, two radio and three TV stations. Lloyd Patterson sums up the busy bird months with a laugh and says, "I learned to get dressed before I opened the drapes in the morning."

Vines

Bean, Scarlet Runner (*Phaseolus coccineus*)
Bougainvillea (*Bougainvillea sp.*)
Butterfly Bush (*Buddleia davidii*)
Butterfly Bush, Fountain (*Buddleia alternifolia*)
Cape Honeysuckle (*Tecomaria capensis*)
Clematis (*Clematis sp.*)
Cross Vine/Trumpet Flower (*Bignonia capreolata*)
Cypress Vine/Morning Glory (*Ipomoea quamoclit*)
Honeysuckle, Coral (*Lonicera heckrottii*)
Honeysuckle, Trumpet (*Lonicera sempervirens*)
Jasmine (*Jasminum sp.*)
Trumpet Creeper (*Campsis radicans*)

Good color and shape for hummers.

Trees and Shrubs

Abelia, Glossy (*Abelia grandiflora*)

Beauty Bush (*Kolkwitzia amabilis*)

Bird-of-Paradise Bush (*Caesalpinia gilliesii*)

Bottlebrush (*Callistemon sp.*)

Black Locust (*Robinia pseudoacacia*)

Buckeye, California/Horsechestnut (*Aesculus californica*)

Buckeye, Red/Horsechestnut (*Aesculus carnea*)

Citrus trees (*Rutaceae sp.*)

Century Plant (*Agave americana*)

Chinaberry (*Melia azedarach*)

Chuparosa (*Justicia californica*)

Crabapple, Flowering (*Malus sp.*)

Currants, Flowering Red (*Ribes sanguineum*)

Desert Lavender (*Hyptis emoryi*)

Desert Willow (*Chilopsis linearis*)

Eucalyptus (*Eucalyptus sp.*)

Fuchsia, Hardy (*Fuchsia magellanica*)

Hawthorn (*Crataegus sp.*)

Hibiscus (*Hibiscus rosa-sinensis*)

Honeysuckles (*Lonicera sp.*)

Lantana, Texas /Calico Bush (*Lantana horrida*)

Lavender (*Lavandula angustifolia*)

Ocotillo (*Fouquieria splendens*)

Red Elderberry (*Sambucus racemosa*)

Rhododendron/Azaleas (*Rhododendron sp.*)

Rose of Sharon (*Hibiscus syriacus*)

Salmonberry (*Rubus spectabilis*)

Silk Tree/Mimosa (*Albizia julibrissin*)

Twinberry (*Lonicera involucrata*)

Quince, Flowering (*Chaenomeles japonica*)

Sage, Autumn (*Salvia greggii*)

Siberian Pea Shrub (*Caragana arborescens*)

Turk's Cap/Wax Mallow/Texas Mallow (*Malvaviscus arboreus*)

Weigela (*Weigela sp.*)

Find out which plants on this list are native to your area and then, with the help of your local nursery or garden center, choose a selection that will give you continuously blooming flowers throughout hummingbird season. In some more temperate regions hummingbirds stay year-round, so try to provide for their needs as well.

Anna's hummingbird on a corkscrew hazel perch.

Butterflies and Moths

———◆———

THE POET ROBERT FROST was so enchanted by these stunning insects that he was moved to poetry. The sight of butterflies in our garden can be an inspiration to us as well, but rather than creating verse, we can be moved to create a hospitable environment. To attract butterflies and moths, you must provide for all the stages of their life cycles with specific habitat requirements. Nectar plants and sunny, sheltered spots in the garden will attract the adult insects. The right choice of host plants will provide egg-laying locations and larval habitat that

Zebra swallowtail.

supplies food for caterpillars. Areas of dense vegetation, leaf litter, unmowed grass, and ground debris will camouflage pupae.

Butterflies and moths are the only two members of the Order Lepidoptera and they can be difficult to tell apart. Moth behavior often mimics that of butterflies which complicates identification and, at a glance, some moths even resemble birds. Butterflies and moths are the only insects with tiny scales on their wings. Butterflies at rest usually keep their wings together and pointed straight out from their backs while moths spread their wings or hold them close to their bodies when motionless. Butterflies have simple knobby antennae, while those of moths are generally plumed, or feathered. Butterflies are seen during the day, but most moths are nocturnal. In North America there are between 8,000 and 10,500 moth species and only about 725 butterfly

Butterfly garden with sign.

species, so moths are likely to be more populous in your garden, just not as readily seen.

Butterflies and moths are best provided for with a carefully planned garden. Butterflies are attracted to more than just sweet-smelling, colorful flowers and leaves, however. Piles of rotting fruit, particularly grapes, are an "intoxicating treat." Urine and feces in small puddles also have their appeal, but such things may be more appropriate in a barnyard than a backyard. Both butterflies and moths need a moist, sandy spot for drinking and absorbing minerals—this is referred to as "mud-puddling," or "puddling," and in areas where damp spots are rare, large numbers of butterflies will congregate in colorful patches on the ground. If it isn't safe for butterflies down low in your yard, water a small patch of earth elevated on a stump, or use a pedestal birdbath.

Provide stones in sunny spots for butterfly basking; being cold-blooded, they need warmth to become mobile. You may even see butterflies lie on their sides to expose a large surface area to the sun in order to remain active throughout the day.

Moths are drawn to light at night. Keep screens and doors closed to avoid attracting them inside. At the same time, you can take advantage of their nearness, and identify individual species. Up close, you'll be able to enjoy the variations of wing shapes and patterns. Moths are partial to sugary concoctions so use your imagination to lure them with sweet mixtures.

You may want to experiment with a butterfly house. According to reports, no

— BUTTERFLY HOUSE NO. 1 —

TOOLS & MATERIALS

- Band saw and table saw
- Jointer
- Strap-clamps
- Sides – two halves of a small red cedar log/large branch
- Front – laminated red cedar strips
- Back – red cedar plank 1½" × 3½" × 12½"
- Bottom – red cedar block 1½" × 3½" × 4½"
- Top – one-half red cedar log
- Water-resistant glue

Butterflies sometimes need a secure, sheltered cavity in which to get out of the wind and cold. They may take shelter in rock and woodpiles, crevasses in rocks and trees, and small spaces in sheds, barns, and other buildings. You can also custom build them a house and place it in your garden. The two different designs given here are both based on splitting a small log and reassembling it with an interior space accessible to butterflies via slots on one side. The dimensions shown are to guide you only. They can be changed to suit the log.

TOP VIEW
(WITHOUT ROOF)

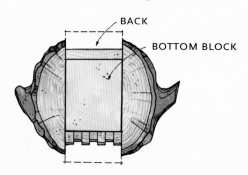

BACK

BOTTOM BLOCK

FRONT VIEW

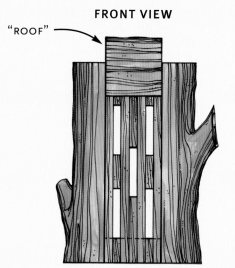

"ROOF"

SECTIONAL (SIDE) VIEW

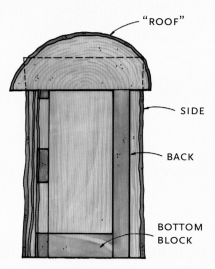

"ROOF"

SIDE

BACK

BOTTOM BLOCK

1. As shown in Figure 1, saw a small red cedar log with the bark still on, in half lengthwise. The log used in this example is 15" long and 6" diameter.
2. Plane the cut faces flat using a jointer (Figure 2).
3. As shown in the front view and Figure 4 make entry slots for the butterflies by gluing narrow pieces of wood together. To make these slots, take a shallow slab of red cedar 12½" long, plane the back and band saw it lengthwise into seven ½" strips as shown in Figure 3. Cut every second strip into pieces to form 3" high slots. Glue these together to form the 3½" wide front face. To add interest, stagger the strips as shown in the top view.
4. Make a bottom block of red cedar 1½" thick × 3½" × 4½".
5. Make a back piece 1½" thick × 3½" × 12½" long.
6. Make the roof from a 3½" length of log cut in half (Figure 4).
7. Glue all of these pieces together with water-resistant glue.

FIGURE 1

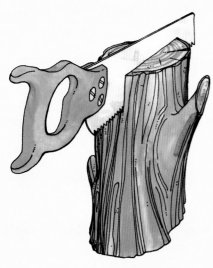

FIGURE 3

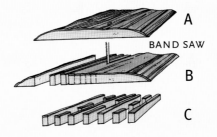

A

BAND SAW

B

C

FIGURE 2

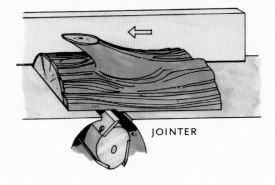

JOINTER

FIGURE 4

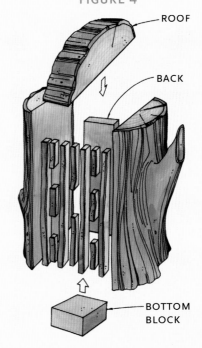

ROOF

BACK

BOTTOM BLOCK

BUTTERFLY HOUSE NO. 2

This house is a variation of Butterfly House No. 1, and the general instructions and dimensions are almost the same. The difference is in how the back is made, as shown in the top view and Figure 4. When the three pieces are assembled, the butterfly house will resemble a round log on end.

TOP VIEW

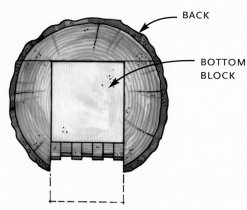

BACK

BOTTOM BLOCK

SECTIONAL SIDE VIEW

ROOF

BACK

FRONT VIEW

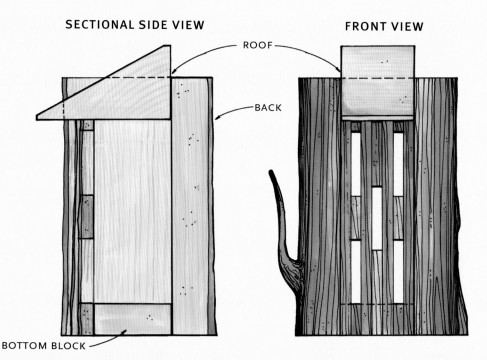

BOTTOM BLOCK

1. To make this variation use two 15" long red cedar logs. Cut both in half and plane as shown in Figures 1 and 2.

2. Select one of the logs to form the sides, and plane the back edge of each piece 90° to the inside face using a jointer. The amount planed off the back will be just enough to match the width of one-half of the second log when the two sides are placed against it, keeping a 3½" gap between them (see top view).

3. Make the front entry holes as described on page 85 (Step 3) and Figure 3. Make the bottom block as described in Step 4, page 85.

4. Make the roof from a 3½" wide triangular piece (Figure 4) or by cutting open small logs and reassembling them in various ways to create interesting, rustic roofs.

FIGURE 1

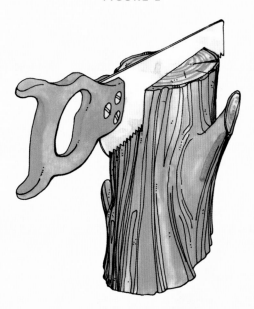

FIGURE 2

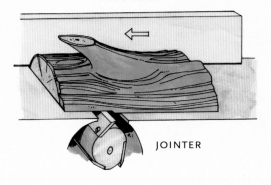

JOINTER

FIGURE 3

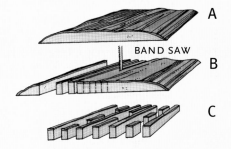

A

BAND SAW

B

C

FIGURE 4

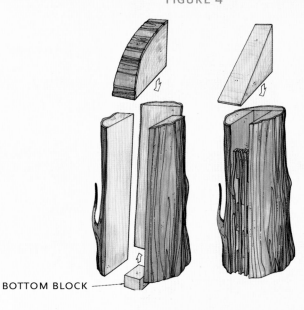

BOTTOM BLOCK

PROJECT 21

— BUTTERFLY LEDGE —

TOOLS & MATERIALS

- Table saw, skill saw, or jigsaw
- Hammer
- ¾" plywood – cut the length of the window opening × 10" wide
- Two-by-three fir – cut the length of the plywood
- Two-by-two fir – cut the length of the plywood
- Small log or large branch
- Several 2" × 4" × ½" plywood dividers
- Tin plate
- Stone, mud, and a selection of plants suitable for feeding local butterflies throughout their life cycles
- Nails
- Water-resistant glue

The butterfly window ledge is designed to provide space for the needs of butterflies throughout their life cycles. It is sectioned off so you can plant weeds and nectar flowers to accommodate butterfly eggs, caterpillars, and the adult insects. To make it even more enticing, it has a place for a sunning rock and a tiny area for a butterfly mudpatch.

TOP VIEW

INSIDE

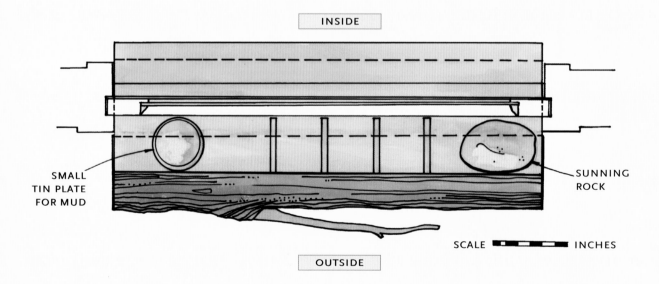

SMALL
TIN PLATE
FOR MUD

SUNNING
ROCK

SCALE ▬▬▬ INCHES

OUTSIDE

88

1. Cut a piece of ¾" plywood the length of the window opening and wide enough to extend 4" to 6" out the window on the outside, and to extend 1½" past the windowsill on the outside.

2. Glue and nail a piece of two-by-three fir under the inside edge of the plywood to act as a "hook" against the sill.

3. Glue and nail a piece of two-by-two fir to the ¾" plywood base, just inside the window. This will act as a draftstop (see sectional view).

4. Cut a quarter out of a small, straight log or large branch lengthwise as shown to add an interesting edge to the outside of the ledge (see sectional view).

5. Glue and nail as many ½" plywood dividers between the log and the window as you like. These will create separate spaces for different plants.

6. Leave room on the ends of the ledge for a large flat basking rock and for a plate to hold a small mound of mud.

SECTIONAL VIEW

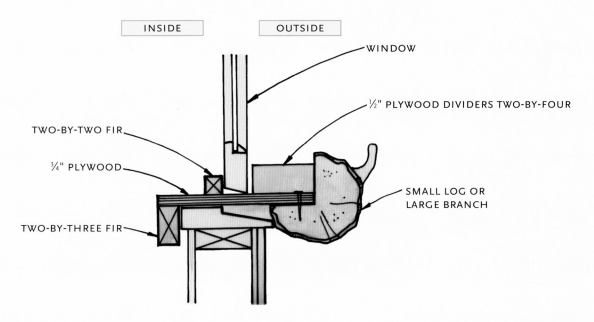

INSIDE

OUTSIDE

WINDOW

½" PLYWOOD DIVIDERS TWO-BY-FOUR

TWO-BY-TWO FIR

¾" PLYWOOD

TWO-BY-THREE FIR

SMALL LOG OR LARGE BRANCH

TOOLS & MATERIALS

- Hammer
- Nails
- Roofing felt
- Small logs

Stack small, uniformly sized logs in layers so they cross one another, leaving a few inches between them. Nail roofing felt onto the top of the pile to keep water out. You can plant larval host plants around your woodpile to assist the emerging caterpillars (see page 43 for a list of appropriate plants). Your sheltered woodpile will be popular with any number of creatures, including beetles, spiders, reptiles, and amphibians.

ROOFING FELT

METAMORPHOSIS OF A BUTTERFLY

1

Egg "glued" to leaf.

2

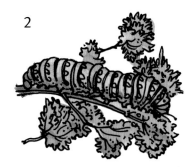

Fully grown caterpillar (larva) eating host plant.

3

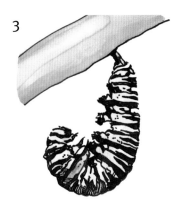

Caterpillar attached to plant.

4

Transforming into pupa, or chrysalis.

5

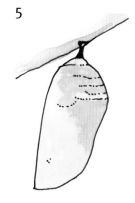

Pupa.

6

Stage before adult emerges—wing pattern is now visible.

7

Adult butterfly emerging.

8

Butterfly waiting for wings to harden enough for flight.

The Valiant Butterfly

For half a mile today as I paddle close to the shore, an anglewing butterfly with silver commas beneath its hind wing – Polygonia progne, the Gray Comma – rides with us. It alights without fear on my hand, the one that is gripping the top of the paddle. With proboscis uncoiled, it dabs at my skin. I shake if off half a dozen times. It merely flutters up and settles down again. The wind strikes it and, at times, forces its wings far over, sometimes almost flat on my hand. For fifteen minutes, the valiant butterfly rides along, rising and falling and turning with strokes of the paddle. It clings there as it would cling to a flower tossing in the wind. Sometimes it holds fast to the back of my hand, sometimes it rides on the upper side of my thumb. I can recall only one other time when I have had a butterfly ride with me so long. That was many years ago, in the long corridor of a blowout in the Indiana dunes. As I walked slowly along, that day, a little copper fluttered down and rode on my shoulder.

Edwin Way Teale – Circle of the Seasons, 1953

one has actually seen a butterfly use one but they are sold commercially as butterfly hibernation boxes. They are not meant for butterfly larvae (caterpillars) which move about and feed themselves after emerging from the egg. Instead, butterfly boxes are meant to give the insects a dry, safe place to shelter over winter. Most butterflies hibernate as larvae or pupae, with only a few species overwintering as adults. Butterflies will hibernate under tree bark, in brush piles and woodpiles (see Project 22 on how to build one), and between rocks in unmortared stone walls. If you would like to try your luck with a butterfly house, see Projects 19 and 20 for how to build one. Even if butterflies don't use your box to hibernate, it will probably be used by other creatures, and will certainly look attractive in your garden.

Creating a Butterfly Garden

Butterfly gardens differ somewhat from hummingbird gardens but contain many of the same plants. The main difference is that butterflies need an open, sunny space sheltered from the wind. Each species of butterfly also requires specific plants for larval habitat, and without these will be unable to reproduce. A butterfly garden should have several flat rocks for basking in the sun. Butterflies cannot drink from open water so your garden should offer a small, moist patch of soil, sand, or mud. You might also want to hang a bag of fermenting fruit to draw them. Both birds and butterflies will enjoy a ripe banana moistened with orange juice hanging from a shrub or tree. Bits of fruit can also be offered in a small dish. A successful

Northern blues puddling.

butterfly garden will provide plants that butterflies can use in all four stages of their life cycles.

Plant your butterfly garden in spring and emphasize hardy flowers, shrubs, and trees. Mass plantings of flowers are the most effective enticement as butterflies are able to sense areas of the garden that have high nectar production. Try to plant the caterpillar food plants in areas where any nibbled appearance won't offend the eye, and use several plants of the same type to help hide damage. Many species of moth caterpillars can be fairly destructive, but they are an important food source for birds. If butterflies overwinter in your area, many will do so as chrysalises or eggs attached to the host plants in your garden. Do not trim or cut back your plants in the fall or you may destroy next year's crop of butterflies.

Each species of butterfly needs specific host plants on which to lay its eggs—the emerging larvae will then be supplied with the necessary food. As in a previous example, Monarch butterflies must lay their eggs on certain milkweed species in order for the larvae to ingest poisons that render the adult inedible to enemies. Some butterflies have a variety of plants on which they can lay their eggs, so try to familiarize yourself with the butterflies in your area in order to choose the right plants for each stage of their life cycles. Most butterfly host plants are categorized as weeds, so get ready to welcome former enemies into the garden in the interests of creating a butterfly haven! Make sure to section off invasive plants or contain

Lorquin's admiral.

them in tubs, dead-heading diligently to prevent seeds from developing and dispersing.

The following is a list of common North American butterflies and their larval host plants:

Admirals (and relatives)

California Sister: Canyon Live Oak (*Quercus chrysolepis*), Coast Live Oak (*Q. agrifolia*)

Lorquin's Admiral: Willow (*Salix sp.*), Poplar (*Populus sp.*), Cherry (*Prunus sp.*)

Viceroy: Willows (*Salix sp.*), Poplars, Aspens (*Populus sp.*), Apples (*Malus sp.*), Cherries, and Plums (*Prunus sp.*)

Queen.

The Primrose Moth

Not far from the straggling cluster of sunflowers at my Insect Garden, a stalk of primrose rises almost as high as my head. It is the lone representative of its species on the slope. There, in the early dawn today, I find two pinkish little moths with white hairs massed behind their heads. Both are in the same position, motionless, their heads thrust deep into the yellow flowers. When first I found such a moth in such a place, I thought it was dead or was being held by some unseen crab spider lurking at the bottom of the bloom. Now I know it was merely fast asleep, already bedded down for the day. For this is the habit of the primrose moth. It sleeps in a yellow bed during the August days.

Edwin Way Teale – Circle of the Seasons, 1953

Pale tiger swallowtail.

Blues

Acmon Blue: Deerweed (*Lotus scoparius*)

Arrowhead Blue: Lupines (*Lupinus albifrons, L. sp.*)

Marine Blue: Leadwort (*Plumbago sp.*), Alfalfa (*Medicago sativa*), Sweet Pea (*Lathyrus odoratus*)

Reakirt's Blue: Mesquite (*Prosopis sp.*), Indigos (*Indigofera*), orn. Acacias (*Albizzia*)

Silvery Blue: Deerweed (*Lotus scoparius*), Lupine (*Lupinus sp.*), Wild Pea (*Lathyrus*), Vetch (*Vicia*)

Sonoran Blue: Stonecrop (*Dudleya sp.*), Live Forever (*Sedum purpureum*)

Spring Azure: Wild Lilac (*Ceanothus sp.*), Dogwood, and Bunchberry (*Cornus sp.*), Viburnum sp., Blueberries (*Vaccinium sp.*), various Cherries and Plums (*Prunus sp.*)

Western Pygmy Blue: Saltbush (*Atriplex sp.*), Pickleweed (*Salicornia sp.*), Pigweed (*Chenopodium album*)

Coppers

Gorgon Copper: Wild Buckwheat (*Eriogonum elongatum & E. nudum*)

Purplish Copper: Docks (*Rumex sp.*), Knotweeds (*Polygonum sp.*)

Tailed Copper: Wild Currants and Gooseberries (*Ribes sp.*)

Fritillaries

Great Spangled Fritillary: Violet (*Viola sp.*)

Gulf Fritillary: Passion Vine (*Passiflora sp.*)

Meadow Fritillary: Violet (*Viola sp.*)

Hairstreaks

Avalon Scrub Hairstreak: Lotuses (*Lotus scoparius & L. argophyllus*)

Bramble: California Buckwheat (*Eriogonum fasciculatum*), Deerweed (*Lotus scoparius*)

Monarch.

Western tiger swallowtail.

Golden Hairstreak: Canyon Live Oak
(*Quercus chrysolepis*) and other
Quercus sp.

Great Purple: Mistletoe *(Phoradendron
sp.)*

Gray Hairstreak: California Buckwheat
(Eriogonum fasciculatum), Cotton
(Gossypium sp.)

Sylvan Hairstreak: Willow *(Salix sp.)*

Western Pine Elfin: many pines including Lodgepole *(Pinus contorta)* and
Ponderosa *(P. ponderosa)*

Metalmarks
Mormon Metalmark: Buckwheat
(Eriogonum sp.)

Northern Metalmark: Ragwort/Ground-
sel *(Senecio sp.)*

Monarchs
Monarch: Milkweed *(Asclepias sp.)*,
Dogbane *(Apocynum sp.)*

Queen: Milkweed *(Asclepias amplexi-
caulis)*, Smooth Milkvine *(Sar-*

costemma hirtellum), Oleander
(Nerium)

Satyrs
Common Ringlet: Grasses

Common Wood Nymph: Oats *(Avena
sp.)*, Needle Grass *(Stipa sp.)*, Sedge
(Carex sp.)

Little Wood Satyr: Grasses

Skippers
Grass Skippers

Fiery Skipper: Bermuda Grass *(Cynodon
dactylon)*, Bent Grass *(Agnostis)*,
Sugar Cane *(Sacchinarum
officinarum)*

St. Augustine grass *(Stenotaphrum
secundatum)*

Juba Skipper: Needlegrass *(Stipa sp.)*,
Bluegrass *(Poa sp.)*

Rural Skipper: Grasses

Sandhill Skipper: Desert Saltgrass
(Distichlis spicata var. stricta)

Umber Skipper: Grasses

Spicebush swallowtail.

Dainty Sulphur: Beggarticks *(Bidens pilosa)*, Marigolds *(Tagetes sp.)*, Sneezeweed *(Helenium autumnale)*

Mexican Yellow: Sennas *(Cassia sp.)*

Orange Sulphur (Alfalfa Butterfly): Alfalfa *(Medicago sativa)*, White Clover *(Trifolium repens)*

Swallowtails

Anise Swallowtail: Common Fennel *(Foeniculum vulgare)*

Eastern Tiger Swallowtail: Wild Black Cherry *(Prunus serotina)*, Tulip Tree *(Liriodendron tulipfera)*

Pale Swallowtail: California Coffeeberry *(Rhamnus californicus)*, Wild Lilac *(Ceanothus sp.)*, Cherry *(Prunus sp.)*

Wandering Skipper: Saltgrass *(Distichlis spicata)*

Spread-wing Skippers

Common Checkered Skipper: Alkali Mallow *(Sida hederacea)* and other mallows *(Malva sp.)*

Funereal Duskywing: Deerweed *(Lotus scoparius)*, Alfalfa *(Medicago sativa)*

Mournful Duskywing: Coast Live Oak *(Quercus agrifolia)*, Valley Oak *(Q. lobata)*, and other oaks *(Quercus sp.)*

Northern White Skipper: Globe Mallow *(Sphaeralcea)*, and other mallows *(Malva sp.)*

Sulphurs

California Dogface: False Indigo *(Amorpha californica)*, Lead Plant *(Amorpha californica)*, Clovers *(Trifolium sp.)*

Cloudless Sulphur: Senna *(Cassia sp.)*, Clovers *(Trifolium sp.)*

True Brushfoots

American Lady: Cudweed *(Gnaphalium sp.)*, Pussytoes *(Intennaria sp.)*, Sagebrush *(Artemesia sp.)*

California Tortoiseshell: Wild Lilac *(Ceanothus sp.)*

Chalcedon Checkerspot: Figwort *(Scrophularia californica)*, Monkeyflower *(Mimulus aurantiacus)*

Common Buckeye: Plantain *(Plantago sp.)*, Monkeyflower *(Mimulas sp.)*

Leanira Checkerspot: Indian Paintbrush *(Castilleja sp.)*

Mourning Cloak: Willow *(Salix sp.)*, Elm *(Ulmus sp.)*, Hackberry *(Celtis sp.)*, Cottonwood *(Populus sp.)*

Painted Lady: Thistle *(Cirsium sp.)*, Lupines *(Lupinus sp.)*

Red admiral on echinacea.

Swallowtail caterpillar on angelica.

Pearl Crescent: Aster *(Aster sp.)*
Red Admiral: Nettle *(Urtica sp.)*, Hops
(Humulus sp.)

Whites
Cabbage White: Mustard (*Brassica sp.*
such as cabbage, cauliflower, broc-
coli)
Mustard White: Mustard *(Brassica sp.)*,
Whitlow grasses *(Draba sp.)*, and
cresses *(Arabis sp.)*
Sara Orangetip: Mustard family such as
Rockcress *(Arabis sp.)*, Wintercress
(Barbarea)

After their remarkable metamor-
phoses into winged creatures, adult
butterflies require nectar plants for nourishment. Try to choose plants that, when
combined, will provide continuous
blooms and nectar throughout the growing season. Three considerations for
choosing flowers should be shape, color,
and fragrance. Butterflies cannot hover
for long so need flower heads that provide places to land—choose composites
with daisy-like petals, panicles with large
bloom clusters, and umbels that have
flat-topped flowers. Strong colors such as
orange, yellow, and purple are preferable
as butterflies are guided to a flower's nectar by ultraviolet patterns on the petals.
Heavy fragrance should be emphasized
in any butterfly garden, as that is what at-
tracts the insects in the first place. Try
old-fashioned "heirloom varieties" for
plants that have retained their heady per-
fume.

Butterfly Nectar Plants

(Includes Flowers, Shrubs, Trees, and
Vines, ***Denotes superior nectar
plants)
Anise, Hyssop *(Agastache foeniculum)*
Aster, New England *(Aster novae-angliae)*
Aster, "Alma Potsche" *(Aster novae-
angliae)* var. 'Alma P.'
Bee Balm *(Monarda didyma)* ***
Black-eyed Susan/Gloriosa Daisy *(Rud-
beckia hirta)* ***

A National Insect

I am surprised this morning, to see a late Monarch, left behind by the tide of migration and flying south alone, pass over the swamp and hillside. What other insect is so widespread in the United States as the Monarch butterfly? I have seen it in Florida and along the St. Lawrence and in Minnesota and at the mouth of the Mississippi, on the Texas coast and in the mountains of California. It is familiar to almost every part of the country. And its fall migration flight has made it famous throughout the world. It is more beneficial than harmful. It is an insect of the New World. It, among all the insect hosts, might well be chosen as our national insect. Thoreau justly complained that legislatures would appropriate money for the study of only injurious insects. The Monarch, beautiful, interesting, and in the main beneficial, deserves the attention of at least one legislature. We have state birds and state trees and state wildflowers. Why not a state insect? I nominate the Monarch!

Edwin Way Teale – Circle of the Seasons, 1953

Buckeye/Horsechestnut
  (*Aesculus sp.*)
Buttercup (*Ranunculus sp.*)
Butterfly Bush (*Buddleia
  davidii*)
Butterfly Bush, Fountain
  (*Buddleia alternifolia*) ★★★
Butterfly Weed/Milkweed
  (*Asclepias tuberosa*)
Candytuft (*Iberis sp.*)
Cardinal Flower (*Lobelia
  cardinalis*) ★★★
Chicory (*Cichorium intybus*)
Clover (*Trifolium sp.*)
Coreopsis (*Coreopsis sp.*)
Cosmos, Common (*Cosmos
  bipinnatus*) ★★★
Dandelion (*Taraxacum sp.*)
Fleabane (*Erigeron sp.*)
Gaillardia (*Gaillardia sp.*)
Globe Amaranth (*Gom-
  phrena globosa*)
Goldenrod, Seaside (*Solidago
  sempervirens*)
Heliotrope (*Heliotropium ar-
  borescens*)

Woolly bear on bracken

Honeysuckle, Japanese (*Lonicera
  japonica*)
Honeysuckle, Trumpet (*Lonicera
  sempervirens*)
Impatiens/Touch-Me-Not/Busy Lizzie
  (*Impatiens sp.*)
Lantana (*Lantana camara*) ★★★
Lantana, Weeping (*Lantana monte-
  vidensis*)
Lilac (*Syringa sp.*)
Lobelia (*Lobelia sp.*)
Marigold (*Tagetes sp.*)
Meadowsweet (*Astilbe sp.*)
Mexican Sunflower (*Tithonia rotund-
  ifolia*)

Anise swallowtail on balsamroot.

Early spring butterfly garden.

Milkweed, Common (*Asclepias syriaca*)

Milkweed, Red-flowered (*Asclepias currassavica*)

Milkweed, Swamp (*Asclepias incarnata*)

Mint (*Mentha sp.*)

Mountain Mint (*Pycanthemum muticum*)

Pear (*Pyrus communis*)

Pentas (*Pentas lanceolata*)

Petunia (*Petunia sp.*)

Phlox (*Phlox sp.*)

Primrose (*Primula sp.*)

Purple Coneflower (*Echinacea purpurea*) ***

Pincushion Flower (*Scabiosa sp.*)

Rhododendron/Azaleas (*Rhododendron sp.*)

Rockcress (*Arabis sp.*)

Sedum (*Sedum spectabile*)

Silk Tree/Mimosa (*Albizia julibrissin*)

Thistle (*Cirsium sp.*)

Trumpet Creeper (*Campsis radicans*)

Verbena (*Verbena bonariensis*)

Viburnum (*Viburnum sp.*)

Wild Bergamot (*Monarda fistulosa*)

Wintercress (*Barbarea orthoceras*)

Yarrow (*Achillea sp.*)

Zinnia (*Zinnia elegans*) ***

Moth Nectar Plants

To attract moths to your garden, try planting fragrant, evening blooming flowers. The following plants have white flowers which are noticable to moths at dusk and on moonlit nights:

Four O'Clock (*Mirabilis jalapa*)

Nicotiana (*Nicotiana alata; Nicotiana sylvestris*)

Night Jessamine (*Cestrum nocturnum*)

A word of warning: ultraviolet "bug zappers," although largely ineffective in the control of mosquito populations, attract and uselessly destroy moths with great effectiveness.

Polyphemus moth.

99

Bugs and Burrowers

Besides the familiar butterflies and moths, a backyard wildlife habitat will be graced with many other tiny and fascinating creatures. Earthworms and slugs, bugs of all sorts, including the insects and spiders, abound in a successful habitat. The term "bug" is used here collectively as a matter of simplification and is not to be confused with the "true bugs" as listed below. There are good field guides available that can help you with scientific details should you wish to study any of these creatures in depth.

Bugs are the backbone of ecology and many are directly beneficial to humans—they pollinate flowers and thereby enhance crop yields, they decompose organic matter, fertilize and build soil, eat weeds and other bugs, and provide food for birds and mammals. Some are responsible for commercially valuable products such as honey, beeswax, and silk. Most bugs are harmless to humans, but you may want to consult local identification guides or your natural history society for the types of bugs in your area. Most insect pests are just a nuisance, but approximately one percent of them cause major damage to crops and gardens. The irony is that the more pesticides used, the worse the insect infestations can become with the pests' natural predators being killed as well.

Bugwatching is becoming popular in its own right, just as birdwatching already is. A bugwatcher will see tiny creatures doing amazing things such as building intricate webs that stretch across roads, or doing the backstroke around a pond, even hiding deep inside a flower to ambush prey. With a change of perspective, the wildlife steward can come to appreciate the role that bugs play in the backyard habitat and acknowledge that even the worst pests have a place in the natural order of things.

Eight-spotted skimmer.

The most important requirement for bugs as well as other wild guests is a pesticide-free environment. A beautifully planted backyard filled with perfect foliage will be a wildlife graveyard if you achieve it by using toxic pesticides and herbicides. When undesirables such as aphids show up, keep in mind that bugs are the beginning of the food chain in any wildlife habitat and most will be eaten by more desirable guests, like birds and ladybugs. Other habitat requirements for most bugs are a source of water, native plants, leaf litter, grass and ground debris, and a woodpile.

There are nearly 100,000 species of insects in North America and about 3,000 spider species, with even more spiders that have not yet been identified. Spiders are non-insects, as are ticks, mites, scorpions, centipedes, and millipedes. The most recognizable differences between insects and spiders are:

Insects	Spiders
6 legs	8 legs
2 antennae	0 antennae
3 major body sections	2 major body sections

Both insects and spiders are invertebrate animals with hard outer coverings (exoskeletons), and are the most numerous creatures on earth, accounting for over three-quarters of all animals.

Dragonflies and Damselflies

Dragonflies and damselflies are great favorites of naturalists and wildlife stewards. If you are fortunate enough to have a pond or bog, or live near a body of slow-moving water such as a stream, you may attract these flying predators. Growing numbers of people like to watch them just as birders watch birds. And the names are alluring—Vivid Dancer, River Cruiser, Cherry-faced Meadowhawk, and Blue Dasher are just a sampling.

Dragonflies have outstanding flying capabilities. A

Dragonfly

Dragonflies patrol for prey near the tiny backyard of one naturalist in a mobile home park, but she had never seen any of the insects around her miniature bog or pond. One hot afternoon, she sat next to the cattails, enjoying the stillness. The woman watched in amazement as a female Paddle-tailed Darner landed on the stem of a cattail, clasped the soft plant tissue, and dipped the tip of her abdomen again and again – the knifelike ovipositor laying each egg precisely into the cattail stem. The greenish-yellow darner, oblivious to its audience, continued her mission amongst the cattails, even as the naturalist stood and walked inside for her camera.

She photographed the dragonfly from less than a foot away with a macro-lens, and continued to observe the insect for the twenty minutes it took to finish its egg-laying. Something to puzzle over: how would the gilled dragonfly nymphs, after hatching, get from the bog to the pond to live out their larval stage? One day she may see it for herself.

large darner can fly up to 40 mph, hover in midair, fly upwards, sideways, backwards and forwards, and reverse directions almost instantly during flight. These insects scoop prey mid-flight with their bristly legs. An amusing bit of folklore is that dragonflies will sew your lips shut, but the reality is that these insects are harmless to people. Dragonflies and damselflies can be very colorful, many in bright turquoises or reds, and they voraciously feed on flies and mosquitoes. Damselflies are smaller and more delicate than dragonflies, and lack the extreme fly-

ing capabilities, but they are intriguing to watch as they hover or perch in the reeds. These insects fly past leaves close enough to snap up resting prey. To attract dragonflies and damselflies to your backyard habitat, nearby water is a must (see Chapter 13 for instructions on making water attractions for wildlife).

Grasshoppers and Crickets

Grasshoppers and crickets provide a soundtrack to summer with their jingly chirping, and are renowned for their jumping prowess. Grasshoppers are not often serious garden pests—just rare exceptions when

Damselfly on loosestrife.
Cardinal meadowhawk.

Grasshopper.

Ground beetle.

Don't step on ground beetles.

they swarm together in some parts of western North America and denude all greenery in their path. Crickets, the most musical among these insects, can also be garden pests and are often destroyed en masse to prevent their nymphal stage from eating garden plants. Adult crickets make up for the damage by feeding on caterpillars and aphids.

Beetles

Beetle species can represent both heroes and enemies to the gardener. Two of the worst pests are the Japanese beetle, an import that has taken up residence in areas of eastern North America, and the Colorado potato beetle. Thankfully, these voracious feeders have many predators that include a variety of wasps and birds. Check with a local identification guide and you will probably find that most of the beetles you see are harmless, even useful, and should be left alone.

The hero among the beetles is the ladybug. They're cheery to look at and have a good reputation—in England, ladybugs mean a good harvest; in France, ladybugs seen in a vineyard signify good weather, and in Canada it's just plain good luck to have a ladybug overwinter in

your garage. Some have shiny, round red, orange, or yellow bodies with black markings, while others have shiny black bodies with yellow or red markings. Ladybugs are champion aphid destroyers.

Some gardeners go so far as to buy ladybugs in bulk to patrol their gardens for aphids, spider mites, mealy bugs, and other pests. Be aware that what you want are native species. The proliferation of non-native species may eventually harm the ecosystem if they out-compete native species. Gardeners who want to encourage ladybugs to take up residence in their

Ladybug on horsetail.

gardens naturally, need only provide a healthy, pesticide-free environment to keep a balance between pests and predators. You can help them through their winter hibernation by keeping a leafy mulch cover on your garden and by allowing them to hide in your house. There are also other helpful beetle species that consume such pests as snails and cutworms.

Flies

Flies are probably the least popular of the insects. This group includes the mosquito, one of the greatest nuisances and health hazards around the world. Also included are bluebottle flies, fruit flies, horseflies, and blackflies. The fact that these unpopular insects are an important food source for many creatures, and that they themselves are effective predators of many pests, is often lost in the "buzz" of hostility. Some flies also pollinate flowers. One can try to remember the positive side when tempted to curse the entire group.

Ants, Bees, Wasps, and Hornets

Ants, bees, wasps, and hornets are some of the most interesting insects to observe in the wildlife garden. Ants are fascinating for their communal approach to survival—an individual ant would not know what to do and would lose its motivation to live. The value of ants in the wildlife garden is mixed. Some cultivate aphids in order to "milk" them of their honeydew, thereby helping them to flourish. However, most North American ants don't have any serious impact in the garden ei-

ther way. Ants are interesting in their own right and you may enjoy watching them parade in long lines while they search for, and transport, food.

The distinction between wasps and hornets can be confusing. It is best to consult an identification guide for your area to determine which species you have. A comprehensive guide will tell you which wasps and hornets are not particularly defensive and which are apt to defend their nests at even minor perceived threats.

Three commonly seen species across North America are bald-faced hornets, yellow-jackets, and paper wasps. The first two are serious defenders of their colonies and will sting repeatedly. Both are notorious for appearing at picnics and barbeques.

Bald-faced hornets build huge paper nests that hang high from trees, and be-

Honeybee on hellebore.

Homemade orchard mason bee box.

A bee box in use.

cause they are added onto throughout the season, these nests can become as large as basketballs. Yellow-jackets build underground nests in abandoned animal burrows, in rotten logs, or under buildings. These are the hornets that will surprise hikers on a trail and swarm black bears foraging in the woods.

Paper wasps are a more human-tolerant species and their nests are small, open constructions usually under an eave. Because paper wasp nests lack an outer covering, the insects can be observed doing the actual building. Most wasps and hornets feed on garden pests, and numerous species parasitize insects and their larvae, making wasps and hornets highly effective predators.

Bees number more than 3,500 species in North America alone. Most of us have been influenced by the many benefits of bees. Their most important function is

pollination which is essential to our commercial fruit and vegetable crops. Yards with beehives tend to be far more productive than yards without. The other obvious benefit is honey from the honey bee.

Bees will use a patch of bare ground for underground nests, branches tied up to a garden shed for nest sites, a mud patch for mason bees, and a water drip (see page 211). If you want to build a honey-producing beehive, make sure to consult a professional beekeeper before you begin. Beekeeping is an old and popular occupation that can be practiced anywhere from farms to urban backyards. Remember, too, that bees require many, many flowers to produce enough honey for themselves as well as for you.

If you want to make your yard even more attractive to bees, consider planting a large number of native nectar-produc-

Spring Bumblebees

At 6:30 this morning, I watch a velvet-coated bumblebee begin her day of hunting for a nest site. In five minutes, as I follow her along the lower slope of the Insect Garden, I see her investigate every possible opening near a pile of moldering fence rails. Zigzagging, hovering, circling, alighting, she covers the slope as thoroughly as a man could do it. I see her alight on a fallen paper and peer under the edges. She explores under a maple root, beneath dead leaves, in four grass clumps, in a knothole in a log, by a weathered glass jar in the weeds, under a fallen branch, in the region of my shoe, at the foot of a cedar tree, along a bit of board lying in the grass. In five minutes, she investigates thirteen possible sites. Multiply this by the hours and days she will continue her searching and we have some idea of the hundreds and even thousands of sites she considers before she comes to the important decision of where she will establish her nest.

Edwin Way Teale – Circle of the Seasons, 1953

ing flowers, particularly in the colors pink, purple, and blue. Try to choose flowers that bees can easily visit (i.e., avoid tubular flowers that bees can't reach down into). Other helpful plantings for bees are alfalfa, clover, soybean, and mustard. If you decide to plant a bird or butterfly garden it will probably be beneficial to bees as well. In addition, bees will visit pussy willows which they are especially fond of, and various herbs and fruit trees. If you really want to attract bees to your backyard, consult a beekeeper to find out about the plants that the bees in your area prefer.

Providing homes for bumble bees in particular is a worthy endeavor as their numbers have been greatly reduced by human development. Bumble bees produce only enough honey for their own use, but they are invaluable in the wildlife garden. The orchard mason bee, also called the blue orchard bee, is a superior pollinator and will make use of homes that we provide. These tiny blue-black bees will pollinate 1,600 flowers in a day compared to a honey bee's 30 flowers. If you have fruit trees, then these bees are the way to go, as they are early spring pollinators and just three or four females will pollinate an entire tree. Many nurseries sell dor-

mant bees (see Projects 23 and 24 for providing shelter for bees).

Most bees are solitary, but honey bees and bumble bees are social and live in colonies where every member contributes to the well-being of the group. Bees, whether solitary or in communities, provide fascinating opportunities for study by the wildlife gardener. The risk of being stung by a bee is small, as they will do so only when surprised or provoked. Honey bees generally die after using their stinger, but bumble bees can sting more than once. Try to avoid interfering with their nests and you are unlikely to find yourself on the wrong end of a stinger.

True Bugs

The "true bugs" are those with sucking, rather than chewing, mouthparts and they typify the pest/predator spectrum that wildlife gardeners usually come to appreciate. Some are responsible for millions of dollars' worth of damage to gardens and crops—squash bugs, many species of stink bugs, and chinch bugs are a few of the better known true bug pests. In the habitat garden, these pests are generally kept in check by their natural predators, which include birds and parasitic and predator wasps. The true bugs that are friend to the gardener, such as the ambush and assassin bugs, prey on other garden pests, such as cutworms and beetle larvae.

Aphids, Cicadas, and Hoppers

These three "true bug" species have a bad reputation with gardeners. The word

Bumblebees will nest in a box similar to the type used by cavity-nesting birds. The box described here is quite small and can be made using a ⅜" plywood bottom and ¼" plywood sides. The sloped roof is designed to shed rain, and the hinge allows easy access to the interior.

TOOLS & MATERIALS

- Table saw, skill saw or jigsaw
- Hammer
- Screwdriver
- Electric drill with ⅝" diameter bit
- Bottom – ⅜" plywood 6" × 7"
- Back – ¼" plywood 6½" × 6½"
- Sides – ¼" plywood 7" × 6½" (at back) and 5" (at front)
- Front – ¼" plywood 6½" × 5"
- Roof – cedar slab 7½" × 8½" long
- One pair of 1" × 1" hinges

1 Cut out the sides, back, front, and bottom to the dimensions shown.

2 Glue and nail the box together, then cut a piece of two-by-three fir to glue behind the front face.

3 Drill a ⅝" diameter entry hole through the front face and the block, angling the hole upward. This provides a tunnel for the bees to crawl through.

4 Drill another ⅝" diameter hole high up on one side of the box. This hole acts as a vent. Staple a small square of wire screen over it from the inside so no other larger insects can get in.

5 Glue a ¾" thick layer of cotton batting over the back wall on the inside for the bees to cling to.

6 Cut a piece of fir or cedar slab for the roof, large enough to overhang the sides by ½" and the front by at least 1". Screw a pair of small hinges to the back of the box and to the end of the slab.

7 The bumblebee nest box can be screwed to a wall or post through the back (under the cotton) or through the bottom.

SECTIONAL VIEW

⅝" DIA. HOLE
WITH WIRE SCREEN
(ONE SIDE ONLY)

TWO HINGES

¾" THICK
COTTON
BATTING

6½"

5"

FIR TWO-
BY-THREE

¼" PLYWOOD
FACE

7½"

⅜" PLYWOOD BOTTOM

FRONT VIEW

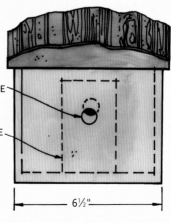

⅝" DIA. HOLE

FIR TWO-BY-THREE

6½"

BEE HOUSES

Solitary bees require a well-defined hole in which to lay an egg and provide nourishment for the growing pupa. This hole is more important than the object it is placed in, so providing such a "home" is a simple matter of drilling $5/16$" diameter holes (the optimum size) at least 3" deep. Using a $5/16$" diameter bit, measure 3" from the end of the bit and mark it with a small piece of masking tape to act as a depth-gauge. Now you can make bee homes in virtually any wooden object in your garden. Old fence posts, trees, and sheds are all suitable. But if you want to monitor these holes and need to remember where they are, you can drill holes in memorable objects and place them in your garden. The following projects are just a few suggestions.

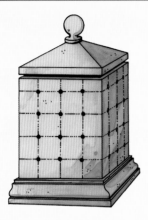

SECTIONAL VIEW (FROM ABOVE)

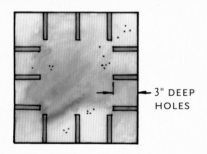

3" DEEP HOLES

Stake House

Sharpen one end of a fir or cedar two-by-two and drill one hole per side in it. Drive it into the ground.

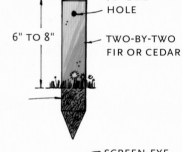

$5/16$" DIA. HOLE

6" TO 8"

TWO-BY-TWO FIR OR CEDAR

Hanging "Apartments"

Put a screw-eye in one end of an 18" long fir or cedar three-by-three and drill four or five holes in each side. Be sure to stagger them so one hole doesn't run into another. Hang the three-by-three from a branch or under the eaves near a window where you can observe it.

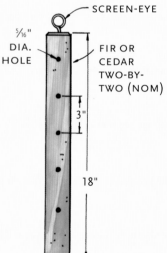

SCREEN-EYE

$5/16$" DIA. HOLE

FIR OR CEDAR TWO-BY-TWO (NOM)

3"

18"

Abandoned Toy

A child's old wooden toy, such as the building block shown, makes an excellent bee home. Drill a hole or two in the toy and place it somewhere accessible for viewing, but high enough up that a child could not grab it.

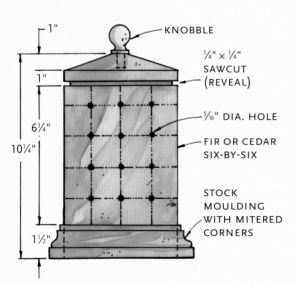

1"

KNOBBLE

1"

$1/4$" × $1/4$" SAWCUT (REVEAL)

$5/16$" DIA. HOLE

FIR OR CEDAR SIX-BY-SIX

$6\frac{3}{4}$"

$10\frac{1}{4}$"

STOCK MOULDING WITH MITERED CORNERS

$1\frac{1}{2}$"

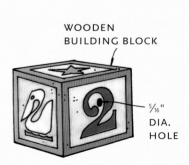

WOODEN BUILDING BLOCK

$5/16$" DIA. HOLE

Jewel beetle.

The larvae of these insects live underground for years, feeding on tree roots.

Hoppers are "true bugs" as well, and include froghoppers ("spit bugs"), treehoppers, and leafhoppers. Some hopper species can be a problem to gardeners and farmers when they appear in large numbers to dine on plants. They have been known to spread plant diseases as they feed. Large numbers of hoppers will attract a variety of welcome predators though.

Spiders

Spiders may fascinate or repel. Their webs are complex constructions of beauty but the creatures can be a fearsome sight to some. Spiders are beneficial in the garden—aggressive hunters helping to balance insect populations. They themselves provide food for

aphid strikes dismay into the hearts of even non-gardeners, such is their fame for plant infestation. Aphids reproduce incredibly quickly; in theory, each female can produce billions of young. On the flip side, aphids are a favorite food for many insects and birds due to sheer number and availablity, and can turn a sickly plant into a place to feast.

The song of the cicada is an announcement of summer in many parts of North America. On dry, hot days the treetops will buzz or clack, depending on the species, as the male cicadas sing with their abdominal sound-producing mechanisms. The mass emergence of these insects from the nymphal stage each year can leave trees laden with shed skins. In some parts of the country, where millions of cicadas emerge at once, their sound can drown out nearly everything else.

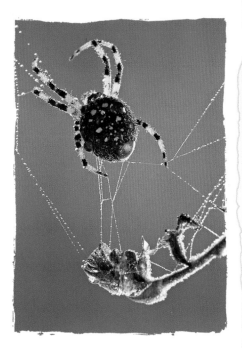

Shamrock spider.

Ambush Bugs

Among the purple flower spires of the butterfly bushes these days, I find secreted the strange little ambush bugs. Hardly half an inch long, they hide themselves among the florets, with enlarged forelegs outward, and thus wait for some insect victim to alight within their reach. I see these little apple-green and dark brown predaceous bugs holding cabbage and grayling and red admiral butterflies, flower flies and even bumblebees. The red admiral has a wing-spread of fully six times the length of its captor. Yet, when caught, it flaps only two or three times; then it becomes quiescent. Apparently, like the robber fly, the ambush bug injects an anesthetic through its sucking beak into the body of its victim.

Edwin Way Teale – Circle of the Seasons, 1953

109

Crab spider on bracken fern.

many birds and some species of insects. Encourage spiders to your wildlife habitat by providing tangled growth and places such as sunny rock walls with lots of crevices in which to hide.

In spite of their good qualities, spiders can instill an irrationally strong fear in many people. Those suffering from arachnophobia (a fear of spiders) are spooked by the idea of being bitten and are unnerved by the appearance and unexpected speed of spiders. It is helpful to remember that of the great many species of spiders you may find in your garden, there are only three species in North America that we should give a wide berth to. These are the black widow (*Lattodectus sp.*), which can have a deadly bite, the violin spider (*Loxosceles sp.*), also known as the brown recluse, whose bite develops a deep, long-lasting crater in the skin of the victim, and the hobo spider (*Teignaria agrestis*), a European introduction whose bite is similar to that of the brown recluse. The black widow, with its hourglass-shaped red marking, has until recently occurred mainly in undisturbed spaces and has been an unlikely visitor to your backyard. However, with housing developments encroaching into so many areas, the black widow is being seen more often around human settlement.

Centipedes and Millipedes

Centipedes and millipedes are neither insects nor spiders but they are beneficial bugs in the wildlife garden. Centipedes have flat bodies, are drab grayish-brown in color, have one pair of legs per segment, and can have as few as thirty legs despite what the name suggests. They prey on earthworms and insects which they kill with a venomous bite. Millipedes have round bodies, are black with yellow markings, have two pairs of legs per segment, and always have fewer than one

Funnel spider's web.

thousand legs in spite of their name. Millipedes feed on plant matter which they then excrete in a form that is easily broken down by bacteria. Both centipedes and millipedes avoid light, preferring to "lurk" under fallen trees, rocks, and bits of wood.

Sowbugs

Sowbugs, also known incorrectly as wood lice and pillbugs, are crustaceans (terrestrial relatives of crabs and lobsters). They have seven pairs of legs and are heavily armored with a segmented shell. Sowbugs feed on decaying plant and animal matter which is then excreted in a form that is easily broken down. You will find sowbugs in the same dark, damp hiding spots you find centipedes and millipedes.

Slugs and Snails

Slugs and snails are molluscs (terrestrial relatives of clams and oysters). These are the creatures that many people, notably gardeners, love to hate. Slugs and snails can cause damage in the garden by eating plants but many are an important food for other wild guests such as box turtles, toads, some birds, snakes, shrews, chipmunks, and field mice. Centipedes will also eat slugs, as will, strangely enough, firefly larva. The following is a list of organic and/or safe slug and snail controls you can experiment with, depending on your feelings toward the creatures:

- remove slug hiding places (weeds, leaves, rocks, mulch);
- sprinkle grit around plants (sand, wood ash, limestone);

Snail on bracken.

- if your family eats a lot of grapefruit, set out the empty halves each evening—collect them full of slugs the next morning and toss into the woods or garbage can;
- patrol your garden at night with salt, a big rock or other weapon, or handpick the slugs;
- commercial slug pots filled with beer;
- put seaweed all around the garden and in between rows (this is only effective until the salt is washed off by rain or watering);
- make slug traps by poking holes around the base of plastic yogurt or margarine containers and then set a small pile of slug bait in the center of the container so that none can spill out the holes (this is about the best way to use poison and still keep children, pets, and wild creatures safe).

Mantis Versus Yellowjacket

This afternoon, about 3:30 P.M., I come upon a green praying mantis, Tenodera sinensis, clinging to the bloom of a butterfly bush at the Insect Garden. It is an adult and winged. In the grip of its spined forelegs it holds a Monarch butterfly, one of a number now drifting along the hillside, beginning the long flight of the fall migration. The mantis commences eating its prize. As I watch, a yellowjacket wasp alights on the butterfly. It, too, is hungry for insect meat. Immediately it falls to with its mandibles. It pays little attention to the predatory mantis, a dozen times its own length and infinitely greater in bulk. To get at choice morsels, it even walks over the head of the feeding mantis. At last, it manages to get a little ball of meat, about the size of its head, stuck to the face of the mantis. This is too much. The mantis rears back, lets go the butterfly, paws at its face like a dog bothered by a fly. The wasp pursues its meat. It alights on the head of the mantis, runs about, seizes the morsel and flies away. Then it returns to the butterfly that has remained wedged among the florets of the buddleia bloom. The mantis retreats six inches and stares at the wasp with the intentness of a Manx cat but, perhaps because it is not especially hungry at the time, it makes no move to drive away the wasp or return to the feast. The little banded insect is undisputed master of the field.

Edwin Way Teale – Circle of the Seasons 1953

Earthworms

Earthworms are annelids, along with seaworms and leeches, and they are the unsung champions of the soil. The two most common worms in North American gardens are the night crawler (*Lumbricus terrestris*) and the field worm (*Allolobophora caliginosa*). Earthworms burrow or tunnel through soil, making openings for air and moisture to penetrate while creating space for other organisms. Worms feed on surface debris such as dead vegetable matter then excrete it back into the soil. Worm castings, as the excretions are called, enrich and help to balance the soil.

By assessing and addressing the needs of your soil, you can assist earthworms in their job. First, check the pH balance of your soil (many nurseries offer this service and there are kits that can be purchased). If it is too alkaline, apply sulfur at a rate of approximately 7 pounds per 500 square feet. Compost is an excellent source of sulfur (see the following for how to build various compost boxes). If your soil is too acid, add ground limestone at a rate of 25 pounds for every 500 square feet of surface. Lime will correct acid soil and add nutrients and minerals.

Vermicomposting

Worms and gardeners both love compost. Composting should appeal to any recycling urges you have as well as to your charitable feelings for backyard wildlife. If you are an apartment dweller, or do not have a backyard, you can compost on a small balcony or even in the house using a worm farm or vermicompost. The worms will make a rich compost you can

This box can be kept indoors or on the balcony. It will help to recycle food wastes, provide housing for hundreds or thousands of worms, and will result in dark, rich compost for your container garden.

1 You will need a plastic or wooden box between 8" and 12" deep. To determine the size of box you need, first calculate how much food waste you generate each week. You will need one square foot of surface area for every pound of food waste. Therefore, a household producing six pounds of compostable waste each week should have a worm box of 2' × 3'. The bin should have a lid or cover to conserve moisture and keep the compost dark. A piece of burlap will also work as a cover. Many people gauge the size of their composter by whether it will fit below the kitchen sink and then feed it accordingly.

2 Drill approximately ten ¼" holes in the bottom for drainage and aeration. If you find your compost getting too wet, drill more holes in the bottom (plastic containers often need more holes). Place your bin on bricks or wood blocks to allow air circulation underneath, and use a tray to catch excess liquid (this can be used as plant fertilizer).

3 For the worm bedding you can use shredded newspaper and cardboard, semi-dry fallen leaves, dried grass clippings, aged manure (if the box is outside), and peat moss. Acidity levels of peat moss differ throughout North America so you may want to check that you're not purchasing an overly acidic type. You should fill the container with a combination of bedding materials to give the worms some variety. The bedding should be as wet as a damp, wrung-out sponge. Add a couple of handfuls of soil or sand to aid the worms' digestive systems, then stir the bedding around to create air pockets.

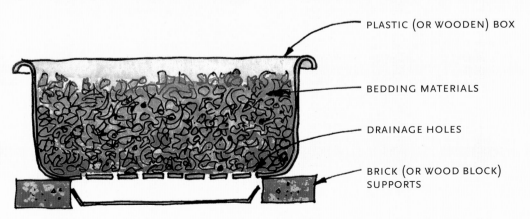

PLASTIC (OR WOODEN) BOX

BEDDING MATERIALS

DRAINAGE HOLES

BRICK (OR WOOD BLOCK) SUPPORTS

Snail.

World's Most Valuable Animal

Underground, the earthworm pushes or literally eats its way through the soil. Its mouth, functioning like a suction pump, draws earth into its body. There it is pulverized and organic particles are digested. The rest is deposited as castings at the mouth of the burrow. In its surface feeding, during the hours of darkness, the creature usually anchors its tail in its burrow and then, elongating its body, moves in a circle like a tethered calf in its search for bits of decayed leaves.

At such times, it is warned of danger by curious senses, amazingly keen. Although it has no eyes, its skin is so sensitive to light that it warns the worm when dawn is breaking. Although it has no ears, it is so sensitive to earth vibrations that it is alarmed by the footfall of even an approaching shrew.

This is the earthworm, that humble and invaluable creature I see so frequently along my way this morning.

Edwin Way Teale – *Circle of the Seasons, 1953*

114

place in your container gardens and window boxes. Vermicomposting will help use up food wastes and clippings from house plants.

You will need a plastic or wooden bin (do not use redwood or other highly aromatic woods that could kill the worms). See Project 25 for how to determine the size of bin necessary. Fill the bin three-quarters full of moist bedding material; this can be a mixture of shredded newspaper (non-glossy), computer paper, or cardboard; shredded leaves, straw, or hay; sawdust; peat moss; or aged manure (if the box is outdooes). Add enough worms to eat all the food waste you produce in a week. If you produce a pound of food waste, you will need approximately two pounds of worms (about 2,000 worms). Use redworms, also known as red wigglers (*Eisenia fetida*) as they are hardy, reproduce quickly, and have a voracious appetite. You can find them in your friends' compost bins, at some garden centers, by mail-order from worm farms, or in old manure piles.

When you add the food waste, pull aside the bedding and bury the food quite deeply into the pile. Put it in different locations each time to make sure no area gets overloaded. Use only fruit and vegetable matter, eggshells, teabags, and coffee grounds. Do not add meat, dairy products, oil, grains, or any items that do not break down (plastic, glass, tin, bones, etc.). Make sure to sprinkle crushed and dried eggshells on the top of the compost regularly to keep it from getting too acidic.

After about two and a half months, you should be ready to harvest your compost. When it seems that there is more dark brown casting material (worm droppings) than bedding, you can move the finished compost over to one side and fill the empty space with fresh, damp bedding. Or you can shine a bright light onto the top of the bin, wait ten minutes for the worms to dive deeper to avoid the light, then remove the top layer. Repeat until you have nearly emptied the compost and then refill with fresh, damp bedding. Leave a bit of the finished compost in the bin and mix it with the fresh bedding. When the worms have moved over to the new material, remove the finished compost and place it in your flower and vegetable containers. The number of worms in the box will be constrained by the size of the box, so there will not be an overpopulation problem. If you do want to release them, give them as a gift to a fellow gardener, for their compost box or manure pile.

If your worm compost begins to smell, you are probably overloading it with food waste. If this happens, gently stir up the compost and stop adding to it until the worms have had a chance to break down the old matter. You can also check that the drainage holes aren't blocked and that the bedding hasn't become too acidic from citrus fruits and other acidic wastes. If so, you can adjust it by adding a small amount of dolomite lime and cutting down on the orange peels.

Keep the worm compost warm, but out of direct sunlight; room temperature or slightly higher is best. If the composter sits on the balcony, bring it in during cold weather.

The corvid family enjoys compost from open bins.

Outdoor Composting

If you live in a rural or suburban area you can add manure, pulled weeds (unless they've just gone to seed, are invasive or diseased), lawn clippings, and fallen fruits. Place your compost box in a sunny corner on bare ground. Layer the compost material with lime and manure if possible.

After your compost pile has been sitting for a month, turn it over and sprinkle with some water. Then a month later, turn the pile again. Your compost will be ready to spread in about six months. You can also compost directly into your garden. Place the compost in trenches, lightly cover with soil, and continue with layers in this way. Direct composting will create vibrantly rich soil conditions just like a compost box will.

A garden filled with rich soil will be inhabited by worms too numerous to count and they will help maintain the health of your soil. Another bonus of a worm-rich backyard is that they are a favorite food for visiting birds such as robins, as well as food for toads and other creatures.

Integrated Pest Management

Integrated Pest Management, or IPM, is a system that emphasizes a balance of natural pest controls in the garden. The system's principles are stated in the context of farming, but can easily be adapted by wildlife stewards for backyard habitats. IPM is defined as a socially acceptable, environmentally responsible, and economically practical method for protecting crops.

The first principle of IPM is to be prepared. This means knowing how to minimize the risk of pests such as insects, diseases, and invasive weeds, and how to deal with them if they occur. If you plan your wildlife garden well, you should find yourself prepared to deal with pests.

Prevention is the second step for practicing IPM in your wildlife garden. To protect your garden you should try to promote biological diversity (a healthy balance of pests and predators), use native plant species that are equipped to resist pests, clean up infestations by removing and destroying sources of disease (infected plants), and plant in suitable areas for each species. If you are maintaining a wildlife food garden such as a bird food patch (see page 196), rotate the crops to break pest life cycles.

Third, keep a close eye on your garden so you know what pests are there and in what approximate numbers.

Based on your observations of pests in your garden, you can decide whether they need to be controlled or not. The basic idea is that crops can tolerate a certain number of pests with a certain amount of loss before any action needs to take place. In a backyard wildlife garden the bottom line will be the health of the majority of creatures in the garden, rather than the loss of a cash crop. For instance, using an insecticide to rid your garden of an infestation of aphids will also rid your garden of many beneficial bugs, and it will harm birds. If you decide to act against a pest, IPM emphasizes choosing the treatment that will work well, but will have minimal harmful effects. The different options for pest control are:

- Cultural: such as crop rotation;
- Mechanical: such as hoeing and weeding by hand to destroy insect cover, draping crops with fine cloth such as Remay, and handpicking larger insects from plants;
- Biological: releasing ladybugs or parasitic wasps;
- Companion planting: for instance, planting marigolds or parsley to deter carrot rust fly, and growing garlic near roses to repel aphids;
- Genetic: planting disease-resistant strains of a particular plant;
- Chemical: using herbicides, fungicides, or insecticides.

In wildlife gardening the emphasis is on cultural, mechanical, and biological pest control and more often, a policy of non-interference. Integrated Pest Management suggests that if action is called for, that it be done at the most opportune

RECYCLED COMPOST BIN

A simple compost bin can be made using old wooden pallets. Screw or wire three pallets together. Attach hook and eyes to the front edge of the bin and the last pallet to create a door that you can remove (Figure 3). You can also add to this bin, making it into a two- or three-bin compost by adding more pallets (Figure 4).

TOOLS & MATERIALS
- Four to six wooden pallets
- 32 wood screws
- Two to three sets of hook and eyes
- Screwdriver

FIGURE 1

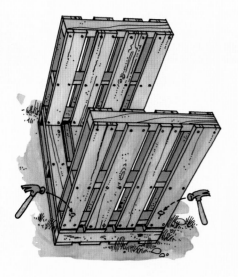

FIGURE 2

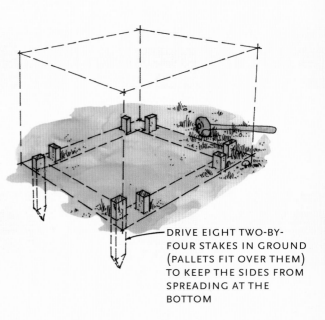

DRIVE EIGHT TWO-BY-FOUR STAKES IN GROUND (PALLETS FIT OVER THEM) TO KEEP THE SIDES FROM SPREADING AT THE BOTTOM

FIGURE 3

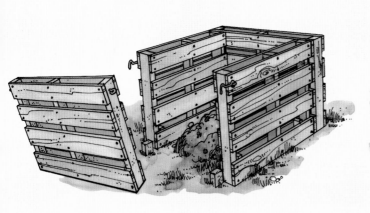

FIGURE 4

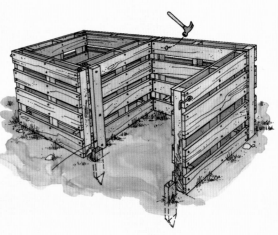

— WIRE MESH BIN —

TOOLS & MATERIALS

- 15 feet of 24" wide ½" hardware cloth
- Plastic-coated wire ties (or metal or plastic clips)
- Wire cutters

Cut five 3' long sections of wire mesh. Make sure to cut through the middle of each square of wire so that you are left with ½" long wires sticking out along the top and bottom. Choose a top and bottom for each panel and then turn the wires over on the top so they won't scratch you when you reach into the bin. Leave the bottom wires so they will stick into the ground and keep the bin stable. Attach the five panels to one another using wire clips and find a suitable place in the backyard to set it up.

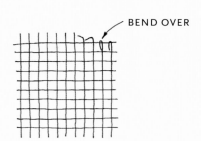

BEND OVER

118

time. For instance, weeds should be dealt with before the seedlings rise much above the surface of the soil.

Finally, IPM suggests re-evaluating actions taken to control pests over both the short term and the long term. At the end of each year or each season, give some thought to the pest control measures you implemented and how well they worked, or if you would approach the problem differently next time.

The basic principles of IPM are essential to the development and management of a wildlife garden. The more diligent you are in planning your garden with the needs of wildlife in mind, the less pest management you will have to do. After all, a successful wildlife garden will contain a healthy population of predators as well as pests. (Information adapted from An IPM Primer by the National Network.)

CHAPTER

7

Reptiles and Amphibians

———◆———

Agood way to remember the difference between an amphibian and a reptile is to ask yourself, Does this creature undergo an amazing transformation from egg to adult? If so, then it is an amphibian with a larval stage, and the most familiar example of this is the change from tadpole to frog. All amphibians hatch from jellyish eggs without

shells, while reptiles lay eggs with leathery shells, and their young emerge fully independent—some reptiles even give birth to live young.

Frogs (including toads) and salamanders (including newts) are the two main groups of amphibians. In the tropics there is a third less common group that are legless. Reptiles are divided into turtles, lizards, snakes, and crocodilians.

Reptiles and amphibians are both cold-blooded vertebrates that rely on external conditions to raise their internal temperatures. You are witness to this when you see a turtle sitting on a log in a lake, or when a frog basks amongst floating plants in a swamp. Skin is a good field mark—reptiles have hard scales, amphibians have soft, moist skin, with most toads looking warty, and some salamanders feeling like sandpaper.

If you maintain a natural landscape, your yard has a greater chance of becom-

Garter snake.

Releasing a garter snake previously injured by a cat.

ing, and remaining, home to reptiles and amphibians than if you landscape with concrete borders and highly maintained plantings. Any nearby undeveloped areas such as greenbelts, fields, vacant lots, plus ponds and marshes contribute to your property's attractiveness as both home and range for reptiles and amphibians.

Human habitation poses many threats to these animals—cats and dogs take a serious toll, children's interest (or fear) can have devastating consequences if not monitored, lawn mowers kill many snakes, cars in driveways kill creatures that have become comfortable basking around humans, and pesticides poison food supplies. It can be difficult to attract amphibians and reptiles, and the temptation to relocate them from elsewhere may seem like the answer, but if a species is not found in a certain area, there is a reason.

Snakes

Snakes are common in the wildlife garden. You will find most of them living under logs, rocks, or boards, down holes, or under dense foliage. If you have ground covers such as St. John's Wort growing in your yard, walk by on a hot day and listen for the rustling of snakes as they slither for cover.

Most snakes you'll find in the garden are harmless animals that prefer to avoid encounters with humans; they will only hiss or strike when threatened. If you have ever nudged a basking snake with a stick to get it off a road, the open-mouthed attack it provoked probably made you jump. As fierce as they may look, it is a thrill to observe a snake in its natural habitat. Field guides and local natural history societies can help with identification of species—especially important if there are poisonous snakes in your area.

Garter snakes, of which there are about a dozen different species, have one of the largest ranges and distribution of any snake in the world and, with the exception of deserts, cover North America. They eat insects, frogs, salamanders, birds, small mammals, and fish (some species of garter snakes swim, so goldfish in a pond may not be safe without a cover).

If you are lucky, you may attract colorful and unusual snakes such as ringnecks, kingsnakes, hognoses, ratsnakes, and corn snakes depending on where you live.

Garter snake species.

Desert tortoise.

Snakes suffer from a bad reputation because so many people are afraid of them, but they are a natural and valuable part of nature. Some larger snakes may climb trees to get at nest boxes, but you can usually prevent them from reaching the boxes by putting up predator guards (see Projects 34 and 35).

To provide homes for snakes, try placing a few boards on the ground in out-of-the-way places, or build a log or brush pile (see page 16 and Project 22), an un-mortared stone wall (see Project 29), rock piles, or a stone or brick pathway for basking (see Project 30). Water sources and

ground cover will also attract snakes. You may be lucky enough to observe snakes catching prey, climbing through branches, or piled high like spaghetti when they come out of hibernation.

Turtles

Turtles are unique. They have existed for approximately 250 million years, and are the only creature whose ribs are fused to their shell, with leg bones tucked inside the body cavity.

Eastern box turtles, snapping turtles (on land, these turtles will defend themselves by biting), spotted turtles, stinkpots (musk turtles), wood turtles, pond sliders, and mud turtles can all be found in North America depending on where you live.

Painted turtles probably have the widest distribution of any North American turtle. Abundance and location of

Painted turtle.

Alligator lizard.

basking sites is an important factor in determining whether your pond will support a painted turtle population. Preferences include full exposure to the sun for most of the day, open views of the shore, closeness to the shore (not too close, not too far away), and surfaces large enough so that turtles do not have to stack themselves on top of each other. Logs, branches, tree trunks, rocks, and floating debris are all used by turtles to bask on, and most species prefer a deep, permanent pond with a soft mud bottom (there are turtle species that frequent streams, and still others that are mainly terrestrial). Some turtles may even make use of a ground-level birdbath. If you have a pond, you can build a simple basking raft in the hope of attracting the local species (see Project 28).

Depending on the species, turtles eat a wide variety of foods—snails, insects, small mammals and birds, frogs and tadpoles, fish, cattail seeds and stems, algae, rotting carcasses, crayfish, earthworms and leeches, fruits, berries, plant leaves, and mushrooms.

Crocodilians

Seven species of alligators are found in North America, the most common being the American alligator which is found in nine southern states. It is restricted to wetlands, canals, and major rivers but can be seen in suburban backyards surrounding these habitats. American alligators were nearly extinct by the 1960s but have recovered in many areas thanks to protected land. Alligators are entirely carnivorous and feed on birds, mammals, other smaller reptiles, fish, amphibians, and

The green anole thrives in suburban and urban areas.

Use any kind of wide board, large enough for several turtles to bask on, and attach a tether of wire or rope to a screw-eye in one end, leaving some excess line. A concrete building block at the bottom of the pond, tied to the board, will work well as an anchor. If you're concerned about the "raft" swinging in the wind, ending up too close to foliage where predators may lurk, attach an anchor at both ends. You can adjust the length of tether to allow one end of the board to be submerged, enabling even small turtles to climb up. An alternative would be to tie a weight onto the screw-eye to get one end of the board low in the water. If you can, position the basking raft where it will get the sun early in the day. You may have to adjust the tether occasionally to allow for fluctuations in the water level of your pond.

Blue spiny lizard.

snails. The young will also eat insects and frogs. If you live in alligator territory and the animals visit your backyard, that may be wildlife enough without attracting creatures that will just end up as easy prey.

Lizards

When you find a lizard, check for claws. It's another good field mark after the "skin test" mentioned previously, if you're still not sure about your discovery. With salamanders being the same general shape as lizards, confusion is common. Of the 3,000 species of lizards in the world, adaptations are remarkable—some live on broiling desert sand, others swim in the ocean, some live their entire lives amongst tree branches, while still other lizards have flaps of skin that enable them to glide short distances through the air. The animals range from three inches long to ten feet in length.

North America is home to about 115 species and, as a sampling, includes the green anole (can be found in urban and suburban areas), five-lined skink (skinks can be quite colorful and are frequently found in backyards), the poisonous and gaudily patterned Gila monster (seen around streams and irrigated farm fields), the toad-like, regal horned lizard (found from desert to mountain slope, often near ant hills), northern/southern alligator lizards (a secretive family often found in dense vegetation and in wood piles), and western/eastern fence lizards (seen on sides of buildings, tree trunks, fences, lumber piles, and rocks).

Lizards will generally hide in stone

Chuckwalla.

125

Red-legged frog.

piles, brush piles, under boards, in stacks of firewood, or in dense foliage. Until you develop your "reptile eyes" it can be difficult to spot the creatures, as they blend in well with their surroundings.

Building an Unmortared Stone Wall

Unmortared, or dry, stone walls provide shelter to various creatures. They are less stable than mortared walls, but the slight gaps between the stones are ideal for basking and resting. A stone wall encircling a pond, or separating one part of a wildlife garden from another, is rustically appealing. About two and a half feet high is adequate if it is intended for division and decoration and use by wild creatures, rather than as an actual barrier. Traditional English stone walls are around four and a half feet high but are used as fences for livestock. The destruction of many of these walls in Britain is proving disastrous for wildlife, including small mammals, birds, insects, and reptiles that have depended on the walls for shelter.

Building a Stepping Stone Path

A stepping stone path will be a hit with worms, beetles, lizards, and many more creatures who like to stay close to the ground. In addition, it will be a traditional focal point for your backyard, one that will help keep human feet away from areas that shouldn't be disturbed. As with a stone fence, a stone path works well as a visual divider between areas in the wildlife garden.

Frogs and Toads

It's easy to recognize frogs and toads by their basic body shapes, but it's not so easy to differentiate between the two. Technically, both are classified as frogs, and the variations in each are astounding. In the broadest sense, though, frogs live in water, are streamlined with long legs and webbed feet for swimming, and have smooth skin. Toads, on the other hand, live on land and have tough, warty skin to prevent moisture loss from evaporation, and are squat-bodied with short legs designed to hop and crawl. Toads are adept at burrowing, frogs excel at swimming. Identification of frogs and toads is simplified by using a local field guide with clear photos or detailed sketches.

To attract these amphibians, and have them reside or breed on your property, you need to offer water. A backyard wildlife habitat with a fish-free pond (fish eat all stages of amphibians), a ground-level rainwater pool, or ground-level birdbath, will help to entice them. It is important that your pond or shallow pool have gradually sloping sides, as young toads head for high ground as

UNMORTARED STONE WALL

1. Dig out and level the soil that will be the foundation for the wall.

2. Begin by piling the largest stones at the base of the wall. Insert smaller stones between the gaps to make the wall more stable.

3. As you layer upwards, each new stone must cover the two beneath it where they join.

4. When you have reached halfway up the desired height of the wall, place long stones across the pile. These are called "through stones" and they serve to hold the wall together.

5. Take your time, and if you make a mistake, don't hesitate to take off a layer of rocks to ensure that the whole structure is stable. Traditional "wallers" spend years learning their craft. One added benefit you will gain from building a dry stone wall, besides a strong back, is added intimacy with your wildlife garden. All that time spent stacking rocks is sure to reveal some new creatures!

TOOLS & MATERIALS

- Enough stone to build to the height and length desired. (A two and a half foot high wall will require approximately three quarters of a ton of stone for each three feet of wall. The stones should be a mix of sizes and shapes. You can gather the stones yourself or buy them from a quarry or cut stone supplier. It is a good idea to consult a stonework book before you begin.)
- A pick and shovel
- A level

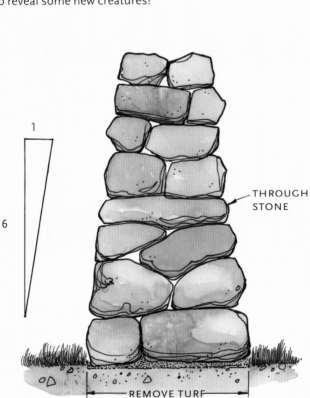

1

6

THROUGH STONE

REMOVE TURF

STEPPING STONE PATH

1. Outline the intended path using stakes and string.

2. Use a shovel to dig all the sod from the path outline. The excavation for the path should be 4" deep and as level and smooth as possible (keep the sod aside to backfill the path where necessary).

3. Fill the dug-out pathway with 2" of sand. This should be angled gradually from the center toward the sides so the water runs off easily.

4. Rake the path and sprinkle it with water to compact the sand.

5. Starting at one corner, place the stones one at a time, one inch apart, inside the path outline. Check each stone to make sure it doesn't wobble. If it does, take it out and flatten the area further until the stone doesn't move when you step on it. Use a level on each stone to make sure it is sitting straight.

6. Once all the stones are in place, fill in between them with damp sand. Let the path sit for a couple of days before using. After the path has set, sweep it thoroughly and enjoy.

FAIRWAY (SECTIONAL VIEW)

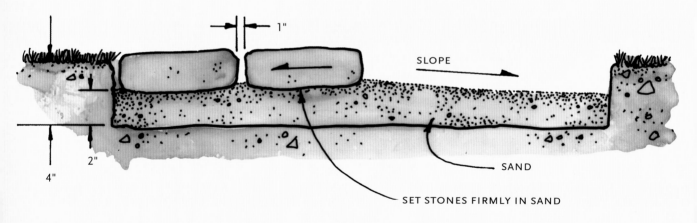

1"

SLOPE

2"

4"

SAND

SET STONES FIRMLY IN SAND

Bullfrogs.

soon as they are able. As well, waterside plants, leaf litter beneath shrubs, patches of unmown grass (especially close to water sources and damp spots), logs, and stumps (which can be brought in) are all factors that make up amphibian habitat. Pesticide- and herbicide-free surroundings are important, and if you are near undeveloped areas and existing breeding spots, the chances of frogs and toads ending up in your backyard are much greater. If you want to make your own homes for toads, dig small depressions in shady areas (preferably near water) and cover the holes with large flat rocks or boards. Or create an amphibian home (see Project 31) from an old clay flowerpot.

Frogs and toads are valuable inhabitants of the wildlife garden. Both tadpoles and young toads are a favorite food for many animals, and they themselves are predators of large numbers of insects (garden pests included). Depending on species, their diets can also include beetles, earthworms, spiders, snails, slugs, and aquatic crustaceans. Bullfrogs are known to eat mice, fish, turtles, birds, snakes, and even other frogs, including their own kind. And both frogs and toads contribute to the chorus of trills, squawks, and croaks that is the music of spring.

Frogs and toads should not ordinarily be handled. Their permeable skin may absorb chemicals from things such as hand lotion or bug repellents. In turn, amphibians' toxic skin secretions can cause illness in humans and pets.

Salamanders and Newts

Conserving natural habitats and creating new ones will go a long way toward helping preserve these unique amphibians that have existed since prehistoric times. Silent, and usually hidden from view, both terrestrial and aquatic salamanders in

Pacific treefrog.

Toad Music

Walking beside the swamp at 3:30 P.M., I heard music of a different kind. There came to my ears, for the first time this year, the metallic, far-carrying bray of a Fowler's toad. The spring peeper, Hyla crucifer, has been filling the marsh-nights with sound since early April. A few American toads, during the past week or so, have been lifting their voices in that sweet, sustained trill that is held for half a minute at a time. Now begins the shorter song of Bufo fowleri. Each year, these batrachian love songs of spring begin in the same order: First the peeper, then the American toad, and finally, fowleri.

Edwin Way Teale – Circle of the Seasons, 1953

North America (including newts) carry out their lives in cool damp places.

As a general rule, salamanders have smooth skin (no scales), four legs, and a tail, and are very similar in shape to lizards. They need moist places to hide—leaf debris, thick grass, rotten logs, and stumps; aquatic species need bodies of water to breed in (temporary ponds are often adequate). All life stages of salamanders are basically carnivorous, and can include a diet of insects, fish, frogs, worms, fish eggs, water fleas, aquatic crustaceans, and snails. It is a thrill to spot a salamander slowly making its way along the ground, or to watch a breeding migration, especially if it is nowhere near a road. Many communities have taken an active part in conserving amphibians by installing tunnels for them to cross highways safely, and by erecting signs warning motorists of their presence.

Long-toed salamander rescued from a cat.

To make a shelter for amphibians, dig a shallow (3" to 4" deep) hollow in the ground about 6" to 8" in diameter. Position a short section of concrete drain tile (pipe) in the ground so it slopes down toward the hollow (Figure 1). Pile large, flat rocks around the end of the drain tile and over the hollow to form a kind of "stone igloo" (Figures 2 and 3).

Homes for toads, salamanders, and newts are easy to create from slabs of firewood set overtop bricks; this gives the animals a safe place to rest (Figures 4 and 5). These homes should stay fairly damp because they're shaded, and placing them on grass will help.

Clay flowerpots, old or new, patterned or plain, make convenient amphibian homes. You can use them upside down with a door chipped out (you may want to sand any sharp edges) and rocks on top to weigh them down if necessary (Figure 6), or lay a pot on its side, pushing it into the ground a little for stability (Figure 7).

A word of caution: Predators can easily overturn flowerpots. Depending on your location, you may want to hide the pots in undergrowth, or secure them to the ground with plenty of soil, rocks, or vegetation.

FIGURE 1

DRAIN TILE

HOLLOWED OUT
AREA BELOW STONES

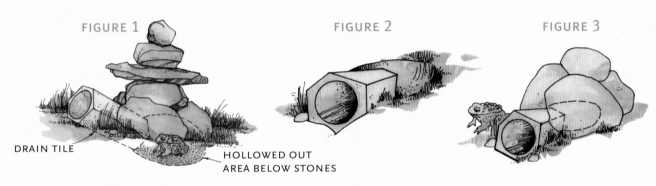

FIGURE 2

FIGURE 3

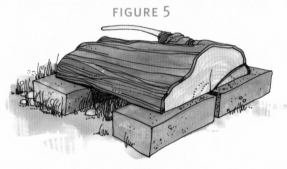

FIGURE 4

FIGURE 5

FIGURE 6

FIGURE 7

Bats and Bat Projects

Bats are unique and beneficial members of the animal kingdom. They are the only true flying mammals, and thanks to a rapid metabolism that requires large amounts of food, a single bat can eat hundreds of insects in an hour; a large colony can devour tons of insects in one night. Bats are an ecologically sound pest control, and to attract these intriguing animals, try planting flowers that moths (a diet staple) favor—Four O'-Clocks, Nicotiana, and Night Jessamine are among the scented, evening-blooming flowers (see Chapter 5). Open water is another powerful bat attractant—the animals scoop up a drink while flying over ponds, lakes, rain barrels, and streams, as well as catch bugs over these sources.

Feared over the ages, bats have long been the target of superstition and ignorance. Their numbers have been decimated by extermination programs, as well as by pesticides, to the point where several species of bats are severely endangered. They do not get tangled in people's hair; rather, they may skim close to your head and catch bugs that are attracted to your body heat and scent. Bats navigate using a sonar-like system called echolocation. The system uses supersonic sounds emitted from the bat's mouth or nose. These then bounce off objects, returning to the bat's ears as echoes.

Adding to the general fear is the bat's reputation for spreading rabies. This has been greatly exaggerated—bats *can* contract rabies, but the stricken animals usually sicken and die quickly. Statistics say you are more likely to be struck by lightning than to get rabies from a bat. If a bat is acting disoriented or strange in any way, you should avoid it completely, and report the sighting to your local conservation office. As well, fear of blood-sucking bats is unjustified, unless you come across any of three particular species found only in tropical rain forests. Even then, the bats prey mostly on other animals, rarely on humans.

An organization called Bat Conservation International has been instrumental in educating people about bats, and encouraging research into providing places for bats to live. According to BCI's guide, *The Bat House Builder's Handbook*, bats living in one cave in Texas eat up to two hundred and fifty tons of insects in the surrounding towns and farmland each year. Imagine the effects of bats in every wildlife habitat—a good case for providing them with homes. Bats are important pollinators for many species of plants, and their role in a healthy ecosystem cannot be underestimated. BCI suggests that people interested in learning about and housing bats join the North American Bat House Research Project. For more information, contact Bat Conservation International, P.O. Box 162603, Austin, Texas 78716, www.batcon.org.

Designing and Placing Your Bat House

Bats range across most of North America, and many species are easily attracted to bat houses. The main factors influencing the success of the houses are location and temperature. As you will see in the following bat house projects, bat houses themselves vary in size and materials. In general, they need to be exposed to at least six hours of sun a day and should be a minimum of twelve feet off the ground. They can be positioned on posts, and protected from predators such as raccoons, cats, and snakes, by using a metal

or plastic sheath (see page 149, Figure 1) or Cone Guard (see Project 34). You can also place your bat house on a building, or mount it on a bare tree trunk. Make sure there are no obstructions near the house, such as overhanging branches. Bats avoid areas that their sensitive echo systems perceive as cluttered.

Bat houses should be designed to maintain as stable a temperature as possible. They should be sealed and caulked to prevent drafts and moisture, problems that will decrease the chances of bats taking up residence, but if you live in a hot area, ventilation slots are necessary. In northern climates, bat houses should be stained or painted a dark color, and in the south, the houses may need a light color, or reflective coating. Many people in cooler climates cover their bat houses with insulation or tarpaper to trap the heat.

It may help to place two or more bat houses in close proximity. A good option is to place two houses on a single post, facing in different directions. Given a selection of locations, bats may move from one house to another as temperature dictates. Before you install a whole series of bat houses, experiment with two to see which placement works best. Keep experimenting until you find a spot that works. Bats like to be near water, such as lakes, ponds, marshes, and rivers. They are also drawn to agricultural landscapes, particularly orchards, and are found in urban areas, proof that they can be attracted to a wide variety of habitats.

You don't have to build a bat house to provide a home for these animals. You

Flittermice

In the long June twilight tonight I watch the bats, the flittermice, zigzag in their wildly staggering flight above the cattails. How beneficial they are; how unearned and unjust is the long enmity that has surrounded them! I wonder if this enmity will be lessened now that the secret of their uncanny ability in avoiding objects in the dark has been exposed as similar to the sonic depth finder man uses at sea. No longer does the skill of the bat seem allied to sorcery. Understanding has replaced mystification. And this, it is to be hoped, may lighten the load of dislike that has descended from ages when the human mind viewed the natural world through superstition's dark and distorting glass.

Edwin Way Teale – Circle of the Seasons, 1953

Erecting a bat house.

summer, or it may be in use for months. Bats in most areas begin to arrive in April or May and leave anywhere from July to October. If the houses and locations you provide for your bat guests are ideal, you may be able to extend the length of their stay.

If you provide a nursery house, the young will be born in late spring. You can check if your bat nursery contains young by waiting outside the bat nursery at dusk and watching all the adults leave for a night of bug-hunting. Look up into the house with a flashlight to see if any young are visible. Never touch the bat house or the pole it is attached to as bats are easily disturbed and may be frightened out of the house. Young bats will be weaned and flying in about a month. You can peer into your bat house for a few seconds each time, but don't overdo it.

Some people are concerned that if they entice bats to their backyards, the bats may decide to move into the house or attic. Don't worry. If your home has an ideal location for bats, they will already be there. If your property does harbor bats in some undesirable place, you can evict them with a minimum of trauma (to yourself and the bats). First, put up at least one or two bat houses. Your bats may decide to move without any prompting from you. If they don't, have the new bat houses in place at least a month before the eviction. Make sure the young are able to fly (early spring or late summer), then wait until dusk when all the bats are away on an evening out-flight. Cover the exit hole or crack with garden netting, leaving a foot of extra netting all the way

can also wrap a tree trunk with about two feet of sheet metal (painted black) or tarpaper, and hope that bats will use the space between it and the tree as a roost (taper the wrap from tight at the top, to a couple of inches open at the bottom for an entrance). Remember to place these homes at least twelve feet from the ground.

Bats and Their Habits

Many bats migrate, up to a thousand miles, while others hibernate, often in mines and caves and other undisturbed places. Your bat house may be occupied for only a few weeks in the spring or early around. Use duct tape to secure it, and leave it loose at the bottom. This will allow bats to leave should any still remain, but won't let them return.

Forty-five species of bats live in North America, and the most likely to be enticed to bat houses are the big brown bat (*Eptesicus fuscus*), the little brown bat (*Myotis lucifugus*), the Mexican free-tailed bat (*Tadarida brasiliensis*), the California myotis (*Myotis californicus*), the long-eared bat (*Myotis evotis*), the pallid bat(*Antrozous pallidus*), and the Yuma bat (*Myotis yumanensis*). Keep watch at dusk for the rapid flutter of wings that say bats!, not birds, and if there is a street light or yard light nearby, all the better to watch these animals hunt.

The Bat

About 3:30 P.M., on this hot and brilliant afternoon, I come upon a little red bat in a wild cherry tree at the garden. It is hanging upside-down from a small branch on a level with my head. Its wings are wrapped tightly about its body. It resembles a reddish, furry cocoon hanging there. In spite of the brightness of the sun, it is sleeping soundly. I photograph it from several angles. Each time the shutter clicks, I notice the little bat gives a convulsive jerk. It is responding to the high-pitched metallic sound even in its sleep.

Edwin Way Teale – Circle of the Seasons, 1953

BAT NURSERY

Yes, this is a nursery for bats; a retreat from the elements and an alternative to a crevice in a rock or tree. The design is a bit elaborate but is intended to be an attractive alternative to the usual man-made bat boxes. This large box, intended to house many families of bats, is actually two identical boxes back to back with a large roof to shed the rain and snow. Each box is mounted on a two-by-four post. The construction may appear complex, but once the slotted two-by-six sides are made, the box is simple to make.

TOOLS & MATERIALS

- Table saw and band saw or jigsaw
- Matt knife (for cutting rigid insulation)
- Hammer
- Drill with ½" diameter bit
- Staple gun with stainless steel staples
- Tin shears (if sheet metal is used on roof)
- Heavy duty scissors (for cutting hardware cloth)
- Sides (4) – two-by-six fir 20½" long each
- Fronts (2) – ½" fir plywood 11" × 18½" each
- Backs (2) – ½" fir plywood 15" × 18 ½" each
- Tops (2) – ½" fir plywood 4"½" × 20" each
- Roofs (2) – ½" fir plywood 9" × 27" each
- Main partitions (4) – ¼" fir plywood 15" × 18½" each
- Insulation covers (4) – ¼" fir plywood, two at 12" × 18½" and two at 10" × 18½"
- Landing panels (2) – ¼" fir plywood 8" × 18½" each
- Cover panels (2) – ¼" fir plywood 5" × 18½" each
- End caps (2) – ½" fir plywood 7" × 14" each
- Battens (4) – one-by-two × 17" long each
- Box spacer – one-by-two × 20"
- Mesh – two square yards
- Insulation – ¾" rigid styrofoam, two pieces: 8½" × 17", two pieces: 10½" × 17", two pieces 4½" × 20"
- Roof ridge cover – 7" × 27" galvanized metal aluminum, duroid roofing
- Roof cap – two-by-three fir 27" long
- General construction caulking
- Galvanized common nails – 1", 1½", and 2½" long
- Bolts (2) – ½" diameter × 8" long with a nut and two washers each
- Posts (2) – two-by-four × 12'-0" long each
- Ladder supports (2) – two-by-four × 4' long each
- Bat decorations (2) – ⅛" plywood 4" × 12"

1 To make each box, first cut two fir two-by-six sizes 20½" long for the sides. To add a decorative flair to the utilitarian nursery, cut the scroll-work at the bottom of each box using the pattern on page 141. Using the dimensions in Figure 1 cut four ¼" slots and two ½" rabbets on the table saw, all 1" deep.

2 Glue and nail a sheet of ½" plywood 15" × 18½" into the back corner rabbet of each two by six, leaving 3" protruding above the top. Now glue and nail a ½" sheet of plywood 4½" × 20" to the top ends of each two-by-six and to the plywood back.

3 Glue and nail a fir one-by-two inside the bottom edge of the back as shown. Fill the resulting space inside the back with ¾" thick rigid styrofoam insulation.

4 Starting at the bottom of the two-by-six sides, slide a sheet of ¼" plywood 12" × 18½" up to cover the insulation. Nail it to the one-by-two batten to hold it in place (Step 3).

5 Glue a ¼" × ¾" × ¾" long piece of wood into the slot below the ¼" plywood sheet (in each two-by-six) as a spacer. Slide a second sheet of ¼" plywood 8" × 18½" up the same ¼" slot from the bottom. This will have to be "toe-nailed" into each two-by-six to hold it in place.

FIGURE 1

SECTIONAL SIDE VIEW

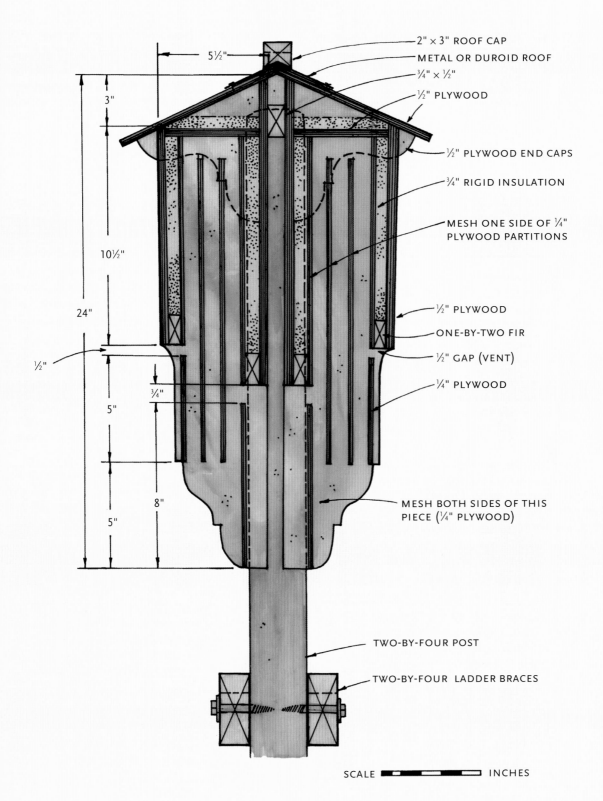

2" × 3" ROOF CAP

METAL OR DUROID ROOF

¾" × ½"

½" PLYWOOD

½" PLYWOOD END CAPS

¾" RIGID INSULATION

MESH ONE SIDE OF ¼" PLYWOOD PARTITIONS

½" PLYWOOD

ONE-BY-TWO FIR

½" GAP (VENT)

¼" PLYWOOD

MESH BOTH SIDES OF THIS PIECE (¼" PLYWOOD)

TWO-BY-FOUR POST

TWO-BY-FOUR LADDER BRACES

5½"

3"

10½"

24"

½"

¾"

5"

8"

5"

SCALE ▬▬▬▬▬ INCHES

137

6 Staple an 8" × 17" sheet of hardware cloth to both sides of this piece of plywood (A2) and one 12" × 17" sheet of hardware cloth to the plywood (A1) above it. The hardware cloth will give all the bats something to cling to while resting in the box and allow them to move about more easily.

7 Now slide the two middle sheets of ¼" plywood 15" × 18½" (B) and (C), but first glue a 1" × ¼" × 1" deep wood spacer right at the top of each slot (on both sides) as shown in Figure 5.

8 Staple a 15" × 17" sheet of hardware cloth to each partition to the side facing the front. To hold the partitions in place, glue long strips of ¼" × 1" wood into the slots below them (on both sides), and trim them off at the bottom.

9 The last two ¼" plywood sheets do not need hardware cloth. However, a one by two fir batten must be glued and nailed along the bottom edge of the top sheet of ¼" plywood (D1), 18" × 18½" and facing outward. This will hold the rigid insulation in place.

10 Slide the top sheet up in place and glue a ½" long spacer in the slot at each side. Slide the lower sheet (D2) 5" × 18½" in place and glue a wooden stop in each slot below it on both sides. Trim them off at the bottom.

11 Lay ¾" rigid insulation in place (Figure 8) and glue and nail ½" plywood 11" × 18½" into the rabbets on each side. This will cover the insulation, be flush with the bottom edge of the one-by-two batten, and extend above the top by ½".

FIGURE 2
SECTIONAL VIEW (FROM TOP)

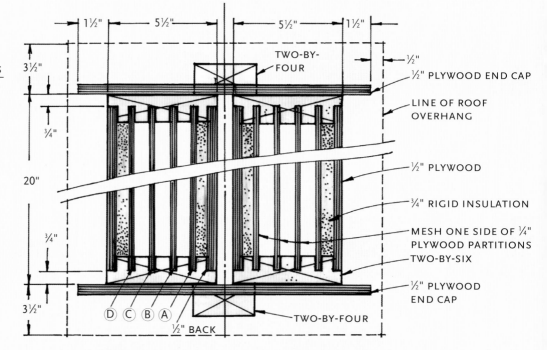

¼" PLYWOOD PIECES

Ⓐ	– 1 – 18½" × 12"
Ⓐ	– 2 – 18½" × 8"
Ⓑ	– 1 – 18½" × 15"
Ⓒ	– 1 – 18½" × 15"
Ⓓ	– 1 – 18½" ×10"
Ⓓ	– 2 – 18½" × 5"

TWO-BY-FOUR

½" PLYWOOD END CAP

LINE OF ROOF OVERHANG

½" PLYWOOD

¾" RIGID INSULATION

MESH ONE SIDE OF ¼" PLYWOOD PARTITIONS

TWO-BY-SIX

½" PLYWOOD END CAP

TWO-BY-FOUR

½" BACK

SCALE ▬▬▬ INCHES

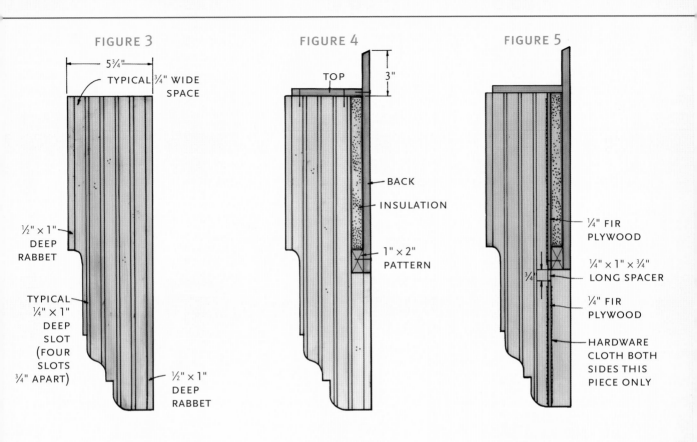

FIGURE 3

5¾"

TYPICAL ¾" WIDE SPACE

½" × 1" DEEP RABBET

TYPICAL ¼" × 1" DEEP SLOT (FOUR SLOTS ¾" APART)

½" × 1" DEEP RABBET

FIGURE 4

TOP

3"

BACK

INSULATION

1" × 2" PATTERN

FIGURE 5

¼" FIR PLYWOOD

¼" × 1" × ¾" LONG SPACER

¾"

¼" FIR PLYWOOD

HARDWARE CLOTH BOTH SIDES THIS PIECE ONLY

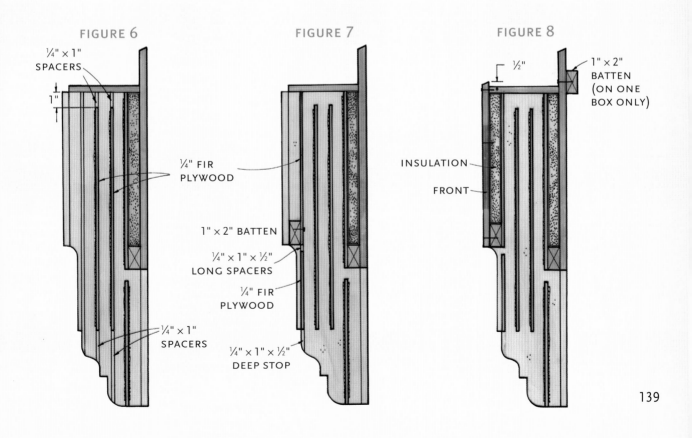

FIGURE 6

¼" × 1" SPACERS

1"

¼" FIR PLYWOOD

¼" × 1" SPACERS

FIGURE 7

¼" FIR PLYWOOD

1" × 2" BATTEN

¼" × 1" × ½" LONG SPACERS

¼" FIR PLYWOOD

¼" × 1" × ½" DEEP STOP

FIGURE 8

½"

1" × 2" BATTEN (ON ONE BOX ONLY)

INSULATION

FRONT

⑫ Nail a one-by-two fir batten on the back of one box only, near the top as shown. This will act as a ¾" spacer between the boxes. Join the two boxes back to back by nailing the second one to the first through the one-by-two batten.

⑬ Using the pattern on page 141, cut out two end caps from ½" plywood 7" × 14". Nail these caps to either side of the boxes, being careful the nails do not go through into the interior. The angles for the roof should be flush with the top angles of the back and front of each box as shown in Figure 9.

⑭ Choose two two-by-four posts, at least 12' long. Use only clear, straight-grain fir for these posts. At the top of each, cut a ½" × 5½" notch (Figure 10) to fit over the end cap and still be flush with the sides of the boxes below. Cut two two-by-four cross pieces to serve as braces as well as ladder supports. The cross pieces should be from 3½' to 4' long; at least long enough to suit the width of the ladder used to inspect the nursery. Use the width of the boxes as a guide to attach the cross-pieces to either side of the two-by-four posts with two ½" diameter × 8" long galvanized bolts. Use two large washers for each bolt.

FIGURE 9
END CAP PATTERN (MAKE TWO)

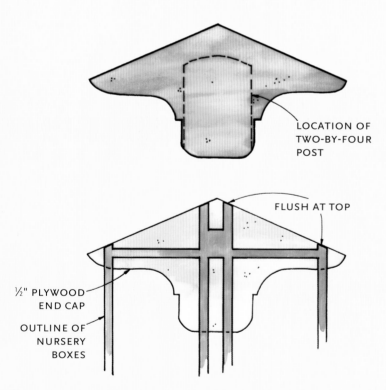

LOCATION OF TWO-BY-FOUR POST

FLUSH AT TOP

½" PLYWOOD END CAP

OUTLINE OF NURSERY BOXES

FIGURE 10

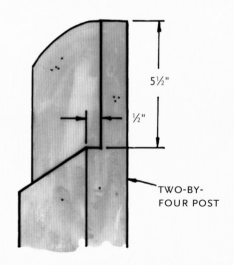

5½"

½"

TWO-BY-FOUR POST

15 Cut two pieces of ½" plywood, each 9" × 27" for the roof. Cut two pieces of rigid styrofoam each 4½" × 20" and lay them on top of the boxes as shown in the sectional view on page 137. The outside edges of each must be beveled so the roofs will fit. Do this by sanding the insulation with very coarse sandpaper on a block of wood. Nail the roof pieces to the top of the nursery boxes, allowing for a 3" overhang at the sides.

16 To cover the center joint, nail a sheet of galvanized metal, aluminum, or duroid roofing 7" × 27" on top. You can also add a 27" length of two by three fir to the ridge to cap off the roofing. If you wish to do this, you must first cut a shallow "V" on the underside (Figure 11). This can be nailed in place after a liberal layer of caulking is placed in the "V."

17 To add interest to the front of the box add the stylized bat design (the Chinese symbol for good fortune). Cut it out of ⅛" plywood and tack it onto the front. Use the pattern (Figure 12).

18 Now fit the completed nursery boxes between the two posts. Fasten the assembly together with a few nails on each side as shown on page 136. To erect the bat nursery, bore, or dig, two holes at a designated location in your yard or garden. These holes should be at least 3' deep. Set the two by four posts into the holes and pack earth, sand, and stones around them until they are solidly planted in place. For extra security, you may also wish to set the posts in concrete.

FIGURE 11

FIGURE 12

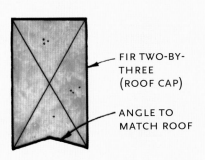

FIR TWO-BY-THREE (ROOF CAP)

ANGLE TO MATCH ROOF

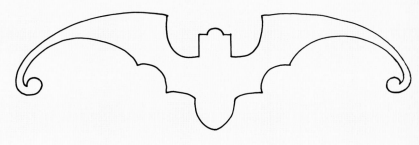

WALL-MOUNTED BAT HOUSE

Wall-mounted bat houses are usually completely built, then hung or nailed in place. If you have a shed or barn wall made of planks, this is probably a good idea, but so many utility sheds are clad with exterior grade plywood now that a simple, one-slot bat house can be built right on the wall.

FIGURE 1

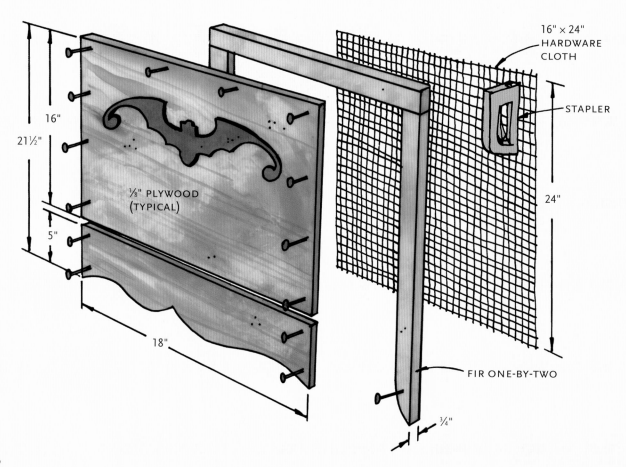

16" × 24" HARDWARE CLOTH

STAPLER

24"

16"

21½"

⅛" PLYWOOD (TYPICAL)

5"

18"

FIR ONE-BY-TWO

¾"

1. Staple a 16" × 24" sheet of hardware cloth on the wall, then nail a three piece/three sided one-by-two fir frame on either side and across the top.

2. Nail a 16" × 18" sheet of ½" plywood over the frame, leaving a ½" gap as a vent.

3. Nail a 5" × 18" sheet of ½" plywood below it.

4. To make the box's appearance less austere, cut a simple decorative edge along the bottom as shown. Another attractive touch is to cut the stylized bat design (Chinese symbol for good luck) out of ⅛" plywood and nail it to the box (see pattern). *Note:* If you prefer to construct the box separately, mount the above construction on an 18" × 24" sheet of ¾" plywood. If the box is not nailed below a roof overhang, caulk both the sides of the one-by-two frame before assembly.

FIGURE 2

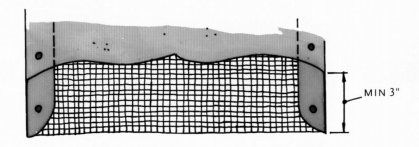

MIN 3"

PATTERN (DECORATION)

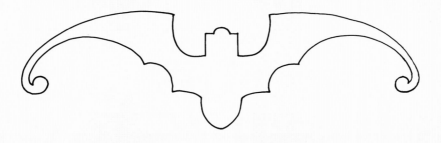

More Mammals in the Garden

K EEPING THE CREATURES you attract to your wildlife habitat safe, as well as enjoying your gardens and keeping them free from damage, will require ingenuity and resourcefulness. Uninvited animals can be a nuisance, but they are just living out their lives from a different perspective than we are. This can pose a challenge when species we've attracted are being chased away, and plants we've nurtured are being eaten. Prevention is always worth a try first, and that may mean burying fence wire, sealing up potential and existing denning sites, taking uneaten pet food indoors, hanging more than one bird feeder, plus a variety of other measures depending on your situation.

As far as predators go, the main threat to birds, amphibians, and other wild creatures is the domestic cat. Next in line is the squirrel, whose damage is not as vi-

olent but will nonetheless take a toll on your efforts to provide a wildlife sanctuary. Squirrels can seriously disrupt a bird feeding program in particular. Raccoons, skunks, coyotes, deer, rats, mice, gophers, woodchucks, moles, opossums, raptors such as hawks and owls, herons, and a host of insects may be considered unwelcome guests by different wildlife gardeners. With the exception of the cat, the other creatures on this list are wild. They all have a role to play. The challenge for the wildlife steward then is to make sure that no species makes your garden uninhabitable for others. The suggestions for dealing with predators include only methods for discouraging them from doing excess damage or from consuming all food. The goal of the backyard wildlife sanctuary is to create an ecosystem in which various creatures can live in harmony.

Cats

Cats are responsible for the deaths of hundreds of millions of wild birds and animals each year. Your friendly neighborhood feline presents as big a danger to migrating songbirds as do pollution, cars, poison, and even loss of habitat. If you want to create a backyard that will attract wild creatures, it should be cat-free. Cats cannot be trained to *not* hunt, and even declawing them does not stop their lethal effectiveness.

The best way to prevent your cat from preying on wildlife is to keep the animal inside. If you are the owner of an outdoor cat, you may be surprised to learn that your cat can be kept indoors with no harmful effects. In fact, indoor cats actually live much longer than outdoor cats. They don't face the same dangers from traffic, predators, and other potentially lethal situations that outside cats encounter regularly. Cats may even contract salmonella from ingesting birds with the illness. Pine siskins are particularly susceptible to this bacterial infection that may be transmitted between the birds at inadequately cleaned bird feeding stations. Cats go missing with alarming frequency in urban areas—ask one of the many cat owners who has lost a cat and never found out what happened to it. If you keep your cat inside you will have peace of mind. If you want to help your outdoor cat make the adjustment to be-ing indoors, consider building it an enclosure where it can bask in the sun and access the house. It is also possible, if somewhat unusual looking, to take your cat for walks outside using a lead and harness.

If your yard is frequented by a neighbor's cat, talk to your neighbors about the wildlife garden you are trying to create, and explain that cats put your wild guests in danger. Try to sell neighbors on the idea of keeping their cat inside. If they're not interested, ask them to put multiple bells around the cat's collar. A cat can learn to keep one bell quiet, but two or more is difficult. Bells are not very effective deterrents, however, and will not prevent young birds and other wildlife from being killed.

Cats are not natural to the North American ecosystem, regardless of what some people believe. Your neighbors may argue that cats are natural predators and that they help to check the pest population by keeping mice and rats under control. Unfortunately, this is not really true. Cats are housed and fed by humans.

Northern saw-whet owl.

Douglas Squirrel Family

Pulling weeds from the tulip bed one spring, a wildlife gardener heard the loud trill of a scolding squirrel inside the nearby shed. She looked up and there it was, staring at her through the window, tail vibrating. Later, she sneaked quietly into the shed and stood still until she heard some rustling. There along the top of the wall, a little head popped up, then another, and another, until three young squirrels were all chirping down at her.

The next day the woman went to the shed and watched as three fuzzy rumps disappeared behind the wall. Daily she visited her resident squirrels and they became braver, staying out longer in the open, ignoring her. In the days that followed, she watched the three chase each other through plastic pipe on the floor, then saw them run in figure-eights along the spare lawnmower belts. Close encounters with young wildlife in an everyday place – her usually quiet shed a playground.

They are non-selective predators, which means that they catch not only pests, but also "desirable" species such as songbirds, which are protected by law in most places. Cats are kept in such large numbers (at least twenty per suburban block by some estimates) that they put a serious strain on wildlife. Natural predators, such as coyotes and raptors, occur at a tiny fraction of these numbers, and cats are actually disruptive of the natural food chain for these creatures as well.

Cat Control

Place chicken wire, or other wire with two-inch or three-inch holes, over brushy areas and around feeding stations to prevent cats from stalking and ambushing birds and other wild creatures.

Use screens made of chicken wire or mesh to block access on heavily traveled cat routes. Cats can climb wooden posts, so if you have feeders on posts, consider sheathing with plastic or aluminum (see Squirrels, page 148).

A fence at least six feet high made of chain link is an effective deterrent, as well as good support for vines, shrubs, and other vegetation. Do not use barbed wire as it can be very harmful to wildlife as well as to domestic animals. The fence must go right to the ground so cats cannot squeeze under it.

Spray a cat repellent around the yard. This could have the effect of keeping other animals out as well, and its effectiveness is limited, but it may be worth a try.

Hide out in your yard and give the cats a blast with a high-powered water gun to let them know they aren't welcome. This won't hurt them, but it will frighten them.

Getting Serious

If you have tried everything, or at least everything you can manage, and cats are still using your wildlife habitat as a hunting ground, you may have to get serious—this would mean trapping the cats. Before you take this step, make sure you give the cats' owners opportunity to curb their pets' wandering. If the cats prowling your yard are feral, you may have little recourse.

First, try posting a notice to let neighborhood cat owners know that cats are killing animals in your backyard wildlife sanctuary. You don't need to be specific about which cats are doing the killing, but your notice should alert cat owners about the problem and warn them that you are going to begin trapping. If the problem continues, buy or borrow a live trap and bait it. Traps are available from the SPCA, animal shelters, and other organizations that deal with animals. If you catch a cat that you recognize, or one that has a name tag, return it to its owners and let them know that if you catch it again, you are going to take it to the local animal shelter or SPCA, which is also where you can take cats that you don't recognize.

If you take this final step, you should be prepared for neighbor relations to suffer. You may want to consider organizing an educational campaign beforehand to let people know the damage cats can do to wild animal populations. Even a printed sheet handed out around a neighborhood can be an encouragement to cat lovers to act in a responsible way. It can also be an opportunity to introduce people to the concept of the wildlife garden, which might help prevent misunderstandings from developing.

Rats and Other Rodents

Almost nobody's favorite, rats are a problem for many creatures, including nesting birds. If you are fortunate enough to have owls visit your wildlife habitat, the rodent population is not likely to get out of hand. Standard cat and squirrel guards on feeders and nest boxes will keep rats from menacing the birds. Rodents will be attracted to spilled birdseed and other fallout from both hanging and ground feeders, and their presence may, in turn, attract coyotes. Try to keep the area around your feeders clean, and promptly remove leftovers from the ground and ground-level feeders.

Co-Existing with Coyotes

Coyotes are a highly adaptable species that has become increasingly comfortable in urban settings. Garbage and compost left uncovered, dishes of pet food on

The Friendly Pigeon

Once in a while, for some unaccountable reason, a wild creature will develop an attachment for some particular human being. I remember reading of a remarkable instance of the kind that occurred at the Amsterdam Zoo in Holland. A caged bittern there preferred the company of the director of the zoo to any of its own kind. It even drove its mate from the nest and tried to induce the director to sit on the eggs.

Some years ago, there occurred near here a somewhat similar attachment of a bird for a human. A friend of ours was in the habit of scattering grain on the lawn near French windows looking out on a terrace. It attracted thrushes, wild sparrows and mourning doves. Soon she noticed that a blue-and-white pigeon was alighting among the other birds to share in the food. It was the only one of its kind to come.

A little later, the pigeon began following her about when she walked on the lawn. Then it commenced appearing at the French windows on the terrace at about five o'clock every evening. It would flutter down and alight near the sill. As soon as she opened one of the windows, the pigeon walked inside. Sometimes it would walk clear around the living room as though on a tour of inspection. At other times, it would fly directly to the top of the fireplace screen. There it would perch motionless, following the movements of the woman with its eyes.

This strange behavior continued for more than two months. Each time the bird would remain in the living room for an hour or so. Then it would return to the French windows. As soon as they swung open, it would fly away. Our friend never learned where the pigeon came from; she never discovered what its history was. But, evening after evening, it arrived as though visiting a friend. It came at about the same time each day, remained about the same length of time on each visit, and, just before dusk set in, it went on its way. It seemed to feel a special friendship for this one human being.

Edwin Way Teale – Circle of the Seasons, 1953

porches, fallen fruit, rats, and small, unattended pets are all food items to a coyote.

Although a fascinating animal to observe, coyotes that become relaxed in urban and suburban yards through feeding have lost their natural timidity—a bold coyote may bite someone and will end up being destroyed. Intentionally attracting and feeding coyotes is prohibited by law in most areas.

If there are coyotes where you live, the best deterrent is to clean up any possible food source and that includes birdseed scattered below feeders—it should be swept or hosed daily as it will attract rats which are a staple of both rural and urban coyotes' diets. Vegetable gardens are prey to coyotes if there is no fence, or if the fence is not flush to the ground, or is less than about six feet high. Coyotes have

even been known to drink milk from cartons that have been delivered to doorsteps, and run away with melons from sidewalk grocers. Keep the garbage can lid on tight, as these animals are very resourceful. For more information on coyotes in urban areas contact your local ecology center or conservation office.

Squirrels

Squirrels can be either an amusement or a headache for the wildlife gardener. Many people enjoy the antics of squirrels and provide for them with feeders and denning boxes of their own. If that describes your attitude toward the "squirrel problem," check out the following squirrel projects to help enjoy these active little mammals. If, on the other hand, you are frustrated by squirrels eating all your birdseed, chewing apart feeders, and taking over nest boxes, you can try some of the effective deterrents that passionate birders have come up with (see the following). These tactics are not intended to eradicate squirrels but merely to manage them. After all, native species of squirrels are natural to the wildlife garden. The key is to co-exist peacefully with animals whose hoarding instincts can quickly wipe out the contents of a feeder.

If your nest boxes and feeders are equipped with squirrel guards and placed at least eight to ten feet from the nearest branch, fence, or building, it is unlikely squirrels will be able to feast at your expense. Or, if you live in an apartment building and the limbs of street trees reach to your balcony, you may want to contact the city or regional district to re-

Douglas squirrel.

Squirrels can use street trees to access balconies.

quest removal, or pruning, of branches to keep squirrels away. Another idea is to keep your feeders and nest boxes on posts sheathed in metal or plastic. The squirrels cannot get a purchase to climb up them this way (Figure 1). Sheets of aluminum or galvanized metal can be placed to extend at least six feet up the posts so squirrels can't jump above them. You can also make squirrel sleeves from metal or PVC piping. If you are covering a live tree, be sure to drive the nails holding the sleeve only halfway in. You can coat the squirrel sleeve with vaseline, spray-on silicone, or non-toxic wax to make the surface even more slippery, but do not use automotive grease as it can be harmful to wildlife.

Trolley feeders suspended on clotheslines should be hung with lengths of plastic pipe threaded over the clothesline on either side of the feeder so the squirrels cannot walk a tightrope to reach the food. You can substitute film cartridges or thread spools on either side as well.

Another approach to keeping squirrels from your bird feeders is to give them a feeder of their own. This will help satisfy the squirrels,

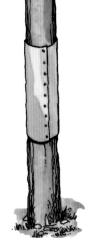

FIGURE 1

Squirrel Ride

A baby squirrel rode across the yard this afternoon. Just as I came out of the back door, the redoubtable Chippy was transporting one of her litter from the hollow silver maple where it was born to another tree. Unlike the carried kitten, it was not held by the scruff of the neck. Instead the young squirrel was curled around its mother's neck, back down, tail tightly wrapped over the top. It looked like a fur neckpiece. In this position, apparently gripped by the loose skin of its underside, it was being transportd on its across-the-yard journey.

Edwin Way Teale
– Circle of the
Seasons, 1953

34

PROJECT

— CONE GUARD —

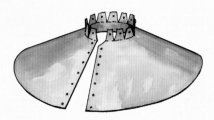

TOOLS & MATERIALS

- Drill with ⅛" diameter bit
- Tin shears
- Work gloves
- Safety glasses
- Drawing compass
- Small common nails
- Rivets
- Galvanized sheet metal 20" square
- Stick ¾" × ¾" × 12"
- Two common nails

A fairly impassable predator guard is a metal cone placed around any post holding a nest box, feeder, or bath. To make a cone guard you will need a large compass or two common nails and a stick.

1 Locate the center of the metal sheet by drawing the diagonals from corner to corner (Figure 1).

2 Where the lines intersect, punch a small hole with a nail or other sharp object and draw a circle the same diameter as the post using a regular compass.

3 Because the outside diameter of the cone is 20" you will require a large compass to scribe the circumference. To make a compass, use a 12" length of fir. Drill a ⅛" pilot hole at either end, exactly 10" apart. Drive a 2" common nail into each hole. One nail will be the pivot point of the compass and the other will be used to scratch the outside circle in the metal (Figure 2).

FIGURE 1

FIGURE 2

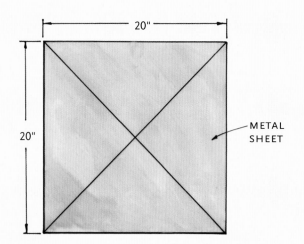

20"

20"

METAL SHEET

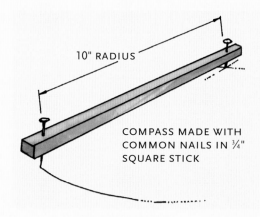

10" RADIUS

COMPASS MADE WITH COMMON NAILS IN ¾" SQUARE STICK

4 As shown in Figure 5, cut a triangular dart in the circle to form the cone. Draw or scratch a straight line from the center to the outside circle (Line A). From the point where this line crosses the post diameter circle, draw another straight line (Line B) from the first one on the outside circle. Now draw a Line C 1" from Line B and parallel to it (Figure 3). Now draw Lines D radiating from the center out to the post diameter circle.

5 Using tin shears, cut along the outside 20" diameter circle, Lines A, C, and D. Do not cut line B. Gloves and safety glasses should be worn for this. Bend up the triangles formed by Lines D and snip off their tips. These tabs will be used to nail the cone to the post. It is best to punch a hole in each tab at this time. Also, punch holes 1" apart and ½" in from the edges of Lines A and C (Figure 5). These will overlap and be riveted together to form the cone.

6 To install the cone, fit it like a collar around the post and then rivet the overlapped edges (Figure 6). Slide the cone high up onto the post (so a predator won't be able to leap on or over it to the post above) and nail it in place (Figure 6).

FIGURE 3

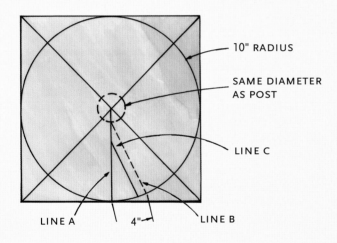

10" RADIUS

SAME DIAMETER AS POST

LINE C

LINE A   4"   LINE B

FIGURE 4

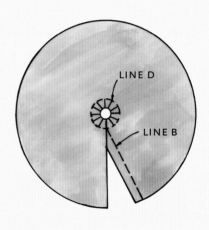

LINE D

LINE B

FIGURE 5

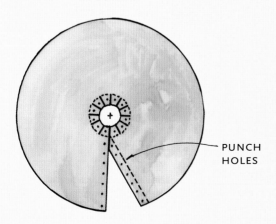

PUNCH HOLES

FIGURE 6

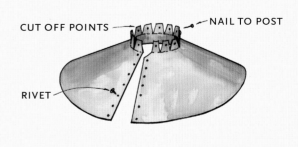

CUT OFF POINTS   NAIL TO POST

RIVET

— BAFFLE BLOCKS —

FIGURE 1 FIGURE 2

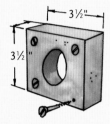

3½"

3½"

COPPER TUBE
INSERTED INTO
WOODEN BLOCK

FIGURE 3

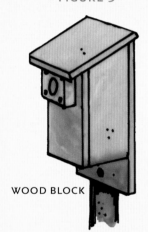

WOOD BLOCK

FIGURE 4

METAL SHEET

FIGURE 5

WIRE MESH
(BOTTOM ENTRY)

To make a baffle block for a nest box, simply cut off 3½" from a two-by-four and drill a hole in the center the same size as the entrance hole in the nest box (Figure 1). Screw or nail it to the front of the box (Figure 3). This will increase the depth of the entrance, making it difficult for larger birds and other predators to reach in to the fledglings.

Some birds will peck at nest box openings to make them larger. To avoid this, screw a 3½" square piece of sheet metal (with a hole the same size as the entrance) to the front of the box (Figure 4) or wood baffle block. Make sure that no sharp edges from the metal are exposed. Birds can be injured,

sometimes fatally, by even mild scratches that become infected.

Another option is to line the baffle block with a piece of metal or plastic tube (Figure 2) that fits the inside diameter of the entry hole.

To protect the nest box from raccoons, cats, or other creatures that may be tempted to reach inside, nail a box of wire mesh outside the opening (Figure 5). This wire mesh box should be the width of the nest box (Figure 6 – A and B) and should be trimmed or folded so that no sharp edges remain. Raccoon guards work by making it difficult for predators to reach in to the eggs or fledglings.

FIGURE 6 – A

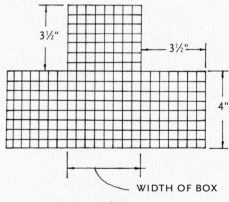

3½"

3½"

4"

WIDTH OF BOX

FIGURE 6 – B

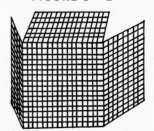

but due to their voracious appetites is unlikely to keep them from raiding your bird feeders as well. The most probable outcome is that you will spend a little more money on seed, have well-fed squirrels to watch, and still have seed left for the birds.

Raccoons

Raccoons do not pose as much of a problem to backyard bird feeding programs as squirrels do because they lack the agility to get at hard-to-reach bird feeders and nest boxes. The precautions you use to keep squirrels and cats away will work to keep raccoons away. One type of baffle is specifically designed to keep raccoons from reaching into nest boxes, and the raccoon guard is made with hard wire mesh (Project 35, Figure 5). Fallen birdseed and open-tray feeders are easy pickings for these animals. Birdbaths may also attract raccoons, as they use water to feel for, and discard, unwanted matter on their food.

People have been known to purposely feed raccoons because they're such fun to watch, but neighborhood cats go missing, dogs are often attacked when a raccoon is cornered, garbage gets dumped, and if a raccoon walks into a house, the destruction can be astonishing in the wake of the animal's search for food (beware of two-way pet doors). A natural diet includes anything from fruit to grasshoppers, and crayfish to small mammals.

Watching raccoons visit in your yard is a privilege, but encouraging them does not usually end well. If raccoons (or

Squirrel Feeder

A professional couple with a home office has several tube feeders outside their windows; watching birds feed and flutter clears the mind. Squirrels, on the other hand, were a problem; a pair would launch themselves from the deck beams onto the feeder trays to feast on birdseed. The couple laughed when squirrels scolded and chased each other, but seed disappeared rapidly and many of the songbirds stopped coming. One experiment was to give the squirrels an old wooden feeder, well stocked with peanuts and sunflower seeds. Set out on the lawn each morning, it was brought in at night before any rats appeared.

That didn't work. One squirrel would chase the other from the feeder, sending it back to the tube feeders. The couple responded to the challenge by taking the bottom tray from each feeder, but the squirrels simply clung to the seed holes and swung while they fed. The couple then stapled aluminum foil around the deck uprights and along the crossbeams, but the squirrels clawed and chewed through. Next, they cut strips of rolled aluminum to replace the foil – the squirrels then hurled themselves onto the feeders from exposed deck areas. Eventually, there were enough pieces of aluminum nailed up to cover all possible launch pads – unique aesthetically, but effective.

On mornings when the wooden feeder is late, one of the squirrels sits on the back of a lawn chair, looks at its hosts through the window and chatters. The day starts off with a laugh and the feeder is promptly put out.

Young raccoons.

skunks, opposums, or marmots) take up residence on your property and it's not working out, you can try motivating them to leave by keeping a radio turned up loud inside the den (as long as it can't be heard by neighbors) and a battery light turned on twenty-four hours a day. When you're sure all animals, including young, have vacated, seal up the entrance holes.

Opossums

Opossums are North America's only marsupial; their young complete their development in the mother's pouch. They are found in cities, suburbs, and towns, as well as rural areas. They'll eat mice, insects, garbage, carrion, small reptiles and amphibians, birds and nestlings, and they favor apples, persimmons, and corn. Opossum mothers sometimes carry their large broods on their backs, which is an exciting sight, especially if it's in the wildlife habitat that you've created.

If you encounter an injured, or recently killed, mother opossum, it's worth checking that she doesn't have a litter of young clinging to her.

Moles

You'll rarely see moles, but you will see where they live. Mounds and ridges of earth on lawns mark where the animals have burrowed for centipedes, beetles, earthworms, snails, or slugs, and where they've dug for shelter and nesting spots. There is virtually nothing that will rid your property of moles, although many unique ideas have been tried (hosing, mothballs, mole "bombs," traps, etc.). The expression, "Live with it" unfortunately seems to apply.

You can manage the problem to a degree by shoveling up, or dispersing, the piles of soil before you mow. This will at least prevent you and your nearby belongings from being covered in dust, and will provide additional soil for the garden. You could also set the soil aside to fill in the inevitable concaves when small areas of the burrows collapse later. The presence of moles makes a good argument for less lawn.

Moles do consume small amounts of vegetable matter, but it is the bulb-eating habit of some vole species using the moles' tunnels that irks gardeners. This can be prevented by lining flower beds, and planting holes, with wire mesh. If frustration is still high, it may be some comfort to know that aeration of the soil by moles is beneficial, allowing rain to penetrate, thereby helping to curb erosion.

Coast mole.

Skunks

Skunks are common in urban, suburban, and rural areas. Spotted skunks, striped skunks, hooded skunks, and hog-nosed skunks are all found in North America. Their powerful defense secretions are so effective that they have few natural predators. Various carnivores such as cougars, coyotes, great horned owls, and foxes will eat skunks but generally as a last choice; vehicles are also responsible for skunk deaths.

Besides berries, garbage, carrion, eggs, and amphibians, skunks eat mice, and many insect pests, and should be welcomed into the backyard habitat; you may get to see them tumbling and rolling in play. Keep your distance and enjoy the antics! Skunks, as a rule, need to be provoked, or have perceived a threat, to discharge their spray (refer to the raccoon section on how to encourage skunks to vacate a den). A word of warning: the striped skunk has been known as a chief carrier of rabies in the United States. Avoid any skunk that is behaving oddly, just as you would with any animal, and report the sighting to your local conservation office.

Woodchucks

You will often see woodchucks in parks and along roadsides, and they do make their way into backyards. Woodchucks are another animal that aerates the soil with their burrowing. In the process, they enhance topsoil-building by bringing subsoil to the surface—over 1,600,000 tons of soil are turned over each year in New York State alone. The animals' excrement is beneficial as well, providing a rich source of fertilizer.

Woodchucks tend to be very destructive to vegetation and foliage, and you will have to fence favorite crops and plants if you want to protect them from these animals. Fences should be a minimum of two feet tall and need to extend at least ten inches underground. It is rumored that nasturtiums are one plant that few foliage-eating mammals enjoy, so you may want to plant them liberally around your yard to experiment.

Despite their voracious appetites, woodchucks are entertaining as they bob up from their holes and scurry around searching for food. When frightened, they give a loud, sharp whistle, and when angry they chatter their teeth, hiss, growl, and squeal. It is in large numbers that woodchucks will damage crops and gardens, and unfortunately it is not possible

Little Ears

As I crossed the hillside this morning, a small patch of dry, yellow grass, beside a green clump, caught my eye. Carefully, I pulled aside the grass and came to a soft, gray blanket of fur. Parting this, I exposed the little ears of a nest full of baby cottontails. Just as carefully, I replaced the fur coverlet and the covering of grass. In a little while, now, I will see new rabbits hopping about on my hillside.

Edwin Way Teale – *Circle of the Seasons, 1953*

to deflect them by offering alternate sources of food.

Rabbits

You can find rabbits living in dense shrubs, brush piles, or burrows, and their diet generally consists of local greens in the summer, and woody vegetation in the winter. Gardens can suffer if rabbits are around, but you can try the following to manage the situation and still enjoy your visitors: Cover tree trunks to a height of about two feet with wire mesh so rabbits cannot "girdle" or chew off the bark all the way around. Vegetable and flower

Black-tailed deer eating birdseed.

gardens can be protected with wire mesh fences two feet or higher, buried a few inches deep. If you want to be hospitable to these animals, you can plant a patch of lettuce, clovers, and other favorites. Rabbits can become quite comfortable around humans and may surprise you by chasing each other around the garden.

Deer

Deer are a serious problem for many gardeners, but will probably be welcome if you are seeking to create a wildlife habitat in your backyard. Found over most of North America, the deer population is now estimated at between twenty and forty million. Deer are a perfect example of an "edge species," and their adaptability is legendary. Squeezed into ever smaller areas, deer learn to forage in parks, lawns, and gardens. Their numbers continue to climb and they put increasing pressure on these unnatural habitats. In some areas, deer will strip gardens and yards of their foliage overnight. Their overgrazing has had a devastating effect on many fragile ecosystems and is detrimental to wildlife that requires low-growing vegetation for food and shelter, such as songbirds and woodchucks.

The features that will

make your backyard a successful wildlife habitat are the same ones that will draw deer. If they become a problem, there are many repellents you can try (see inset on page 158). Chicken wire cages placed around young plants will deter deer, as will electric fencing or fences that are seven to nine feet high. You may want to try using a scarecrow, especially one with clothing that will flap in the wind. If you have a dog, keeping it outside at night, either tied up or confined, is effective if it barks, but letting a dog run loose can be disastrous for deer.

You can also landscape to emphasize plants that deer dislike but that are popular with less voracious wildlife. These include Buddleia sp. (butterfly bush), boxwood, California wax myrtle, Christmas berry, holly, pine, spruce, hawthorn, eucalyptus, jasmine, lilac, and vinca vine. Check with the nursery on invasiveness of plants before purchasing. Deer are actually repelled by some fragrant herbs such as catmint, catnip, chives, garlic, onion, lavender, sage, spearmint, thyme, mint, oregano, parsley, and rosemary.

Another option is to hide plants that deer love, behind those less favored. Deer favorites include fruit trees of all kinds, as well as yew and tea roses. They also enjoy produce from the garden including beans, broccoli and cauliflower, peas, sweet corn, and flowers such as chrysanthemums, daylilies, and particularly spring bulbs with the exception of daffodils and hyacinths. Keep in mind, though, that if deer are hungry enough they will eat almost any plant and their tastes vary from place to place.

Caterpillar species.

Insects

Wildlife gardeners learn to see insects in a whole new light. As Charlotte Seidenberg writes in her book *The Wildlife Garden*, "There's always someone eating someone in the wildlife garden!" In a balanced ecosystem, every creature has a role to play.

The trick with insects, as with mammals, is to try to nurture a system in which no species overwhelms the rest. An annoying insect may be key in the diet of one of the most charming wildlife guests. If insects are allowed to chew on a few leaves, their growing population will attract predators, which will in turn keep the insect numbers, and damage, in check.

We tend to think of insects as almost universally harmful, but the truth is that only a small number, less than two percent by some estimates, cause harm. Even serious pests, such as aphids, are consumed by birds and preyed upon or parasitized by other insects such as ladybugs, lacewings, various wasp species, and/or

Deer Repellents

The following repellents may be effective in discouraging deer from feasting on your wildlife habitat:

- Bars of strongly scented soap hung from trees (within three feet of each other)
- Human or dog hair hung from trees in cheesecloth bags or nylon stockings (within three feet of each other)
- Crushed garlic hung in bags from shrubs and trees
- Predator urine (this will likely be expensive and hard to find)
- Predator feces (going on a hike in wolf country, or planning a trip to the zoo?)
- Blood meal sprinkled on the ground, or placed in bags, and hung on trees and shrubs (caution: this may draw predators)
- Hot pepper spray
- Strips of highly scented fabric softener sheets
- Strips of white fabric that will flutter (or try white plastic bags)
- Scarecrows with movable parts
- Shiny noise-makers such as pie plates, tin cans on a string, pieces of aluminum

their larvae. Cutworms are consumed by birds as well, and mealybugs are eaten by birds and the tachina fly.

If an insect is doing significant damage in your wildlife habitat, avoid resorting to the use of chemical pesticides. These poisons kill indiscriminately and will upset the ecological balance you are trying to attain. Poisoned insects can poison birds. Try to be patient and let the natural cycle play itself out. Your garden may have a few signs of insect damage,

Harmless ladybug pupa.

but flawlessness is not natural and is often maintained at great cost to wildlife and the environment.

10

Attracting Wildlife to Balconies and Rooftops

———✦———

So you want to provide wildlife habitat, but barely have room for yourself? Fortunately, some form of stewardship is possible in almost any space. If you understand the basics of habitat creation in a yard, you won't have any trouble applying the principles to containers for your balcony or deck (check page references at the end of this chapter for where in the book to find further information on most topics covered).

Birds, and insects of many types, especially butterflies, are the most likely visitors to container gardens. Even one planter filled with carefully chosen bird food plants or butterfly nectar plants, can thrive with activity. Assess which bird and butterfly species are most common in your area (with the help of a field guide), and what they like to eat. Creating wildlife habitat on your balcony or rooftop can encourage other people to do

the same, and in turn extend the city's greenways.

Diversity

Create diversity on your deck by growing plants with a variety of bloom times, shapes, foliage, and seed types. As in a backyard, diversity is the key to attracting a wider variety of wildlife. You may want to try growing a tiny wildflower meadow or patch of native plant species with the hope of attracting butterflies. This will be more likely to succeed if the spot you have for the plants is also sunny and sheltered from the wind. If creating diversity on your balcony is not feasible, you can still attract wildlife, just not as wide a range.

Layering and Edge Zones

Try the principle of layering on your balcony as well. Although on a small scale, wildlife (most likely birds in a balcony

Surrounded by rooftop foliage.

setting) still have preferences in vertical habitat. For instance, you could plant native grasses in a low container or small raised bed on the deck, followed by taller wildflowers, with several potted shrubs (preferably berry-producing) in behind. Then if space and sun allow, a dwarf fruit tree, or ornamental such as Japanese maple, where birds can shelter and find insects and seed.

Try experimenting with nectar-bearing flowers and native plants around the base of your trees. You can create edge zones in miniature, and when paired with a small water feature, the area could be very alluring, especially to birds.

Tree Considerations

Many trees are exceptional in providing for the needs of birds. Just keep in mind when making your choices that there could come a day when the tree requires repotting. A tree can become heavy and awkward, and if its removal becomes necessary because of size or weight, there could be costs in lowering it from the balcony. Taking a tree out through your apartment on a dolly is also no fun, and the worst scenario would be eventually having to cut up the tree and dispose of it in pieces. Besides the initial cost, it's easy to become attached to a tree over a period of time. You've watched buds and blooms appear every year, seen leaves turn color and shimmer with rain, admired the bare branches in winter, seen songbirds hopping amongst the leaves, and possibly nursed the tree back to health from some infestation. You've also regularly watered, weeded, and fertilized, perhaps for many years. Check with a nursery, or comprehensive gardening book, about which species and varieties are best in pots.

Efficient Use of Space

If you have a *tiny* balcony, diversity need not be your first consideration—just aim for plants most likely to attract the birds in your area. The best use of space should be a priority. This is where climbing plants are useful—on back walls, on railings, and on trellis work at either end of your balcony. There are a number of flowering vines that will attract hummingbirds, and will leave desirable seedheads and berries for other bird species. Many varieties of vines have dense foliage, offering shelter for birds and windbreaks for other plantings if grown along railings. Hanging baskets are also an efficient use of space; they add an abundance of greenery that will help catch the attention of birds on their flights through the city.

Simple for a bird to choose.

Container Gardening

You can build moss hanging baskets, and brim them full of plants you choose yourself, or you can adhere to the suggestions in Project 41. In lieu of using moss from the wild, you can use coconut fibre inserts, cultivated sphagnum moss, or "Super Moss," made of plastic and recycled fibres; most nurseries carry these products. If you're after something simpler, yet still want to create your own plantings, there are different shaped wooden, terra cotta, and plastic hanging planters of nearly any size you want; with these, just add soil and bedding plants, and hang them up. "Growing Bags" are another hanging planter option. They are green plastic cylinders, commonly two feet long by nine inches wide, with ten pre-made holes for stuffing annuals through. You layer these bags with soil and plants the same way you do moss hanging baskets, and when they've filled

out, the plastic is hidden except for the top handle. Petunias are a good choice as they fill out and cover very well, and are also attractive to hummingbirds.

Besides traditional plant containers, try something unusual. Wooden grocers' crates have folk-appeal, and are often available; collector tins of varying sizes can be found at second-hand stores, as can jars, buckets, old kettles, and pots. Hollowed-out logs make sturdy, rustic planters (although may not last too many years), or you can undertake woodworking projects to build your own planters, then stain or stencil the outsides. These unique containers will need drainage holes, and if that is not an option, one container can always be set inside another. Just keep in mind the weight of the filled, watered container when you embark on your balcony habitat project. Most buildings have by-laws in this regard. Better to check with the building

Plants of varying heights.

superintendent first, than to have to dismantle or discard your garden later. This would be especially true if you have a large deck or rooftop and plan to install raised beds (which are usually constructed from heavy planks, railway ties, or bricks). Remember to keep your containers at least an inch or two off the deck to increase air circulation to the roots; this will help avoid a variety of pests, and deck rot.

Watering Container Plants

Watering is a concern when gardening with containers. The smaller the container, the faster it will dry out. Some gardeners prefer to use nothing smaller than the equivalent of a two gallon pot; something to consider, especially if you are gardening on a south-facing balcony, or a windy rooftop. Watering isn't usually an issue if you're home, as it gives a great excuse to be close to what's growing—see new shoots come up, or watch buds form. It's when you go away, you may not want

someone walking through your apartment to get to the balcony or rooftop to water.

Irrigation systems on a timer are the best, and although they may sound elaborate and expensive, they don't have to be. Vinyl tubing can be purchased at building supply stores and nurseries, as can simple timers. If you don't possess the basic wiring savvy, it wouldn't take an electrician long to hook things up. Another watering device available at nurseries is a terra cotta cone. They come in several sizes and the principle is to wick water up from a dish through a small hose into the soil. Other options are out there as well. And you can try the old stand-by of dishes or tubs of water that you set your plant containers in.

An advantage of container gardening is the variety of miniature habitats you can achieve from one container to the other. There are bog gardens, natural grasslands, ponds, damp woodlands, wildflower meadows, and many other ecosystems you can attempt to replicate with plants, depending on the season and where you live. It's fun to experiment, just to see what wildlife may be attracted.

Space Maximizers

A ledge, or shelf, built to fit along the top of your balcony railing is a good way to maximize space, and depending on what container plants you fasten to it, you can create a privacy screen as well. A tier of potted plants up a wall on a purchased stand, or on bricks or blocks of wood of varying heights, works well as a space-saver. Many gardening guides now have

Use of existing features.

directions on how to create a "tapestry wall" formed from chicken wire against a sturdy wall, lined with plastic, and filled with soil. You then poke holes where you want to grow your annuals.

An alternative could be a wall devoted to brackets for various plant pots, and if you have a staircase, bright, potted flowers make a stunning display (for people and hummingbirds) when lined up one pot per step. Espaliered trees and shrubs (especially fruit- or berry-producing species) are a possibility too. This is a method of cultivation whereby branches are trained to grow in a flat pattern against a wall or trellis, along horizontal wires. A maximum of branch surface is exposed to the sun, contributing to heavier flower and fruit production. Dwarf fruit trees are a good choice to espalier for balconies and rooftops (many gardening guides have sections on how to espalier).

When your area is limited, don't worry about trying to use *all* native plants. Your knowledge of ecology can al-

ways help friends who want to know more about creating habitat in their backyards.

Window Boxes

If you have only a window ledge to work with, you may want to put up a planter box for butterflies, and fill it with plants that meet the needs of their entire life cycle. This type of box may not be the most

Efficient use of railings.

163

A Flicker Attacks a Starling

It is now more than half a century since the first European starlings were released in Central Park in New York City. They have multiplied and spread until they have reached the Pacific Coast and Churchill, on Hudson Bay, and Mexico City. They have taken over nesting territory from bluebirds and flickers. On our part of Long Island, bluebirds no longer nest and I have seen starlings perched on limbs of a tree waiting until a flicker finished making its nesting hole which they then appropriated. Twice I have found holes cut in trees at the bottom of a flicker hole, thus rendering the nests useless to the starlings. This seemed to be a form of flicker revenge. But I have never seen one of the big woodpeckers make a direct attack upon a starling until today. This afternoon a female flicker landed in our yard to feed upon ants. As I watched it from a window, a starling came walking up with its characteristic swinging swagger and pushed close to see what the flicker was finding in the grass. It walked completely around the feeding woodpecker at a distance of hardly a foot. As it came closer from the rear, the flicker suddenly leaped like a cat. A hop or two and it was hammering the starling in a flurry of wings that suggested a cockfight. In a moment, the melee was over. The starling flew away squawking and the flicker returned to its ant-hunting. Perhaps, in the end, flickers will learn how to cope with starlings.

Edwin Way Teale – Circle of the Seasons, 1953

lavish on your block, but it will have the potential of being the most active and entertaining. A butterfly ledge will require five to eight hours of sun a day and must be free of direct wind.

Another option for a ledge is a bird food garden in a planter box. Attracting birds close to a window will require precautions against them hitting the glass. This type of planter box will require fewer flowering plants than the butterfly garden, as it is mainly seeds that you will be offering, but a few dwarf sunflowers, if you're in a sunny spot, will brighten up your ledge in the summer.

You might also enjoy a window box full of flowers for hummingbirds. You can plant directly or set in individual potted plants. The latter offers seasonal flexibility as well as room for error or accidents. Many people in urban apartments derive a lot of joy from feeding birds in this way, and it is also an opportunity to garden, in however small a space, right from the planning stages.

Bird Feeders and Baths

A bird feeder or two is a good way to augment your balcony or rooftop habitat, especially in winter. You may be surprised to hear, though, that large numbers of wildlife stewards in cities have never hung a feeder; they first began gardening on their decks for the love of gardening, and not purposely to attract wildlife. That came later, and with it, a whole new love, but the birds arrived strictly because of the foliage, and in many cases, because of available water. This is good to know if you live in a building where feeders are not allowed. Even if they are allowed at present, be cautious about your feeding habits because by-laws in buildings can change. There was an incidence of this in a brand new strata complex by a river, where many unit owners fed birds from their balconies. Unfortunately, hulls and seed landing on the ground drew rats. It didn't take long for the building's management to veto feeders. If everyone had fed hulled seed, or kept trays below feeders and emptied them regularly, the outcome may have been different (or at least delayed).

Posting an educational bulletin in the lobby of your building about the joys and responsibilities of feeding birds would be helpful to any new wildlife stewards. Rather than going it alone on this, a local natural history society or wildlife group may be interested in writing a notice and putting it on their letterhead to display in buildings. The notice could briefly include information on cleanliness (to avoid both salmonella poisoning in birds, and rat problems), cat control (err on the side of caution here, as anyone who is, or has been, a pet owner knows the topic can be touchy), feeding ideas, and possibly a contact number to have questions answered.

As in a yard situation, water can be a more powerful attractant to birds than either plants or feeders. Thanks to its reflective qualities, water is easily spotted as birds fly through the city, even more so when you have a drip rigged up. As in a backyard, a birdbath is most enticing if it is placed near a group of shelter trees or shrubs, as birds have no way of knowing

A variety of new habitat.

that your balcony is free of predators. Of course, hawks can still swoop down from the sky and seize songbirds.

Nest Sites

If you have space on your balcony or deck for a nest box or nesting shelf, great. Determine which species are around, then build or buy your box accordingly. House sparrows and starlings will nest in any sort of box as long as they can fit through the hole. There was a case of a pair of finches nesting right on the front door of someone's house, in a wicker basket of plants (this example should serve to illustrate how adaptable the birds can be—how many times must that door have opened?). Finches will also nest in flower boxes and hanging baskets. Robins as well are known to build their homes among flowers, and near people.

One city wildlife steward had a pair of house finches nesting in a flower box on her balcony for several years in a row, but one spring a pair of robins showed up, fought for territorial rights, and replaced the finches. It's interesting to note that this space would only support one pair of nesting birds, regardless of species. The wildlife steward then discovered that robins are notorious for pecking at their own reflections in window glass. As amusing as this may look to an unsuspecting observer, this behavior can result in serious damage to the bird. Use whatever you can to rid the glass of reflection until the mating season is over, when the birds will no longer be protecting territory from "intruders."

Nesting Responsibilities

There are responsibilities involved in having birds nest on your deck. Although most species that end up doing so will become used to your daily watering routine and activities, they generally need undisturbed time when the young hatch, or are being fed, and when they fledge (leave the nest). A young bird learning to fly will spend a great deal of time on the ground, and it is very exciting to watch this stage of a bird's life. Unfortunately, it is a danger to the birds to have people, especially children, walking around them. It is also a great aggravation to the parent birds, who will swoop and dive at the unwanted visitors, trying to get rid of them. Pets are deadly to fledglings. There's nothing like a flopping bird to attract the attention of dogs and cats, even old, docile pets who would never bother otherwise.

When you have birds nesting among your flowers, either in planter boxes or hanging baskets, it's up to you to decide whether you will keep watering around the outside of the nests, or give the planter entirely over to the birds. Most wildlife stewards keep watering, after they've gauged how adapted the birds are to human disturbance. There is an important point to consider in your choice. If the birds have nested amid foliage, and it ceases to be watered, both nestlings and adults will then be exposed to hot, summer sun, and could suffer or die. Unless other plants will shade the nest, or you can move your planter elsewhere, it would be best to continue with careful watering.

Common Balcony Birds

The following is a list of commonly seen "city" birds across North America. If you are not attracting what you'd hoped for to your balcony or rooftop, but are instead being visited by wildlife that is considered a nuisance, it may be worth reconsidering what is desirable or interesting, and give yourself credit for enticing the wild visitors that you do have. Included are tips on how to discourage these common birds so that you can first attempt to attract other species, before you decide to set up feeding programs for the messier and introduced birds that your neighbors may not enjoy. You will also find references at the end of the chapter for information elsewhere in the book on dissuading "nuisance" birds.

Introduced species are here to stay; in fact, they are so familiar that they have a place in field guides alongside native species. Should you consider attracting them, keep in mind that they are not appreciated by everyone, not even by all bird enthusiasts. There is well-founded concern over introduced species keeping native birds from nest spots and food sources, which prevents many people from encouraging them. Even North American native birds, such as the crow, are deemed pests by many people. Remember to have respect for neighbors when it comes to mess and noise created by your wildlife habitat.

Skylight garden.

Crows (*Corvus sp.*)

Crows are clever birds. In laboratory settings, they have learned to differentiate between shapes, and to count to six. Crows are recognized for their ability to learn from experience, and for their sharing in the welfare of their flock—when a group is feeding, there are "sentinel" birds posted to alert the others of danger. Studies are being done on the incidence of corvids purposely alerting each other to available food sources, which would indicate a remarkable degree of sharing in these highly evolved birds.

It's this adaptable intelligence that makes crows less than endearing to most people. They're deemed "nuisance" because they go through garbage, steal dog food, grab groceries from bags, pick seed from newly planted gardens, and eat crops, fledglings, and small animals. But it is this very intelligence that makes the crow worthy of respect. Crow behavior is fascinating, and if the birds visit your balcony or rooftop, it's an opportunity to observe them—you can be sure they will be observing you. Do respect your neighbors, though. Crows are noisy, and the droppings are messy, especially when there are a few of the birds together. Some people are awakened happily in the morning to the sound of crows, but most aren't.

Crows play in the wind, use twigs as tools, tease pets, use passing cars to crack nuts and shellfish, defend territory, mimic other animals, steal from knap-

A Starling Swings a Rival

A pair of starlings have taken over the nesting box on the grapevine trellis. This morning, there was a great commotion at the box. A stranger starling had tried to enter while one of the owners was at the nest. By the time we trained our glasses on the spot, the owner had its bill clamped on one leg of the interloper and was jerking and swinging its rival this way and that. The moment it could break free, the intruder fled pell-mell in squawking terror over a garage, beyond maple trees and out of sight.

Edwin Way Teale – Circle of the Seasons, 1953

sacks, use ants to rid their feathers of parasites, caress each other's beaks and heads during courtship—to name only a few of their unique behaviors. Crows also regurgitate pellets as owls do, so you may be the lucky recipient of one on your deck. Few people come across crow pellets, and with the aid of tweezers you could find hair, bone, and shell fragments, and any number of surprises inside that will give a clue to what your visitor was eating. Crows are omnivores who constantly change their food habits according to season and available supply, very much like humans. If you're trying to discourage crows, don't put out foods such as cracked corn, suet, bread, berries, or pieces of fruit. And if you have an open compost, you'll have to cover it, at least until the crows find another area to feed.

European Starling (*Sturnus vulgaris*) Starlings were introduced to North America in 1890 by an individual attempting to bring all of the bird species mentioned in Shakespeare's works to the United States. His eccentricity and ecological naiveity were also to thank for the introduction of the birds north into Canada and up into central Alaska. The birds' adaptability is legend, with huge flocks congregating wherever the hand of humans has left its mark—agricultural areas, orchards, and cities are all places where starlings feed, gather, roost, and become "pests."

Starlings are reviled for taking over native birds' nesting cavities, as well as for building their own messy nests in inappropriate places, such as aircraft engines and building fans; large flocks also dam-

Water features help to attract birds.

age crops. Starlings are not the only species to practice these behaviors, but they are the most commonly credited with them, probably due to sheer number.

During nesting season, the birds pair up in lieu of flocking, and they eat large numbers of insects. Their behaviors in spring are especially interesting, and include the wing-wave (done vigorously by the male during courtship), sidling (along a branch to rid the area of an intruder), bill-wipe (done aggressively against a branch when intruders appear), squeal-call (high-pitched call done with wing-wave), crowing-call (continuous, unmusical chortling over territory), and many others that are easily observed wherever starlings are found. Their aggressive displays are frequently seen at feeders.

These iridescent black birds are dazzling in spring and summer sunshine, and sport yellow bills. In winter, their plumage becomes speckled with white, and the bill dulls to brown. Starlings are good mimics, and besides imitating the songs of other birds, much to the confusion of the listener, they have been heard "wolf-whistling" and doing guinea pig impressions. If you have starlings visit your balcony habitat, it is worth considering their interesting qualities and remarkable success at flourishing, especially if they are your main visitors.

If you do not want starlings at your nest boxes, make sure entry holes are less than one and a half inches in diameter. If you wish to discourage these birds from your feeding program, switch to tube

Small balcony habitat.

feeders instead of hoppers or tray feeders, and provide black oil sunflower seed and niger thistle seed, which starlings tend to avoid. They may also avoid sunflower seeds, whole-kernel corn, thistle, buckwheat, and peanuts in the shell. You can also attempt to divert starlings from your songbird feeders by setting out food especially for them, such as table scraps, dry and canned dog food, suet, hulled oats, and cracked corn, away from the songbird food. Starlings usually feed late morning and early afternoon, so once

American robin eggs.

Young birds.

you have established their times in your own habitat, try working around them when setting out food for other birds.

House Sparrow (*Passer domesticus*)
House sparrows are attracted to any areas settled by humans, especially cities. They are an introduced species from Britain that has prospered throughout North America. Very adaptable birds, house sparrows are not actually sparrows at all, but Old World weaver finches that are similar looking to many native sparrow species, but with shorter legs and thicker bills.

When you walk down a city street and hear birds chirping from the eaves of stores, ledges of buildings, or from boulevard trees, you are generally hearing house sparrows. They are the birds commonly seen

hopping along sidewalks, searching for crumbs or bits of seed. You can hear house sparrows chirping noisily en masse from their daytime or evening roosts in hedge rows or other dense plantings, such as ivy-covered walls. These little birds are part of city life across North America and are easily attracted to balconies and rooftops.

Most people do not relish house sparrows as visitors because of their aggressive behavior toward other birds at feeders and nest boxes, but they do have a brash charm all their own. They are so attuned to human life that they've been seen greeting newly arrived vehicles at campgrounds and gas stations in order to pull insects from radiators. If they are the only species attracted to your habitat, there is

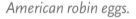

Rock dove.

170

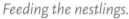
Feeding the nestlings.

Ready to leave the nest.

plenty about them to enjoy. If you have other species that are being harrassed by house sparrows, try setting up a ground or platform feeder with white proso millet, canary seed, cracked grain, and sunflower seeds for the house sparrows, and hanging feeders for the other birds. House sparrows will usually avoid the hanging feeders but will eat from a platform or from the ground.

House Finch (*Carpodacus mexicanus*) This sociable finch is native to the southwest United States, but its range has come to include the eastern United States, as well as southeastern and southwestern Canada. The expansion to new territory within its own country was aided by the hand of humans in 1941, with the export of the birds from California, to pet shops on the east coast.

The house finch is equally at home in urban, suburban, and rural areas. City behavior of the bird is similar to that of the house sparrow, except that it has a pleasing song and attractive red plumage in the male. The birds are easily enticed to feeders, and are known for building nests in flowerpots and hanging baskets. They also drink nectar solution from hummingbird feeders, much to the shock of many new birders. If they're keeping the hummers away, just remove the perches. House finches prefer small sunflower seeds from feeders, but during the growing season feed mainly on buds, seeds, and fruits. In some western areas, these birds are considered pests, due to the amount of fruit they consume.

Rock Dove (*Columba livia*) The "city pigeon" or "carrier pigeon" was brought to the United States by settlers in the early 1600s. Originally kept and raised for food, the birds were later used for message-carrying during emergencies and war, when it was discovered they possessed homing skills. Rock doves were, and still are, a popular bird to race and to raise for unusual, multi-colored forms. They are not popular for their messy, pushy behavior at feeders. If by chance you live high above the usual habitat of other birds, you may welcome rock doves as your only avian visitor.

The rock dove adapted nicely to cities, following human expansion, and began using nooks and crannies of buildings and bridges for nesting, in lieu of the natural rock ledges of their wild predecessors. Besides many interesting courting and nesting behaviors that can be observed, pigeons possess two unique qualities: both parent birds produce "pigeon milk," similar to mammals' milk, to feed their young, and they drink water by sucking it up, rather than having to tilt their heads back like other birds.

Rock doves are attracted to any height window ledge feeder, even in busy downtown cores. Many urban apartment dwellers enjoy feeding and watching pigeons; their flashy, iridescent feathers, bobbing heads, and soft cooing can be soothing.

Other City Birds to See

Besides the above listed birds that occur commonly on balconies, there are many other species seen in cities, just not as close to people as a rule. Common nighthawks range over most of North America, and their nasal *peent* call can be heard as they swoop and dive to catch insects. Owls are becoming more common in cities. For example, in the Pacific Northwest, in Canada, a spotted owl was recently seen roosting on the outside of a downtown art gallery during the day, and two weeks later, just across the U.S. border, another was seen, also roosting on a downtown building.

In the east, chimney swifts are regular city visitors, but are also seen in southern California, and as the name implies, they do nest in chimneys. Colorful budgerigars, natives of Australia, have established wild breeding populations in Florida where they are commonly seen at feeders and birdbaths. These birds must compete with house sparrows for nesting sites, so if you are providing boxes for budgies, check with your local birding group on the size of entrance hole that will work.

Many people find that the larger birds, such as gulls and crows, sit on railings and observe their surroundings, but don't do much else. They become comfortable around people and are not usually the "nuisance" that is expected. Their excrement is messy, but easily taken care of with a hose. The bigger birds are attracted to bakery goods, so if you don't want those birds around, don't put bread out, and because of the volume of excrement, neighbors' decks and property should be respected.

Take a walk around your city and scout out other people's balconies; you might get some good ideas for plantings. You might also see which birds are visiting which trees and shrubs. There could come a time when a new wildlife steward will be eyeing up your habitat for inspiration.

Where to Look in the Book for Further Information

CHAPTER

11

Planning and Designing Your Wildlife Habitat

As a backyard wildlife steward, you will get the opportunity to try your hand at landscape design, naturalist-style. The first step is to identify your wild guests and determine their needs. Then you can take stock of your garden habitat as it stands. This will include making a detailed map of your property, and matching the possibilities with the wildlife in your area. To do this, you will need to carefully plan out different landscaping "scenarios." Then comes the rewarding work of planting and constructing your wildlife garden.

Feeding chickadees.

Determine Needs

So which wild guests might be attracted to your habitat? What are their requirements for food, water, and shelter? Spend some time in your yard and around your neighborhood with a planning book and take notes on the birds, insects, reptiles, amphibians, and mammals that you see. If these creatures live near you, they are likely to visit your yard once it offers them a suitable habitat. Take your list and look through nature guides to discover food preferences and shelter needs for each species, keeping detailed notes (see Chapter 3 for bird nesting and feeding preferences).

Think about how you use your yard. Do you play badminton or croquet on

the lawn? Do you host garden parties and barbecues? How about a play area for the kids? Once you have determined the space you need, you can do an analysis of the current conditions.

Mapping Your Site

Take a detailed inventory of your backyard, and sketch a map. What are the exact dimensions of the property you have to work with? The larger and more accurate you can make the scale, the better for getting down detail. Adding compass points and a legend to your map helps, as does using graph paper, a ruler, and colored pencils. Indicate on your map the location, shape, and relative size of your house and all other buildings. Add windows and other vantage points that will influence where you locate various plant-

Wildlife tree sign tells the story.

The Mouse and the Chickadee

Hanging on the suet-feeders, flying away with sunflower seeds, investigating crevices in the bark, a little band of chickadees has filled the old maple with life on this cold winter day. It is chickadee time all across the northern states. The friendliest and most open-mannered of the winter birds, the little black-cap is performing invaluable service through his consumption of insect eggs.

Many a boy has first become interested in birds through some sociable chickadee that came close, hopping from branch to branch, stopping confidingly only a few feet away, cocking its head and peering intently into his face with its bright little eyes...

Among birds, I suppose the black-capped chickadee ranks close to the top in inquisitiveness. It is always investigating, always coming closer to see what is happening. A friend of mine was once standing quietly in the winter woods when a mouse appeared from a hole at the base of a tree, scurried about among the fallen leaves, then darted back into its tunnel again. A chickadee, investigating the bark of a limb overhead, spied the little animal. It followed its every movement. When it disappeared, the chickadee darted down and peered into the entrance of the tunnel Then it flew away only to return again, hop about the hole, cock its head on one side, peer again and again into the burrow. It even perched at the top of the tunnel entrance and hung upside-down to get a better look inside.

Edwin Way Teale – Circle of the Seasons, 1953

Backyard Habitat Checklist

STRUCTURES & INSTALLATIONS

____House and outbuildings

____Doors and windows (particularly those with views of the backyard)

____Porches, decks, patios

____Paths, driveways, sidewalks

____Fences

____Play or recreation areas

____Overhead or underground utilities

VEGETATION

____Trees and shrubs (show size)

____Vegetable and flower gardens, window boxes

____Lawn

____Garden structures such as gazebos, latticework

WILDLIFE FEATURES

____Existing feeders and nest boxes

____Burrows

____Dead trees and snags

____Nesting areas (in existing shrubbery)

____Perching areas

____Drinking and feeding areas

____Shelter areas

____Travel paths

____Potential hazards for wildlife

PROPERTY CONDITIONS

____Sunny areas

____Shady areas

____Wet areas

____Dry areas

____Streams and ponds

____Hills and slopes

____Prevailing winds in winter, summer, fall, and spring

____Sources of noise

ADJACENT CONDITIONS

____Trees

____Shrubs

____Roads

____Buildings and structures (neighbors' houses, sheds, patios, balconies, driveways)

SOIL CONDITIONS

____Soil composition

____Acidity

____Nutrients

____Drainage

ings, feeders, and garden items. Show your property line and existing vegetation, such as trees and shrubs, as best you can. Use the preceding checklist to help make sure your map is complete.

Plant and Soil Identification

Try to find out exactly what types of vegetation are growing on your property. If you can't identify a plant, take samples of leaves and flowers, place them in plastic bags, and refrigerate until you are ready to search through field guides, or until you can take them to a local nursery. If you can't figure out what species a plant is, you can probably send it to an agricultural branch of your local government that specializes in plant identification. It isn't necessary to go too far down the path of plant identification though, unless it piques a particular interest. The basic idea is to figure out whether the plants are native to your area or not, and determine their usefulness to wildlife.

For a detailed analysis of the soil conditions on your property, take a sample to the branch of your local agriculture department for soil testing, or to a nursery that offers the service. Check the drainage of your soil by digging a hole and filling it w i t h

Indigo bunting.

Posts for wildlife.

water to monitor how quickly the water drains. If you live in a wet area, the hole you dig will probably fill with water on its own. If you live in an area with dry, compacted conditions, the water will stay pooled in the hole. Well-drained soil will filter water at a rate of approximately one inch per hour.

Detailed soil analysis is more interesting than necessary. No matter what your soil conditions, there are almost always some species of plants that will flourish in it. Don't be in too much of a hurry to correct poor soil. Instead, try to find native plants that will do well in the given conditions, and will in turn provide food and shelter for wild guests. These hardy, "grow in anything" kind of plants are called pioneers. They prepare the soil to receive more delicate and specialized vegetation.

Wish Lists and the Master Plan

Once you have your base map complete, it is time to start planning the wildlife garden you've envisioned. You can begin by drawing bubble diagrams over top of your base map. These are circles and other shapes that indicate areas of use on your property.

You can also cut out pieces of paper in the shape of habitat features you wish to incorporate— pond, butterfly garden, tree islands, log piles, stone wall—and try arranging them in various ways. The principles to keep in mind

Edible Homes

Imagine yourself living in a globe-like room with greenish walls bulging outward and upward and then arching in to meet above your head. Imagine such a room constructed of succulent, edible material, forming a house that at once provides food and shelter, plenty and protection. That is what you would find if you traded places with one of those gall insects that now live in the globular swellings on the stems of my hillside goldenrod.

Sometimes the galls are on the stems and twigs, sometimes on the leaves themselves. They resemble seeds and cones and fungi and insect eggs and masses of fuzz and burs and nuts and flowers and cockscombs and fruit. Some are green and some are red and some are shaded with delicate tintings of color. If you are in doubt whether some odd formation on a plant or leaf is a gall, split it open with your thumbnail. If there is a grub inside or evidence that there has been a grub there, you can be sure your surmise is correct.

Edwin Way Teale – Circle of the Seasons, 1953

The Insect Garden

Once more, today, as I have done for nearly fifteen years, I drop seeds, cover them up, set out plants, bring pails of water from the swamp stream, and thus start my Insect Garden on another cycle of its existence. From this activity will come leaves and flowers that will be hosts to the summer insects that I will watch with interest.

Edwin Way Teale – Circle of the Seasons, 1953

when creating designs for your wildlife habitat are simple. If necessary, review the material in Chapter 1 to refresh your understanding of the processes involved.

• Try to model your backyard on natural areas as much as possible. Take a look at undisturbed habitats in your area. Look at the plants by the side of roadways; not the manicured roadways, but areas that are allowed to grow wild. Check out plants growing beside natural ponds and streams.

• Try to keep as much area as possible free of traffic and commotion. Group your "people" activities into one area to minimize the disturbance to wildlife.

• Keep existing trees if possible, even if they aren't native. A mature, non-native species is more beneficial to wildlife than a native sapling.

• Try to arrange habitat areas to view from convenient spots such as your kitchen or living room, patio, or deck.

Once you have done as many bubble diagrams as necessary to get all of your ideas down on paper, begin to compile them into one master plan. This will outline your needs, and show the overall concept of your wildlife garden.

Begin with lists of specific plants that will work. For instance, if you want to maintain a small area of lawn and border it with shrubs, go through the guide books for your area and decide which native shrubs are best for the space you have allotted, and which are useful to wildlife.

Plantings should provide a combination of seeds, berries, fruit, nectar flowers, and shelter.

Refer back to your list and take note of existing conditions such as amount of sunlight, soil quality, and drainage. Include as many plants for each specific area as possible.

Look at your list of possible wild

Black-tailed deer.

Clematis trimmings provide good shelter.

guests, particularly birds and butterflies, and note the plants they prefer. Where your two lists overlap is where you can narrow your choices.

Remember to try and use plants with staggered flowering and growing times so that your habitat is productive throughout the gardening season. Cost and availability will naturally affect many of your plant choices.

Getting Ready

When you have completed your map and are satisfied with plant selections and landscaping ideas, you need to prepare for planting. Before you dig anything up, call local nurseries and find out if they carry the items on your list. If not, you will have to substitute plants, or order from catalogs. When ordering by mail, try just a few items to begin with to ensure that healthy plants arrive. Gardening catalogs are often advertised in gardening magazines, and many suppliers are now specializing in native plants. Most people plant their wildlife gar-

dens in the spring when there is the greatest plant selection available. Keep in mind, though, that certain plant species can be started in the fall, and if you live in a rainy climate you won't have to water them to help them get established. Talk to any knowledgeable growers you can find, including other wildlife gardeners and experts in native vegetation.

Consider in advance how much time and money you can afford to spend on creating your wildlife habitat. Any type of landscaping is expensive, and if you are doing it yourself it can be very time-consuming. You may be able to implement only part of your garden in the first year. Perhaps only the shrubs and ground cover will go in. Maybe you will wait to plant the wildflower meadow until the pond is in. The main thing is not to dig up your entire property and then realize that you cannot complete the job. There is nothing wrong with planting and building in stages. Try to plan it in such a way that new projects won't entail disturbing or destroying older areas.

Community Meadow

City officials posted a warning sign next to a colorful tangle of wildflowers growing in an empty suburban lot. A local resident had planted the flowers, and now they had been designated as "untidy." The notice proclaimed that the lot had to be mowed and restored to its previous state (which was rubble-strewn) or a fine would ensue. After a barrage of protest letters from people in the neighborhood, the notice was revoked. The wildflower meadow continues to burst with blooms every summer, providing a haven for wildlife and an enjoyable focal point for people.

179

Construction of a Townhouse Garden for Wildlife

Top left: *Beginning construction of a townhouse garden for wildlife.*

Top right: *Intermediate phase of construction.*

Right: *Completed habitat garden, lush with growth.*

12

Backyard Landscaping and Gardening for Birds

Remember to plant your yard to provide different levels of habitat. Start at grass level (from two inches to one foot), then increase to a combination of short and tall shrubs, then up to short and tall trees if possible. Try to mix deciduous and evergreen species wherever you can. Planting shrubs and trees in clumps, or groups of five or so, makes them more inviting to birds. It also helps increase the chances of pollination. These groupings will provide layers and windbreaks for birds and other wildlife. The distance between your trees and shrubs should be determined by the size of the plants at maturity.

The following list emphasizes plant species that are particularly prized by wild birds for either food, shelter, nesting, or a combination of these uses. Your plant choices should be made according to what is native to your region (regional advice is available at any good gardening center), soil conditions, site exposure on your property (shady north face, sunny south slope, etc.), and space available. Watch that your choices do not include invasive species that can overwhelm native plants. Some can spread to such an extent as to destroy natural habitat. Your local agriculture department or natural history society can provide a list of plants to avoid for your area. You can also go to www.for-wild.org for downloads of invasive and exotic species.

Trees and Shrubs for Birds

Evergreen Trees

Arborvitae, American (*Thuja occidentalis*)

Ash, Velvet (*Fraxinus velutina*)

Blackhaw, Rusty (*Viburnum prunifolium*)

Cedar, Eastern Red (*Juniperus virginiana*)

Cherry, Catalina (*Prunus lyonii*)

Farkleberry (*Vaccinium arboreum*)

Fir, Balsam (*Abies balsamea*)

Fir, Douglas (*Pseudotsuga menziesii*)

Fir, Grand (*Abies grandis*)

Fir, Noble (*Abies procera*)

Fir, Shasta Red (*Abies magnifica*)

Fir, Alpine (*Abies lasiocarpa*)

Fir, White (*Abies concolor*)

Hemlock, Canada (*Tsuga canadensis*)

Hemlock, Mountain (*Tsuga mertensiana*)

Hemlock, Western (*Tsuga heterophylla*)

Holly, American (*Ilex opaca*)

Holly, Dahoon (*Ilex cassine*)

Holly, English (*Ilex aquifolium*)

Juniper, Alligator (*Juniperus deppeana pachyphlaea*)

Juniper, Ashe (*Juniperus ashei*)

Juniper, California (*Juniperus californica*)

Juniper, One-seed (*Juniperus monosperma*)

Juniper, Rocky Mountain (*Juniperus scopulorum*)

Juniper, Utah (*Juniperus osteosperma*)

Juniper, Western (*Juniperus occidentalis*)

Laurel, California (*Umbellularia californica*)

Magnolia, Southern (*Magnolia grandiflora*)

Magnolia, Sweetbay (*Magnolia virginiana*)

Oak, Blue (*Quercus douglasii*)

Oak, Coast Live (*Quercus agrifolia*)

Oak, Engelmann (*Quercus engelmannii*)

Oak, Gambel (*Quercus gambelii*)

Pine, Digger (*Pinus sabiniana*)

Pine, Eastern White (*Pinus strobus*)

Pine, Jeffrey (*Pinus jeffreyi*)

Pine, Limber (*Pinus flexilis*)

Pine, Loblolly (*Pinus taeda*)

Pine, Lodgepole (*Pinus latifolia*)

Pine, Longleaf (*Pinus palustris*)

Pine, Monterey (*Pinus radiata*)

Pine, Pinyon (*Pinus edulis*)

Pine, Pitch (*Pinus rigida*)

Pine, Ponderosa (*Pinus ponderosa*)

Pine, Red (*Pinus resinosa*)

Pine, Sand (*Pinus clausa*)

Pine, Scotch (*Pinus sylvestris*)

Pine, Shore (*Pinus contorta*)

Pine, Short-leaf (*Pinus echinata*)

Pine, Slash (*Pinus elliottii*)

Pine, Sugar (*Pinus lambertiana*)

Pine, Torrey (*Pinus torreyana*)

Pine, Virginia (*Pinus virginiana*)

Pine, Western White (*Pinus monticola*)

Pine, Whitebark (*Pinus albicaulis*)

Redbay (*Persea borbonia*)

Spruce, Black Hills (*Picea glauca var. densata*)

Spruce, Colorado (*Picea pungens*)

Spruce, Red (*Picea rubens*)

Spruce, White (*Picea glauca*)

Yew, Pacific (*Taxus brevifolia*)

Northern saw-whet owl young.

Deciduous Trees

Alder, Arizona *(Alnus oblongifolia)*
Alder, Red *(Alnus rubra)*
Alder, Sitka *(Alnus sinuata)*
Alder, Thinleaf *(Alnus tenuifolia)*
Alder, White *(Alnus rhombifolia)*
Apple, Common *(Malus pumila)*
Ash, Black *(Fraxinus nigra)*
Ash, Green *(Fraxinus pennsylvanica)*
Ash, Oregon *(Fraxinus oregona)*
Ash, White *(Fraxinus americana)*
Aspen, Bigtooth *(Populus grandidentata)*
Aspen, Quaking *(Populus tremuloides)*
Beech, American *(Fagus grandifolia)*
Birch, Gray *(Betula populifolia)*
Birch, Paper *(Betula papyrifera)*
Birch, Sweet *(Betula lenta)*
Birch, Water *(Betula occidentalis)*
Birch, Yellow *(Betula alleghaniensis)*
Black Tupelo *(Nyssa sylvatica)*
Buckthorn, Carolina *(Rhamnus carolinianus)*
Buckthorn, Cascara *(Rhamnus purshiana)*
Butternut *(Juglans cinerea)*
Buttonbush, Common *(Cephalanthus occidentalis)*
Cherry, Bitter *(Prunus emarginata)*
Cherry, Black *(Prunus serotina)*
Cherry, Pin *(Prunus pensylvanica)*
Chokecherry, Common *(Prunus virginiana)*
Cottonwood, Black *(Populus trichocarpa)*
Cottonwood, Eastern *(Populus deltoides)*
Cottonwood, Fremont *(Populus fremontii)*
Cottonwood, Narrowleaf *(Populus angustifolia)*
Crabapple, Flowering *(Malus sp.)*

Migration Fly-way

Ever wonder what living on a migration fly-way might be like? Aurora Paterson, an RN from Scotland, found out when she moved to Tofino on the west coast of Vancouver Island, British Columbia. She went from being an average to a very knowledgeable birder, thanks to a stream of vagrant and transient species that kept "dropping in." Paterson's first exotic sighting was of a Laysan albatross — exotic not because it originated from another country, but because it lives its life exclusively in the open ocean. The Laysan was also rare along that particular stretch of the ocean, seen more commonly off of California and Alaska.

Paterson had a tropical kingbird use the power line in her yard as a hunting perch for two weeks. She also watched a rustic bunting, a Eurasian species, with two hundred and eleven other birders who visited her yard. She was also host to an oriental turtle-dove that was later officially classified as a vagrant for continental North America.

Paterson's feeders have been stop-overs for many first and second species sightings to her West Coast location. Included are a common redpoll, black-headed grosbeak, common grackle, western bluebird, white-throated sparrow and a bluejay. As a result of Paterson's occupation, she has ended up tending sick, injured, and orphaned wildlife that people bring to her and now operates "Rory's Refuge," a volunteer wildlife rehabilitation center specializing in birds.

Golden Asters

Across the swamp and the hillside, as summer advances, new flowers appear in their appointed time. The shaggy white blooms of the American great burnet now hang heavy with dew at the foot of the hill where the purple of Joe-pye-weed is beginning to appear. The great butter-yellow disks of the sunflowers shine at the tops of stalks that rise higher than my head. And north of the apple trees, like an island in a sea of open sand, the clump of golden asters is now in full bloom. For a decade and a half, I have seen it there. Only here do the golden asters grow; nowhere else along the swamp edge or up the hillside do I find them. Here they are rooted and here, slowly expanding their clump with the years, they seem as stable, as enduring as the trees around them

Edwin Way Teale – Circle of the Seasons, 1953

Crabapple, Oregon *(Malus fusca)*

Dogwood, Alternate Leaf *(Cornus alternifolia)*

Dogwood, Flowering *(Cornus florida)*

Dogwood, Pacific *(Cornus nuttallii)*

Dogwood, Western *(Cornus occidentalis)*

Elm, Slippery *(Ulmus rubra)*

Fringe Tree, Chinese *(Chionanthus retusus)*

Fringe Tree, White *(Chionanthus virginicus)*

Hackberry, Common *(Celtis occidentalis)*

Hackberry, Sugar *(Celtis laevigata)*

Hackberry, Western *(Celtis reticulata)*

Hawthorn, Blueberry *(Crataegus brachyacantha)*

Hawthorn, Cockspur *(Crataegus crus-galli)*

Hawthorn, Douglas *(Crataegus douglasii)*

Hawthorn, Downy *(Crataegus mollis)*

Hawthorn, Fireberry *(Crataegus chrysocarpa)*

Hawthorn, Fleshy *(Crataegus succulenta)*

Hawthorn, Parsley *(Crataegus apiifolia)*

Hawthorn, Washington *(Crataegus phaenopyrum)*

Hickory, Mockernut *(Carya tomentosa)*

Hickory, Pignut *(Carya glabra)*

Hickory, Shagbark *(Carya ovata)*

Hickory, Water *(Carya aquatica)*

Woodland habitat in a container.

Hop Hornbeam, American *(Ostrya virginiana)*

Hornbeam, American *(Carpinus caroliniana)*

Larch, Eastern *(Larix laricina)*

Madrone *(Arbutus menziesii)*

Maple, Amur *(Acer ginnala)*

Maple, Box Elder *(Acer negundo)*

Maple, Norway *(Acer platanoides)*

Maple, Red *(Acer rubrum)*

Maple, Rocky Mountain *(Acer glabrum)*

Maple, Silver *(Acer saccharinum)*

Maple, Sugar *(Acer saccharum)*

Mesquite, Screwbean *(Prosopis pubescens)*

Mountain Ash, American *(Sorbus americana)*

Mountain Ash, European *(Sorbus aucuparia)*

Mountain Ash, Northern *(Sorbus decora)*

Mulberry, Red *(Morus rubra)*

Mulberry, Texas *(Morus microphylla)*
Mulberry, White *(Morus alba)*
Myrtle, Wax *(Myrica cerifera)*
Oak, Arizona White *(Quercus arizonica)*
Oak, Black *(Quercus velutina)*
Oak, Blackjack *(Quercus marilandica)*
Oak, Bluejack *(Quercus chapmanii)*
Oak, Bur *(Quercus macrocarpa)*
Oak, Chestnut *(Quercus prinus)*
Oak, Gambel *(Quercus gambelii)*
Oak, Laurel *(Quercus laurifolia)*
Oak, Live *(Quercus virginiana)*
Oak, Northern Red *(Quercus rubra)*
Oak, Oregon White *(Quercus garryana)*
Oak, Pin *(Quercus palustris)*
Oak, Post *(Quercus stellata)*
Oak, Scarlet *(Quercus coccinea)*
Oak, Southern Red *(Quercus falcata)*
Oak, Swamp Chestnut *(Quercus michauxii)*
Oak, Valley White *(Quercus lobata)*
Oak, Water *(Quercus nigra)*

Oak, White *(Quercus alba)*
Oak, Willow *(Quercus phellos)*
Osage Orange *(Maclura pomifera)*
Palmetto, Cabbage *(Sabal palmetto)*
Pecan *(Carya illinoensis)*
Pepper Tree, California *(Schinus molle)*
Persimmon, Common *(Diospyros virginiana)*
Plum, Wild *(Prunus americana)*
Poplar, Balsam *(Populus balsamifera)*
Possum Haw *(Ilex decidua)*
Sassafras, American *(Sassafras albidum)*
Sycamore, Arizona *(Platanus wrightii)*
Sycamore, Western *(Platanus racemosa)*
Sweet Gum, American *(Liquidambar styraciflua)*
Tulip Tree, North American *(Liriodendron tulipifera)*
Viburnum, Smooth Withe Rod *(Viburnum nudum)*
Walnut, Black *(Juglans nigra)*
Willow, Black *(Salix nigra)*

Removal of lawn and creation of berm for native shrubs and perennials.

Willow, Coyote (*Salix exigua*)
Willow, Diamond (*Salix rigida*)
Willow, Pacific (*Salix lasiandra*)
Willow, Peach-leaved (*Salix amygdaloides*)
Willow, Sandbar (*Salix interior*)
Willow, Scouler (*Salix scouleriana*)

Evergreen Shrubs

Blueberry, Ground (*Vaccinium myrsinites*)
Buckthorn, California/Coffeeberry (*Rhamnus californica*)
Buckthorn, Holly-leaved/Redberry (*Rhamnus crocea*)
Cactus, Prickly Pear (*Opuntia sp.*)
Cherry, Carolina Laurel (*Prunus carolinia*)

Living archway.

Cherry, Holly-leaf (*Prunus ilicifolia*)
Christmasberry (*Photinia arbutifolia*)
Currant, Golden (*Ribes aureum*)
Dahoon, Myrtle (*Ilex myrtifolia*)
Gallberry, Large (*Ilex coriacea*)
Grape, Oregon (*Mahonia nervosa*)
Hackberry, Spiny (*Celtis pallida*)
Holly, Chinese/Inkberry (*Ilex glabra*)
Holly, Japanese (*Ilex crenata*)
Holly, Yaupon (*Ilex vomitoria*)
Huckleberry, Box (*Gaylussacia brachycera*)
Huckleberry, Evergreen (*Vaccinium ovatum*)
Juniper, Chinese (*Juniperus chinensis*)
Juniper, Common (*Juniperus communis*)
Manzanita, Green-leaf (*Arctostaphylos patula*)
Manzanita, Mexican (*Arctostaphylos pungens*)
Oak, Palmer (*Quercus palmeri*)
Palmetto, Dwarf (*Sabal minor*)
Saltbush, Big (*Atriplex lentiformus*)
Saltbush, Brewer (*Atriplex brewerii*)
Saltbush, Desert Holly (*Atriplex hymenelytra*)
Snowberry, Common (*Symphoricarpos oreophilus*)
Snowberry, Mountain (*Symphoricarpos rotundifolius*)
Sumac, Laurel (*Rhus laurina*)
Sumac, Lemonade (*Rhus integrifolia*)
Sumac, Sugar Bush (*Rhus ovata*)
Thimbleberry (*Rubus parviflorus*)
Yew, Canadian (*Taxus canadensis*)

Deciduous Shrubs

Acacia, Mescat (*Acacia constricta*)
Alder, Hazel (*Alnus serrulata*)
Alder, Speckled (*Alnus rugosa*)

Ash, American Mountain (*Sorbus americana*)

Ash, Green Mountain (*Sorbus scopulina*)

Barberry, Japanese (*Berberis thunbergii*)

Bayberry (*Myrica pensylvanica*)

Beautyberry, American (*Callicarpa americana*)

Bilberry, Bog (*Vaccinium uliginosum*)

Blackberry, Allegheny (*Rubus alleghe-niensis*)

Blackberry, California (*Rubus macropetalus*)

Blueberry, Highbush (*Vaccinium corymbosum*)

Blueberry, Lowbush (*Vaccinium angustifolium*)

Blueberry, Western Bog (*Vaccinium occidentale*)

Buckthorn, Alder (*Rhamnus frangula*)

Buckthorn, Alderleaf (*Rhamnus alnifolius*)

Buckthorn, Cascara (*Rhamnus purshiana*)

Buckthorn, Common (*Rhamnus cathartica*)

Buffalo Berry, Silver (*Sheperdia argentea*)

Bugleweed (*Ajuga reptans*)

Bunchberry (*Cornus canadensis*)

Ceanothus, Fendler (*Ceanothus fendleri*)

Cherry, Bessey (*Prunus besseyi*)

Cherry, Bitter (*Prunus emarginata*)

Cherry, Dwarf Sand (*Prunus pumila*)

Chokeberry, Black (*Aronia melanocarpa*)

Chokeberry, Red (*Aronia arbutifolia*)

Coralberry (*Symphoricarpus orbiculatus*)

Cotoneaster, European (*Cotoneaster integerrimus*)

Cotoneaster, Rockspray (*Cotoneaster horizontalis*)

Crabapple, Sargent (*Malus sargentii*)

Crabapple, Toringo (*Malus sieboldii*)

Currant, American Black (*Ribes americanum*)

Currant, Buffalo (*Ribes odoratum*)

Currant, White Field (*Ribes cereum*)

Dangleberry (*Gaylussacia frondosa*)

Deerberry, Common (*Vaccinium stamineum*)

Dewberry, Northern (*Rubus flagellaris*)

Dogwood, Brown (*Cornus glabrata*)

Dogwood, Miner's (*Cornus sessilis*)

Dogwood, Red-osier (*Cornus stolonifera*)

Dogwood, Silky (*Cornus amomum*)

Elder, American (*Sambucus canadensis*)

Elder, Black-bead (*Sambucus melanocarpa*)

Elder, Blueberry (*Sambucus caerulea*)

Elder, Bunchberry (*Sambucus micro-botrys*)

Elder, Scarlet (*Sambucus pubens*)

Elderberry, Pacific Red (*Sambucus callicarpa*)

Euonymus, Winged/Burning Bush (*Euonymus alatus*)

Fig, Common (*Ficus carica*)

Firethorn, Scarlet (*Pyracantha coccinea*)

Gooseberry, Missouri (*Ribes missouriense*)

Gooseberry, Prickly (*Ribes cynosbati*)

Hackberry, Western (*Celtis reticulata*)

Habitat garden in winter.

Rooftop trees beckon to birds.

Hawthorn, Douglas (*Crataegus douglasii*)

Hawthorn, One-flower (*Cratageus uniflora*)

Hazel, American (*Corylus americana*)

Honeysuckle (*Lonicera quinquelocularis*)

Honeysuckle, Fly (*Lonicera canadensis*)

Honeysuckle, Hairy White (*Lonicera albiflora*)

Honeysuckle, Morrow (*Lonicera morrowii*)

Honeysuckle, Swampfly (*Lonicera oblongifolia*)

Honeysuckle, Tatarian (*Lonicera tatarica*)

Honeysuckle, Twinberry (*Lonicera involucrata*)

Honeysuckle, Utah (*Lonicera utahensis*)

Honeysuckle, Winter (*Lonicera fragrantissima*)

Huckleberry, Black (*Gaylussacia baccata*)

Huckleberry, Dwarf (*Gaylussacia dumosa*)

Huckleberry, Red (*Vaccinium parvifolum*)

Juneberry, Roundleaf (*Amelanchier sanguinea*)

Meadowsweet, Narrowleaf (*Spiraea alba*)

Mesquite (*Prosopis juliiflora*)

Mountain Ash, Alpine (*Sorbus occidentalis*)

Mountain Ash, Green (*Sorbus scopulina*)

Mountain Ash, Sitka (*Sorbus sitchensis*)

Myrtle, California Wax (*Myrica californica*)

Olive, "Cardinal" Autumn (*Elaeagnus umbellata*)

Olive, Russian (*Elaeagnus angustifolia*)

Osoberry (*Osmaronia cerasiformis*)

Partridge Berry (*Mitchella repens*)

Pea Shrub, Siberian (*Caragana arborescens*)

Plum, Sandhill (*Prunus angustifolia*)

Raspberry, Black (*Rubus occidentalis*)

Raspberry, Boulder (*Rubus deliciosus*)

Raspberry, Red (*Rubus idaeus*)

Raspberry, Whitebark (*Rubus leucodermis*)

Rose, Baldhip (*Rosa gymnocarpa*)

Rose, California (*Rosa californica*)

Rose, Meadow (*Rosa blanda*)

Rose, Multiflora (*Rosa multiflora*)

Rose, Nootka (*Rosa nutkana*)

Rose, Pasture (*Rosa carolina*)

Rose, Prairie Wild (*Rosa arkansana*)

Miniature yard habitat created on a rooftop.

Rose, Rugosa (*Rosa rugosa*)

Rose, Swamp (*Rosa palustris*)

Rose, Virginia (*Rosa virginiana*)

Rose, Woods (*Rosa woodsii*)

Sagebrush, Common (*Artemesia tridentata*)

Salmonberry (*Rubus spectabilis*)

Saltbush, Big (*Atriplex lentiformis*)

Saltbush, Four-wing (*Atriplex canescens*)

Serviceberry, Allegheny (*Amelanchier laevis*)

Serviceberry, Bartram (*Amelanchier bartramiana*)

Serviceberry, Downy (*Amelanchier arborea*)

Serviceberry, Running (*Amelanchier stolonifera*)

Serviceberry, Saskatoon (*Amelanchier alnifolia*)

Serviceberry, Shadblow (*Amelanchier canadensis*)

Serviceberry, Utah (*Amelanchier utahensis*)

Serviceberry, Western (*Amelanchier florida*)

Snowberry, Common (*Symphoricarpos albus*)

Spicebush, Common (*Lindera benzoin*)

Sumac, Dwarf (*Rhus copallina*)

Sumac, Fragant (*Rhus aromatica*)

Sumac, Smooth (*Rhus glabra*)

Sumac, Staghorn (*Rhus typhina*)

St. John's Wort, Shrubby (*Hypericum prolificum*)

Viburnum, American (*Viburnum trilobum*)

Viburnum, Arrowwood (*Viburnum dentatum*)

Viburnum, Black Haw (*Viburnum prunifolium*)

Taut Silk

This morning I came upon a thread of spider silk, straight and taut, stretching between two adjacent apple trees at the Insect Garden. One end anchored almost exactly opposite the other end, the fine, glistening line bridges a gap of eight feet or more about seven feet above the tangled grass. How has the little spider stretched the thread across the open air? Only one hypothesis – and it is the true explanation – solves the riddle. Sitting at the very twig tip of a branch, the spider lets the silken thread play out in the breeze. Even the slightest movement of the air is sufficient to carry the spider's silken cable. When the end of the drifting silk becomes entangled with the leaves and twigs of the opposite tree, the spider pulls the line taut, makes it secure, and thus is equipped with a roadway in the air from tree to tree.

Edwin Way Teale – Circle of the Seasons, 1953

Viburnum, Hobble Bush
(*Viburnum lantanoides*)

Viburnum, Maple-leaf
(*Viburnum acerifolium*)

Viburnum, Nannyberry
(*Viburnum lentago*)

Viburnum, Northern Arrow
Wood (*Viburnum recognitum*)

Viburnum, Southern Arrow
Wood (*Viburnum dentatum*)

Vibernum, Withe Rod
(*Vibernum cassinoides*)

Willow, Purple Osier (*Salix purpurea*)

Willow, Pussy (*Salix discolor*)

Winterberry, Common (*Ilex verticillata*)

Winterberry, Smooth (*Ilex laevigata*)

A Note About Fruit Trees

Fruit trees are particularly useful to wildlife. Many species of birds and mammals eat the fruit and buds of the trees, and pollinating insects are attracted to the blossoms. To make sure you are getting the most wildlife benefit from your fruit trees, ensure that they aren't crowding each other out. As well, if a tree is young and has only a few side branches, trim the top to encourage branching or, if it is older, remove dead branches and any small stems competing with large healthy stems. Consult a grower, or nursery worker, for specific information on your type of tree and how you can best care for it.

If you are in a suburban area where jays, crows, and other large birds visit, or where raccoons, opossums, or deer pass through, there may not be much fruit left when they're done, but you will have had

Native woodland garden with container features.

Vines are a good addition to any balcony habitat.

a glimpse of wildlife in action. There are many methods to try if you want some fruit for yourself, such as tightly pulled netting, loud noises, scarecrows, and electric fencing. You may want to protect certain trees and leave others for the animals and birds.

Ground Cover

Ground covers are more useful to birds than tidily clipped lawns, particularly in dry or desert climates. Many varieties of cover are effective in attracting ground feeding birds, especially when grown on slopes. Consider building up small hills for planting on, and incorporating rock edging, or a rock garden around the base. Logs and brush piles at the foot of small planted slopes are also favorites of ground feeders, giving them a protected place to dart into. Ground covers come in various heights, and there are types for virtually every growing situation, from the deep shade beneath conifers, to scorching sun.

Ground Covers to Grow

Bearberry/Kinnikinick (*Arctostaphylos uva-ursi*)

Bilberry, Bog (*Vaccinium uliginosum*)

Bilberry, Dwarf (*Vaccinium caespitosum*)

Black Crowberry (*Empetrum nigrum*)

Bugleweed (*Ajuga reptans*)

Bunchberry (*Cornus canadensis*)

Cotoneaster, Bearberry (*Cotoneaster dammeri*)

Cotoneaster, Creeping (*Cotoneaster adpressus*)

Cowberry (*Vaccinium vitis-idaea*)

Crowberry, Black (*Empetrum nigrum*)

Juniper, Creeping (*Juniperus horizontalis*)

Juniper, Sargent (*Juniperus sargentii*)

Manzanita, Pine-mat (*Arctostaphylos nevadensis*)

Partridge Berry (*Mitchella repens*)

Rose, Ground (*Rosa spithamea*)

Strawberry, Cultivated (*Fragaria ananassa*)

Strawberry, Scarlet (*Fragraria virginiana*)

Whortleberry, Grouse (*Vaccinium scoparium*)

Wintergreen, Alpine (*Gaultheria humifusa*)

Wintergreen, Checkerberry (*Gaultheria procumbens*)

Vines

Ampelopsis, Heartleaf (*Ampelopsis cordata*)

Bittersweet, American (*Celastrus scandens*)

Creeper, Trumpet (*Campsis radicans*)

Creeper, Virginia (*Parthenocissus quinquefolia*)

Wildlife Barrel

Outside a small storefront on a busy city street, hordes of birds plunder a sorry-looking rambling rose that climbs up a trellis in a half-barrel. During spring and early summer, the rose is visited by a twittering, fluttering assortment of birds, bees, and butterflies. The attraction? Aphids – each year the rosebush harbors an infestation. The store owner and office workers on that street probably derive more pleasure from the thriving wildlife at the half-barrel than they would from a healthy, aphid-free rose.

Creeper, Winter (*Euonymus fortunei*)
Grape, Bush (*Vitis acerifolia*)
Grape, California (*Vitis californica*)
Grape, Canyon (*Vitis arizonica*)
Grape, Fox (*Vitis labrusca*)
Grape, Frost (*Vitis vulpina*)
Grape, Mustang (*Vitis mustangensis*)
Grape, Riverbank (*Vitis riparia*)
Grape, Summer (*Vitis aestivalis*)
Greenbrier, Cat (*Smilax glauca*)
Greenbrier, Common (*Smilax rotundifolia*)
Greenbrier, Laurel (*Smilax laurifolia*)
Honeysuckle, Chaparral (*Lonicera interrupta*)
Honeysuckle, Orange (*Lonicera ciliosa*)
Honeysuckle, Pink (*Lonicera hispidula*)
Honeysuckle, Trumpet (*Lonicera sempervirens*)
Moonseed, Common (*Menispermum canadense*)
Snailseed, Carolina (*Cocculus carolinus*)
Supplejack, Alabama (*Berchemia scandens*)

Brambles

Brambles are tangled, mostly thorny, berry-producing vegetation; blackberry, dewberry, raspberry, and thimbleberry all come under this heading. Bramble bushes are different sizes and heights, and provide cover, food, and nesting habitat for many bird species and other wildlife—even the most determined predator is usually unwilling to risk the thorns or denseness of a bramble patch. Pruning and occasional fertilizing will keep brambles healthy and productive.

Flowers for Birds

Asters/Michaelmas Daisy (*Aster sp.*)
Bachelor Buttons/Cornflower (*Centaurea cyanus*)
Basket Flower (*Centaurea americana*)
Blessed Thistle (*Carduus benedictus*)
Calendula/Common Marigold (*Calendula officinalis*)
California Poppy (*Eschscholzia californica*)
Campanula/Bluebells (*Campanula sp.*)
China Aster (*Callistephus chinensis*)
Chrysanthemum (*Chrysanthemum sp.*)
Coneflower/Black-eyed Susan (*Rudbeckia hirta*)
Coreopsis (*Coreopsis grandiflora*)
Cosmos (*Cosmos sp.*)
Dayflower (*Commelina sp.*)
Dusty Miller (*Centaurea cineraria*)
Echinacea (*Echinacea purpurea*)
Love-lies-bleeding (*Amaranthus caudatus*)
Marigolds (*Tagetes sp.*)
Phlox (*Phlox sp.*)
Portulaca (*Portulaca grandiflora*)
Prince's Plumes (*Celosia cristata*)
Rock Purslane (*Calandrinia umbellata*)
Royal Sweet Sultan (*Centaurea imperialis*)
Silene (*Silene sp.*)
Sunflower, Common (*Helianthus annuus*)

American robin.

Sweet Scabius *(Scabiosa atropurpurea)*
Tarweed *(Madia elegans)*
Verbena *(Verbena hybrida)*
Zinnia *(Zinnia elegans)*

Lawn

Lawns can play a valuable role in a natural garden that has been landscaped and planted to attract wildlife. A small patch, or swaths, of lawn clipped short will create edge in your habitat. Native grasses are preferred by birds, and are much easier to maintain than non-native lawns. After all, natural grasses are supposed to be there, but birds are attracted to the openings and layers that lawns provide. Certain birds use grassy lawn as a hunting ground, most notably robins for earthworms, and flickers for insects.

The problem with lawns lies partly in the way they are maintained, and in the plants used to create them. A neatly manicured, uniformly green blanket of non-native turf grasses usually entails the use of pesticides and herbicides. Large amounts of water, fertilizer, and maintenance are generally needed as well.

Dustbath

For some birds, a good dustbath seems to be as satisfying as bathing in water. If you're lucky, you may see birds preen, splash, and flutter in the dust, cleaning their feathers and ridding themselves of parasites.

To include a dustbath in your habitat garden, clear as large an area as you can, given the scale of your yard (three feet square is ideal for those with sufficient space). Locate the dustbath in an open

Swaths of lawn.

area, perhaps at the edge of a lawn. Dig a hole approximately six inches deep and line the outer edges with bricks, rocks, or pieces of log, making sure they are securely in place. Find the best quality sand you can (or make your own mix with one part sand, one part ash, and one part loam). As a simple alternative for those with dryish soil, just find a spot along a

Phases of a Front Yard Habitat Creation Project

Getting rid of lawn.

Creating beds and borders.

Habitat sign amidst new plantings.

194

Yard project in
early spring.

Birdbath and
perching branches.

Bench tucked
in at edge.

Rocks and posts
for wildlife.

Yard project in winter.

The Concord Ant

Across the street from the Colonial Inn this evening, I see a Concord (Massachusetts) ant engaged in Herculean labors. I first notice the white wing of a moth traveling across the sidewalk, seemingly supported by magic. Then I observe a small, dark ant. Although it is less than one-eighth the length of the moth wing, it is gripping the base of the wing in its jaws, holding its burden straight out in front of it, and thus running at top speed across the concrete of the sidewalk. How fabulously strong must be the neck of such an insect

Edwin Way Teale – Circle of the Seasons, 1953

fence or shed, and scrape off the first few inches of earth.

Nesting Cavities

Many birds are dependent on dead trees (snags) for nest holes. Consider yourself a fortunate wildlife steward if you own dead trees. They are prime woodpecker habitat as well as valued perching sites. As an alternative, you can create a snag from a living tree by having the top third or so professionally removed, along with some of the side branches (leave short perching branches near the top). This is a better method than girdling, as the latter results in an intact top on a dead tree, leaving it susceptible to wind damage. Girdling just a large branch or fork in a tree is another option. As well, you can create cavities in a living tree by drilling holes one to two inches in diameter at a ten-degree angle, sloping towards the tree's center. Try spots where water will pool up, below crotches, or above a burl or old branch site, to speed up the decay process.

Weeds

Endless hours and tremendous amounts of energy are spent by gardeners trying to rid their property of weeds. But the weeds persist. And that's good news for birds. The prolific and hardy nature of weeds makes them an essential food source of wild birds, butterflies, and many insects. Weeds are plants that for one reason or another, we have deemed unworthy of space in our gardens or lawns.

Weeds such as bristlegrass (*Setaria sp.*), doveweed (*Eremocarpus*), knotweed (*Polygonum argyrocoleon*), lamb's quarter (*Chenopodium album*), bush clover (*Lespedeza violacea*), pigweed (*Amaranth*), pokeweed (*Phytolacca americana*), sheep sorrel (*Rumex acetosella*), and sunflower (*Helianthus annus*) grow in a variety of situations. Try cultivating a weed patch in a quiet corner of your backyard and see how popular it is with wildlife. To encourage weeds in a certain area, just till or otherwise disturb a patch of soil and wait for the weeds to "activate." For more information on planting a weed patch, see bird food gardens below.

Bird Food Gardens

Just as you would keep a vegetable garden to feed your family, you can grow a food patch to feed the birds. A bird food garden is an area where you plant and rotate possibly unattractive crops of high yield that have maximum food value for birds. Ideally, your bird food garden should contain a few different crops. You can grow cultivated plants like millet and sunflower, as well as native species of weeds and wildflowers. Bird food gardens should be located near water and cover, and will be a welcome addition to the other food offered in your wildlife habitat.

Caterpillars on dandelion.

Plants for a Bird Food Garden

Buckwheat *(Polygonum convolulus)*

Clover, Honey *(Melilotus alba)*

Delar, Small Burnet *(Sanguissorba minor)*

Foxtail *(Setaria sp.)*

Millet *(Panicum sp.)*

Milo *(Sorghum sp.)*

Oats, Wild *(Avena fatua)*

Panic Grass *(Echinochloa crusgalli)*

Pigweed *(Amaranth sp.)*

Ragweed *(Ambrosia artemisiifolia)*

Rye *(Lolium temulentum)*

Smartweed *(Polygonum hydropiper)*

Sunflower *(Helianthus annus)*

Wheat *(Triticum aestivum)*

A rotten urban tree with woodpecker hole.

A Wildflower Meadow

You can create a wildflower meadow in your own backyard or on your balcony, in miniature, using any number of containers. All you need is a site with good drainage and plenty of sun. For humans, a meadow is an ideal addition for its burst of color, and soft, country feel; different wildlife will feed, bask, and carry out pollination in a wildflower meadow.

There is a decided contrast between traditionally manicured patches of lawn and the untamed appearance of a wildflower meadow. Before you plant a meadow on your property, you could talk to your neighbors about it, and look into local by-laws regarding yard maintenance. Some areas dictate neat and tidy lawns for all homes; if this is the case, you may need to convince officials before they accept the more wild appearance of your flower meadow. Misunderstandings in your neighborhood can sometimes be avoided by posting a small sign describing the purpose of *any* backyard wildlife habitat that varies from the tidy-lawn norm. Wildflowers are a picturesque transition between lawn and forest, and serve edge species especially well. Meadows are also very appropriate at the end of a pond or other water feature, such as a bog or a stream.

Preparing to Plant

First, choose an appropriate spot for your meadow, keeping in mind the large amounts of sun needed, and good drainage required, as well as proximity to a hose for getting your meadow established. If you are replacing lawn with wildflowers, you'll need to hoe, or rototill, just deep enough to dig up the old roots from your lawn. This is best done in early fall or late summer the year before, to

Windfall used for wildlife posts.

avoid using herbicides in eradicating weeds and grasses. Another option is to remove the turf and compost it, or use it piled upside down to contour the ground. Let the soil overwinter with no crops unless your meadow is going to be grown on a steep slope, then you could plant a cover crop such as rye grass to hold the soil until spring. You would then turn over the new growth before planting.

Sowing the Seeds

You will want to plant your wildflower meadow just before the vegetable gardens in your region are planted. If you live in a warm climate, you can plant in spring or fall, but not full summer. Try to time it so that your meadow benefits from rainfall and warm soil. In colder climates, you can plant your wildflowers during the summer, but consistent watering will be necessary. There are many good sources for wildflower seed at nurseries. As with all the plants in your wildlife habitat, try to choose seed mixes native to your area. They should be composed of approximately half wild grass seeds which will prevent soil erosion, support tall flowers, give food and protection to wildlife, and fill in the spaces around the wildflowers. Choose a combination of mat-forming and bunch-forming grasses.

When your ground is ready, choose a windless day to plant. Divide the seed into two batches and pour it into clean containers (cans are good). Mix plenty of sand with the seeds until completely blended. For a very full, flowering meadow, you can sow up to two or three times the minimum seeding recommendation on the seed packages (any more than that will keep your wildflowers from reaching their full growth due to crowding). Take the first can of the seed/sand mixture and scatter evenly over the entire area. Repeat the procedure with the second container, scattering the seeds crosswise to the first. Push the seeds into the ground (but do not rake or cover them) using a lawn roller or a piece of plywood laid down and walked on.

Maintenance

Your wildflowers will appear at different rates. The annuals will sprout and bloom quickly, predominating the first year, and will need to be reseeded every one or two

Family can participate in wildlife activities.

years. Biennials will take two years to bloom and they will reseed themselves, making them nearly as permanent as perennials, although they will die in the first frost. Perennials will appear every year and progress to more impressive displays after their first year.

At the end of every growing season, mow your wildflower meadow, keeping the mower on its highest setting. This will discourage native shrubs and trees from establishng themselves. You may want to do some hand weeding to discourage in-vaders, but be careful, as it is often difficult to distinguish between a weed and a wildflower.

As your meadow matures, its displays will be increasingly full and you will need to do less weeding because of this. Do not mow (or scythe) until your late-blooming flowers have dropped their seeds. If you can, try to leave tall grasses uncut in the meadow over the winter to give interest to the area and provide cover for wild creatures.

Water Features for Wildlife

W ATER IS ONE of the most sought-after, and important, features in any wildlife habitat. Insects, birds, mammals, and amphibians are attracted to water sources—even those that do not come to our yards for food may arrive because of water. It is especially valued in dry regions and during winters when most sources are frozen, and if you keep a reliable supply, chances are you will be rewarded with visitors. If you are not able to provide a pond, a birdbath will be welcomed. Even a simple drip can bring interesting activity to your yard.

Ponds

Ponds range from simple half-barrels, to sophisticated and durable ponds made of concrete. Take care when deciding on the type and the location. Is your pond going to be the focus of your wildlife habitat, or will it be an accent? If you live in an urban area, what are the regulations regarding ponds? In some communities, any depths greater than eighteen inches must be surrounded by a fence. In addition, you should check to see whether ponds in your area are required to have filtration; local authorities can supply you with information before you build. Other considerations include locating your pond in a spot that receives at least five hours of sun each day, and not locating it beneath a tree. Shedding leaves or needles make maintenance much more difficult. Try to keep the size of your pond in proportion to the rest of your wildlife habitat.

When planning your pond, remember that it is a habitat in its own right. After you build, plant, and perhaps stock it, the pond will continue to develop and mature. After becoming established, it should be a balanced system of inter-related life forms. Until then, your pond will go through stages, and a likely one will be an algae bloom in which the water turns a slimy green. Don't despair and don't clean it out. Too much cleaning in the early stages of a pond's cycle will upset the equilibrium. Snails, aquatic plants, and/or fish should eventually control algae growth, and large-leaved plants around the edges will help by shading the water. Over time, bacteria build up and contribute to waste removal. You will know your pond is balanced when the water is fairly clear.

A good filtration system is an option, especially if you prefer the water to be completely clear for viewing fish. Pumps are a possibility too if you enjoy moving water, or want to keep the water from freezing over in the winter. It's a good idea to consult local experts before you install your pond, and if you have any questions while it is becoming established. Pond dealers can be located through the phone directory, aquarium supply stores, plant nurseries, and hardware stores that stock pond supplies.

Take precautions against West Nile virus by eliminating water on your property. If there is nowhere for mosquitoes to breed, you will be contributing to a healthy environment. Change water in birdbaths every three to four days, or

Pacific treefrog.

even daily during the summer months. Depending on the incidence of West Nile virus in your area (check with your local health board), you may want to aerate ponds or stock them with fish to assure the absence of mosquito larvae.

Water Barrel

Half-barrel ponds are a great way for wildlife stewards with limited space to enhance their habitat. With a combination of floating and submerged plants, the barrel should attract birds and various insects, and fit well onto a balcony or small patio.

A plastic barrel liner will prolong the life of your barrel. Place six inches of soil in the bottom and fill with water (preferably rainwater, filtered water, or tapwater aged for 48 hours to allow chlorine to dissipate). Select your aquatic plants from a pond supply center and nestle them, still in their pots, in the soil at the bottom of the barrel. Add a thin layer of gravel. Float a small log or arrange a rock

Red-winged blackbirds frequent cattail marshes and lush vegetation around ponds.

36
PROJECT

TOOLS & MATERIALS

- Shovels (round point, square point)
- Pick
- Crowbar
- Level
- two-by-four long enough to lay across the center of your pond (to check level)
- String
- Stakes
- Wheelbarrow (or plastic sheeting for holding excavated dirt)
- A liner – either flexible PVC or rubber – durability varies (buy only the kind that is safe for plants and fish)
- The basic formula for determining how much flexible liner you will need is:

Length of hole + depth of hole x 2 = liner length / Width of hole + maximum depth x 2 = liner width

- Sand – enough to place at least 2" between the liner and the excavation
- Safe water – use stored rainwater runoff from your roof, or treat your tapwater to ensure it is safe. Your local water authorities will be able to tell you whether your water supply is treated with chlorine or chloramine. For chlorine, allow water to stand for 24 to 48 hours to gas off. If it is also treated with chloramine, you can purchase chemical solutions to treat it (stores specializing in pond supplies will carry this). You can also purchase inexpensive water quality test-kits from aquarium supply stores and pond suppliers.
- Edging material – bricks, rock, etc.

A flexible liner pond is a permanent feature of the backyard habitat and is relatively simple to install, although more work and expense than a half-barrel. Ponds should be at least 18" deep if fish are to survive, with pockets of depth to 36" deep if they are to overwinter in temperatures to minus 40°F. Plan to build steps or tiers into your pond for plants that require varying depths. With a flexible liner, you can build your pond any size you like, but keep in mind that generally the smaller the pond, the more difficult to maintain a healthy biological balance.

1. Lay out the pond using a string and stakes. Look at it from a variety of angles to make sure it is suitable.

2. Dig out the turf and sod in the shape you want plus 2" extra width and depth to accommodate a layer of sand beneath the liner. Dig out a space for the edging materials as well (Figure 2).

3. Lay a two-by-four across the pond and place a level on top of it (Figure 1). Make sure that the edges around the pond are level. Measure in all directions. Make any necessary adjustments and then measure out the rest of the pond's depths with confidence that these outside edges will give you a standard measurement.

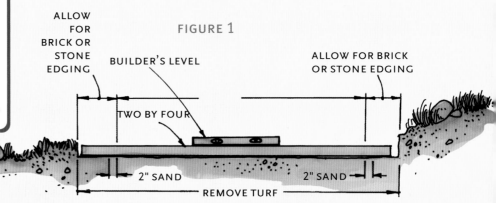

FIGURE 1

ALLOW FOR BRICK OR STONE EDGING

BUILDER'S LEVEL

ALLOW FOR BRICK OR STONE EDGING

TWO BY FOUR

2" SAND

2" SAND

REMOVE TURF

4. Now, beginning in the center of the pond, dig out toward the edges, allowing for shelves if these are included in your design. Pile the soil in a wheelbarrow or on a plastic tarp (this soil may be used later to create a raised bed or some other garden project). All shelves should be 9" to 12" wide and they should move about 1" toward the center for every 3" down (about 20° off vertical).

5. Once all the soil has been excavated, remove any sharp objects such as sticks or stones that could puncture the liner and cause a leak.

6. Pour a 2" layer of damp sand around the bottom and sides of the pool, packing it in as tightly as possible.

7. Warm the liner by spreading it out on a driveway or lawn (even better if it's a sunny day). This will make it more flexible and easier to work with.

8. Roll up the liner again and carry it to the pond.

FIGURE 2

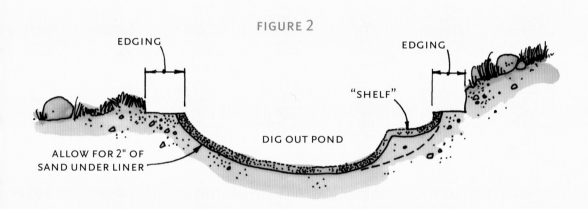

EDGING

EDGING

"SHELF"

DIG OUT POND

ALLOW FOR 2" OF SAND UNDER LINER

FIGURE 3

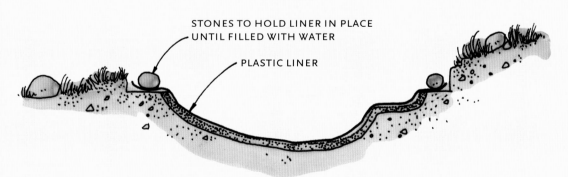

STONES TO HOLD LINER IN PLACE UNTIL FILLED WITH WATER

PLASTIC LINER

9. Carefully unroll the liner and place it in the pond so that it fits into the contours and extends over the edges (there will be folds and creases). Place some stones on the liner extending up onto the edges to keep it taut as it fills with water (Figure 3).

10. Begin filling the pond. As the liner creases in the curved areas of the pond, fold the excess material neatly into flaps.

11. When the pond is full, cut away the excess liner around the edges. It can be used for patching or for added protection under heavy plant pots.

12. Place the edging materials around the pond so that the rim of the liner is hidden (Figure 4). If you are using bricks, have their lengths face the center of the pond.

FIGURE 4

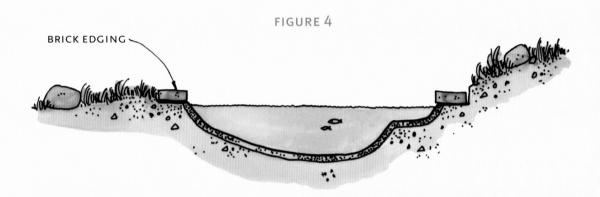

BRICK EDGING

FIGURE 5

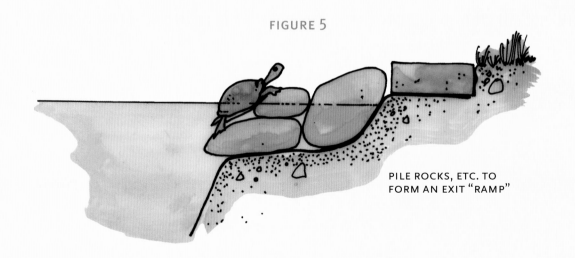

PILE ROCKS, ETC. TO FORM AN EXIT "RAMP"

Spider web by pond.

"island." This will enable birds to access the water and will provide an essential escape route for smaller creatures that need to climb out.

Pumps and Filters

Pumps and filters are optional; they *can* be necessary, but are often just pleasant to have. A pump will prevent your pond water from becoming stagnant. The size of the pump will depend on the size of your pond, so check with a supplier for what is best in your situation and the options available. The pump you choose should be capable of recirculating all the

Rough-skinned newt.

water in the pond through a filter at least once every two hours and preferably every hour. Filters will rid the water of particulate matter, and range from simple mechanical systems to complex biological systems.

Soil

Soil for your pond should not contain fertilizers, herbicides, or pesticides. After placing your soil directly on the bottom of the pond, cover it with a one- to two inch layer of coarse gravel to keep it from muddying the water.

Fertilizer

Use a fertilizer on your aquatic plants with extreme caution as it can upset the biological balance of your pond, cause algal blooms, and injure fish and other aquatic life. Slow-release aquatic pellets are best. Talk with a pond specialist before proceeding.

pH Kits

These are available at aquarium stores and will tell you if the pH of your water is in the acceptable range for the fish and plants you are keeping. You can also have your pond water tested at many aquarium stores and gardening centers.

Concrete Ponds

A concrete pond will last for many years, but it must be built properly. You can pour your concrete into a shallow depression for a "free form"

Winter Bathing

The mercury this morning is in the mid-twenties and a cutting wind blows out of the northwest. Yet as soon as we put out a pan of water in the backyard, starlings are splashing and bathing in it, ruffling their feathers and sending the water flying. This is a thing we notice each winter: of all the birds that visit the yard, the starlings bathe the most during the months of cold. Can it be that they are hotter birds? I turn to my library. A starling, I find, has a temperature of 109 degrees F. An English sparrow runs from 107 to 109. The bluejay exceeds the peak of both at its maximum body temperature. It ranges between 106.2 to 110.2. Yet a bluejay bathes much less frequently than a starling. So the explanation lies elsewhere than in the temperature of the bathing birds.

Edwin Way Teale – Circle of the Seasons, 1953

PRE-FORMED FIBERGLASS PONDS

37 PROJECT

TOOLS & MATERIALS

- Shovels (round point, square point)
- Crowbar
- Level
- two-by-four long enough to lay across the center of your pond (to check level)
- String
- Stakes
- Wheelbarrow (or plastic sheeting for holding excavated dirt)
- Pre-formed fiberglass shell
- Sand – enough to place at least 2" between the liner and the excavation
- Safe water – use stored rainwater runoff from your roof or treat your tapwater to ensure it is safe. Your local water authorities will be able to tell you whether your water supply is treated with chlorine or chloramine. For chlorine, allow it to stand for 24 to 48 hours to gas off. If it is also treated with chloramine, you can purchase chemical solutions to treat it (stores specializing in pond supplies will carry this). You can also purchase inexpensive water quality test-kits from aquarium supply stores and pond suppliers.
- Edging material – bricks, rock, etc.

Something to keep in mind with both pre-formed fiberglass shells and PVC pond liners is that they are slippery, and may be difficult for animals to scale. To avoid scenarios where creatures drown in ponds made for their benefit, make sure to include objects such as bricks or rocks that rise out of the water at a gentle angle—you want a bridge between the slick sides of the pond liner and the ground that will allow creatures such as baby toads and frogs to climb up and out.

1 Place the pond shell where you want it to go and outline the shape with rope or twine.

2 Remove the shell and then enlarge the rope outline approximately 3" to 4" in all directions to accommodate the backfill.

3 Remove the top layer of turf as you would for a PVC liner (see Steps 2 and 3 on page 202) and then check that the edges are level. Use topsoil to level the area if necessary.

4 Dig out starting from the center of the pond, making space for any shelves built into your liner shell. The excavation should be 2" deeper than the liner in order to fit a layer of sand underneath. Dig out a shallow area around the perimeter of the pool to accommodate any edging material you want to use. If the pond is going to be surrounded by grass, make sure the rim of the pool is higher than the lawn.

FIGURE 1

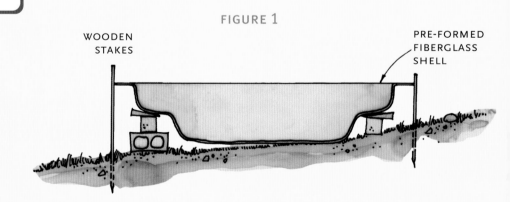

WOODEN STAKES

PRE-FORMED FIBERGLASS SHELL

5 When the pool has been dug out, cover the inside with a 2" layer of sand. Place the pond shell in the hole to check the fit. Remember that you will be backfilling the space between the pond and the hole.

6 Begin to fill the pond with water while filling the remaining space between the shell and the excavation with soil.

When the soil and the water level are even, tamp down the soil with the shovel handle. Do not tamp it down too hard, just make sure it is compacted enough to support the sides of the shell.

7 When the pond is full, add edging as desired.

FIGURE 2

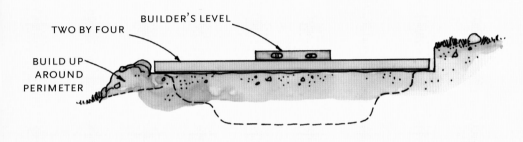

TWO BY FOUR

BUILDER'S LEVEL

BUILD UP AROUND PERIMETER

FIGURE 3

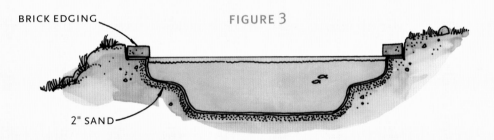

BRICK EDGING

2" SAND

FIGURE 4

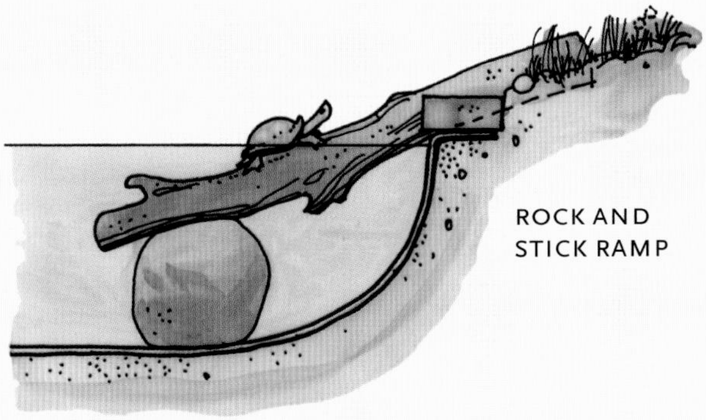

FIGURE 5

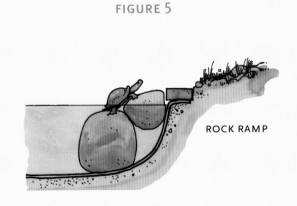

ROCK AND STICK RAMP

ROCK RAMP

207

CONCRETE PONDS

TOOLS & MATERIALS
- Shovels (round point, square point)
- Pick
- Crowbar
- Level
- Wooden form work
- Reinforcing bars
- Wire mesh

Concrete ponds have the potential to be the most desirable of all the backyard ponds. They have the added advantage of a non-slip surface to aid frogs, toads, insects, and birds to come and go safely.

1. Dig out the area for the formed concrete pond as you would for the liner ponds.

2. Build the forms in place to hold the concrete. Reinforcing bars should be cut to size and placed both vertically and horizontally at 20" intervals to prevent the bottom from cracking when the ground freezes.

3. The floor or the footing should be poured first, then the sides, shelves, and finally the top and any edging you want to include.

4. Concrete is highly acidic so you will need to leach it out before adding plants or fish. To do this, fill the pond and flush it at least once a day for four days. The last rinse water should stand for ten days.

5. After the final rinse, let the pond dry and then, if desired, paint it with a dark-colored pool paint to hide the bottom. Painting will also help to stabilize the pH which can be altered by unfinished concrete.

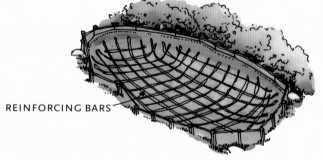

REINFORCING BARS

Raccoon visits pond.

pond, but this type lacks the depth that many aquatic plants require. However, these shallow ponds make ideal baths for birds, with easy access for amphibians, reptiles, mammals, and insects. There are also some varieties of fish that are able to survive in shallow water if an outdoor goldfish pond is what you're after.

For a deeper concrete pool, you will probably want to use a builder's form, into which wet cement is poured. Before you begin construction, it's a good idea to speak with a concrete or pond specialist to get some advice. A badly built concrete pond will be a problem to maintain, and may end up costing more to fix than it cost to build. Choose a builder who has proven experience building ponds. Look at samples of previous work, and talk to other people who have had ponds built for them.

Planting the Pond

The plants you choose for your pond should be dictated by the region in which you live, the size of your pond, and what creatures you are hoping to attract. You can generally find a selection of aquatic plants at nurseries, through mail-order catalogs, and at aquarium and pond supply stores. A healthy pond requires a combination of submerged and floating plants. Investigate the individual requirements of each plant you choose, and make sure that the amount of sunlight, average temperature, and depth offered by your pond is suitable. As with the rest of your backyard habitat, try to purchase native species whenever possible. Planting is simple—just partially submerge the pots in the gravel on the bottom of the pond.

There are invasive and noxious aquatic plants that should never be planted, such as purple loosestrife (*Lythrum salicaria*), Eurasian water milfoil (*Myriophyllum spicatum*), Brazilian elodea (*Egeria densa*), parrot's feather (*Myriophyllum aquaticum*), and reed-canary grass (*Phalaris arundinacea*). Your local natural history society, or agriculture branch, will be able to tell you what to watch for. As well, there are aggressive plants such as common cattail (*Typha latifolia*) that you might want to use with caution, checking that their root systems stay in their containers.

Submerged plants oxygenate the water of the pond, while floating plants

Northern pintail.

A Myrtle Warbler Drinks Maple Sap

Each winter, the gray squirrels nip twigs on our maple trees and obtain liquid from the sap that oozes from the opening. One such squirrel-produced spigot has been dripping on the driveway for several days. This morning, a myrtle warbler alighted on the twig and drank the drops of sap as they collected below it. Here was another source of winter water.

Edwin Way Teale – Circle of the Seasons, 1953

April sunshine

At Milburn Pond, in the April sunshine, a painted turtle has clambered up the side of the swan's nest and is resting there, its neck outstretched, its body soaking up the warmth, its sluggish winter blood reviving in the spring. It is between one swan sitting on the nest and the other pulling up waterweeds and adding them to the pile. Neither pays any attention to the turtle. The blackbirds are more quiet now. They seem to be settling down. They are less noisy and more serious — as befits persons of property.

Edwin Way Teale – Circle of the Seasons, 1953

provide basking sites for frogs, plus shadow and protection for fish and insects. Limited light reaches the bottom through these plants, and prevents most algae growth. You may also want to include free-floating plants which move with the water and provide more cover for fish. Spring is the best time to plant.

Stocking the Pond

Fish are a popular addition to a backyard pond; they can be soothing to watch and will keep the mosquito population down. Be aware though that they eat all stages of amphibians and may be eaten themselves by snakes, birds, and other pond visitors. Try to find minnows that would occur naturally in your area. Other fish to consider are Koi, or Japanese carp (only suitable for large ponds) that have been bred to provide flashes of color. You can also stock your pond with goldfish, but they become too numerous fairly quickly for most small ponds (the extras could be given away).

Do a bit of research before adding fish to your pond. Avoid fish that have voracious appetites for plants because they will quickly denude your pond of foliage. Stock fish at densities of no more than one inch of fish to five gallons of water. It is better to understock than overstock your pond. Check with the local aquarium dealer for information about the overwintering of permanent pond residents.

Great blue heron.

Baths

A birdbath can be the site of your most entertaining wildlife-watching. Birdbaths are available commercially in a wide variety of styles, or you can create your own. The basic requirements are a non-slip surface, a water depth of no more than two and a half inches, gradually sloping sides, and clean, fresh water. Probably the safest birdbath is the standard concrete pedestal model, as the water is out of reach of cats and other predators (see Chapter 9 for more details on keeping birds safe from cats). If you are unconcerned about appearances, you can nail an aluminum garbage can lid to a post and keep that filled, or sink a lid into the ground. Remember to place a small rock or two in it for birds to stand on, and line the bottom with gravel. Another option is a ground level concrete birdbath (see concrete ponds on page 208). It is best to fill your birdbath with fresh water each day and spray it out with the hose at the same time. Once a week or so, go over it with a scrub brush.

Birdbath amid foliage.

Drips

Adding a drip is a sure-fire way to attract birds and other interesting visitors to a water source. A "drip" is just what it sounds like—a device that drips water, making the gently audible burbles and tinkles that birds and other wildlife find appealing. You can purchase sophisticated drips or fountains with recirculating pumps in many styles. If you want to keep it simple and inexpensive, just punch a tiny hole in a bucket (on the side, about half an inch up) and suspend it so the drips fall into the birdbath or pond. You can also suspend a garden hose, clear plastic tube, or small irrigation hose from a tree branch. Keep the drips to a minimum, about ten or twenty per minute, as rushing, splashing water can frighten songbirds.

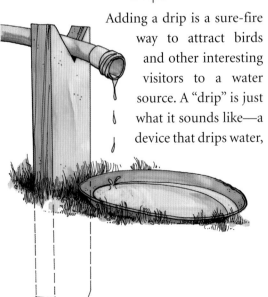

Bog Garden

Natural bogs are wet areas containing a cover of sphagnum moss, flowering plants, heathers, sedges, and grasses. The moss growing under the surface dies due to oxygen-poor conditions, and forms

A Discovery

A boy called this afternoon excited by the discovery of a rare, beautiful, exotic bird in his backyard. It shone in the sunlight with brilliant metallic sheens. It seemed iridescent. He thought it must have escaped from some zoo as he had never seen a bird like it before. The bird was a purple grackle in full breeding plumage. It is relatively common. But the boy had made an important discovery. He had – for the first time in his life – really seen a grackle.

Edwin Way Teale – Circle of the Seasons, 1953

211

Phases of a Native Woodland Garden with Waterfall

Top: Initial digging and forming.

Right: Liner and rock in place.

Below: Preparation of soil for planting.

Left: Incoporating native plants and moss-covered logs saved from excavation of site.

Below: Established woodland garden.

Natural variation on a bog garden.

peat. Rainwater-fed bogs are home to a wide variety of delicate plants and animals that thrive on the acidic, mineral-deficient conditions. They may also contain fascinating insect-eating plants such as sundews (*Drosera sp.*). Boglands are valuable not only for supporting sensitive vegetation, but for providing homes to many birds and insects. Not the dreary places you might think, bogs are rich in subtle color and scent.

With a bit of commitment and some work you can create a bog garden in your backyard (see Project 39), and although it will not truly resemble a natural bog, it will be a flourishing wetland habitat. You may wish to build a bog garden as part of a habitat creation initiative in your community, as an example of what can be accomplished to aid and enjoy wildlife.

Place your wooden platform or stepping stones at the edge of the bog to act as a viewing station, and put your watering system in place (the water needs to be kept level with the surface of the peat during the summer). You should use rainwater, but aged tap- or well-water is fine; fresh tapwater can be used in emergencies. The water can be pumped into the bog from your collection source. Planting the bog in spring or fall is best, and you can fertilize periodically with compost (avoid slow-release fertilizers).

Bog Maintenance

Never let your bog dry out or be disturbed by people or pets. You can do clean-up and major weeding during the winter months when it is dormant, and every couple of years the plants will need

Bog gardens are miniature ecosystems whose creation offers the wildlife steward a chance to grow moisture-loving plants, and to attract wildlife that frequents a wetland habitat. If you have an existing wet spot in your yard so much the handier, but a bog garden can be made anywhere with a little digging. Apartment dwellers may wish to experiment in creating a scaled-down bog garden, using a shallow plastic tub instead of lining a depression in the ground.

1. To begin, decide what sort of bog community you want to build. You can include some wet bog, a bog pool, and a peat hummock. The location should be the lowest part of your garden, in an area that receives a lot of sun. It should be away from overhanging trees and shrubs to avoid leaf litter. Choose an area away from traffic, keeping in mind the safety of children and pets. You may want to store up as much rainwater as you can over the year for watering the bog during the summer.

2. Once you have decided where to place your bog, mark out the shape and size with pegs and string. The total area should be at least 4' by 4' and at least 2' deep.

3. Once you have dug out the bog, dig a small trench around it for burying the liner. Make sure the hole is at least an inch or so deeper than you want it so that you can place some padding between the ground and the liner. Remove sharp stones and debris from the excavation to prevent liner damage.

4. After you have dug the hole, line it with the padding, then add the liner, pulling it up to extend over the trench around the bog.

5. Punch holes in the shallow point of the bog if you want to put in ferns or other perimeter plants.

6. Fill the depression with the wet peat moss and soil, and saturate it with rainwater.

7. Trim and bury the edges of the liner with rocks and soil. Make sure no part of the liner is exposed to sunlight for any length of time, as light may damage it.

8. To create a bog pool, dig a hole in the peat approximately 12" deep and set the peat aside.

9. To build a hummock, use the excess peat and soil to form a hump.

PEAT

GRAVEL

The Seeing Eye

Thinking of that sea meadow pool and the mood it evoked last night, I have been remembering a time when my Insect Garden was invaded by experts. Between thirty and forty of them arrived for the annual outing and field trip of the New York Entomological Society. They had brought their naturalist friends and some came from as far away as Philadelphia. Each in his own way saw a different facet of the garden activity.

Beetle experts began peering under bark and lifting up old logs and making a harvest among the goldenrod of the hillside. Butterfly enthusiasts worked the open fields and moth-men hunted among the wild cherry leaves for unusual larvae. A mosquito collector immediately investigated all the knotholes in the old apple trees. The life of the swamp stream absorbed one entomologist; a termite nest under a decaying board interested a second; leaf-hoppers among the sunflowers, a third. There was an authority on mayflies, another on wasps, another on stink-bugs. There was even a snail collector in the group.

The thing that fascinated me all day long, as I watched these friends of mine in action, was the functioning of the seeing eye. Side by side, two of the specialists would look at the same bush. One would see leaf-hoppers, the other slug caterpillars. They were concentrating on their special fields, seeing mainly what they were interested in seeing. Although I have known this area intimately for a decade and a half, have walked back and forth and up and down its paths far more than the equivalent of a pedestrian tour from coast to coast, I had missed many of the things these men and women saw on their short visit. Their specialized knowledge gave them seeing eyes I did not possess. In truth, no matter how much we know, there will always be someone who will see what we overlook, someone who will understand what we gaze upon without comprehension.

Edwin Way Teale – Circle of the Seasons, 1953

to be pruned. As well, your bog may need to be thinned of sphagnum, and perhaps other plants, about every three years. If you want to divide plants, spring is the best time.

Bog Plants

Bog Arum (*Calla palustris*)
Bog Bean (*Menyanthes trifoliata*)
Bog Lily (*Crinum americanum*)
Cattails (*Typha sp.*)
Cotton Grass (*Eriophorum angustifolium*)
Iris (*Iris laevigata*)
Marsh Marigold (*Caltha palustris*)
Monkey Flower (*Mimulas luteus*)

14

Nature Activities and Projects

Interesting nature activities are available in most communities, and there are many ways to enjoy nature on your own. Photography clubs are popular, and besides going on field trips with people who share your interest in nature, there are generally contests, guest speakers, and workshops.

Lists are fun to keep. A favorite with birders is a yard list, and from there, a life list can be kept to include birds you identify away from home. Keeping a record of first sightings on your calendar is rewarding—you'll have an idea when to expect the return of bird species each spring (and marvel at how close or far apart those returns are); you can observe late or early snowfalls and freeze-ups, watch the differences in bloom times of shrubs and trees from year to year, hold friendly competitions on who sees the first bat arrive, or the first hummingbird.

Ideas are everywhere, even simple ones like these that can make nature a part of your daily life.

Volunteer Activities that Aid Wildlife

The following is a list of ways you can enjoy wildlife while contributing to research. Each state, province, and community will differ in programs offered, but generally you can contact a natural history society or museum, a local Audubon Society, wild bird food stores, nature federations, universities, wildlife societies or rescue associations, and government agencies for information, or at least for some help in who to contact next.

Bluebird Conservation

In appropriate areas, promote conservation of bluebirds by building, erecting, and monitoring bluebird boxes, then

Moss baskets beckon to butterflies.

submitting data to the North American Bluebird Society. You can be instrumental in bluebird recovery by taking an active part in the Transcontinental Bluebird Trail. NABS, The Wilderness Center, P.O. Box 244 Wilmot, OH 44689-0244. www.nabluebirdsociety.org.

Butterfly Counts

Butterflies across the continent are counted each summer by volunteers who provide their tallies to the North American Butterfly Association (NABA) 4 Delaware Rd., Morristown, NJ, 07960. www.naba.org.

Christmas Bird Counts

Once a year, in communities across North America, bird species are counted by volunteers. Each locality organizes groups made up of beginners and experienced birders, so anyone can participate. National Audubon Society, www.audubon.org.

Frog Watch Programs

Help to identify ecological changes that affect frog populations by monitoring their calls each spring. www.naturewatch.ca; www.nwf.org/frogwatchUSA.

Great Backyard Bird Count

Where are the birds in winter? Contribute data that will add to a "snapshot" of North American bird populations. Bird Studies Canada and Cornell University join forces to use this information in conjunction with Christmas Bird Count and Project Feeder Watch to give the big picture. www.birdsource.org.

Ladybug Surveys

Biodiversity is being compromised by the introduction of non-native species of ladybugs. Contribute to databases of information on these insects' numbers and distribution. Check with regional groups.

Nest Record Schemes

Contribute important information on the breeding habits of birds by keeping records of nests and broods you find. Check with regional groups.

Plant Watch Monitoring Programs

Flowering times of predetermined plant species are recorded by "citizen scientists" to aid in tracking the effects of climate change and, in particular, global warming. Check with regional groups.

Project Feeder Watch

A North American bird-monitoring program through Cornell Lab of Ornithology, 159 Sapsucker Woods Road, Ithaca, NY 14850. www.birds.cornell.edu/pfw.

Brewers blackbird.

Worm Watch Programs

Provide scientists with information on species and distribution of earthworms to assist in learning more about historical disappearance of worms, and the health of soil. Check with regional groups.

Volunteer Activities In Your Community

- "Green Streets" programs (volunteer gardening on city traffic circles, boulevards)
- Invasive plant removal from eco-reserves, lakes and marshes, riverbanks, parks
- Native plant re-introductions to urban areas
- Parks trail maintenance
- Stream restoration
- Tree planting projects in urban natural areas

Nature Journaling

Keeping a journal is one of the ways we document our passions and explorations. We keep journals about our interior lives, about the sports we play, the vacations we go on, and about various other interests. Written records of our interactions with nature are a time-honored tradition which have produced an abundance of knowledge, as well as some excellent prose.

Your journal may consist of daily observations:

May 3: First pussy willows out! Planted currant bush in northwest corner. Pileated woodpecker flew over, calling. Scanned pond, no tadpoles yet, eggs still there.

219

Bird Count

This is the day of the winter bird count. Each year, the same five square miles are covered intensively by members of the Baldwin Bird Club. Twenty-two of us were out today. The skies were clear and cloudless over the snow-covered earth. It was dawn when I began at Milburn Pond. It was dusk when we all got together to compare notes. During this day, in the five square miles, we had seen more than 4500 individual birds belonging to sixty-seven different species. They ranged from common loons and Canada geese to European widgeon and greater scaup and from marsh hawks and short-eared owls to northern horned larks and slate-colored juncos.

Among them all, the cowbirds presented the most puzzling paradox. For several days, larger and larger flocks of cowbirds have been building up in our backyard. Today, 200 came in to feed on the scattered grain. Yet this was the only record for this bird in the area. Not one of the 200 was seen by any of the twenty-two trained observers on the alert for any bird that flew. Apparently, all the cowbirds in the region – concentrated into this single flock – came directly to our yard and then left the area unseen.

Edwin Way Teale – Circle of the Seasons, 1953

Or your journal may be a personal exploration of events: the elation you felt when the first swallow returned in the spring, or the excitement of watching a migration of salamanders. Many people include a mixture of words and drawings, and some nature journals focus on the development of the wildlife garden from initial planning to mature, productive habitat.

A soothing spot for nature journaling.

You can keep mementos of your garden, right in your journal. Press and mount leaves from a productive berry bush, or save a jay feather found under the feeder. You can keep records of your bird box nestlings, and include the behavior and feeding routine of the adult birds. Photos in a nature journal are a good record of habitat events and details— squirrels running along a fence, or a chickadee on a snow-covered branch. The creative possibilities for your journal are limitless, inspired by a habitat garden rich with life.

Yellow-throated warbler.

PAPER FROM THE GARDEN

A piece of paper, made with pressed flowers and leaves from your garden, is a perfect mount in a wildlife journal. If you don't own a plant press, try flattening an assortment of flowers and leaves between sheets of waxed paper and heavy slabs of hardwood weighted down with bricks. For some of your sheets of paper, you may want to place each botanical treasure by hand to create patterns or pictures (this would be a variation on Step 4).

TOOLS & MATERIALS

- Sheets of white paper
- Selection of pressed dried flowers and leaves
- 2 Tbsp white glue
- 3 cups water
- Food processor or blender
- Sink or a large tray
- Nylon stockings
- 16 or 18 gauge wire (wire coat hangers will work; one per piece of garden paper)
- Electric iron

1. Bend the wire into a square frame, slightly larger than the desired size of paper (Figure 1).
2. Pull nylon stockings over the wire frame and knot them in place so they lie tight and flat (Figure 2).
3. Tear the white paper into small pieces and put approximately 1 cup of them into the blender. Add a few tablespoons of water and turn the blender on high. Continue adding paper and water until you have a large, wet mass. Add as much water as you need to keep the blender moving. Make sure all of the paper has been mixed into a pulp.

4. Add white glue to a sink or tray filled with 3 cups of water, and add the paper pulp. Stir the flowers and leaves into the mix.
5. Slide a nylon/wire frame to the bottom of the sink or tray, then slowly lift the frame out and allow the water to drain off (Figure 3). There should be a layer of wet fibers on the nylon wire frame.
6. Repeat until you have filled as many frames as you desire.
7. Place the frames in a warm place to dry.
8. When the pieces of paper on the frame are completely dry, gently peel them off. Place a dry dish towel on an ironing board and iron the pieces flat using high heat and steam.

FIGURE 1

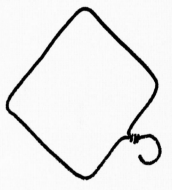

FIGURE 2

FIGURE 3

C.J.'S MOSS HANGING BASKETS

Sun basket.

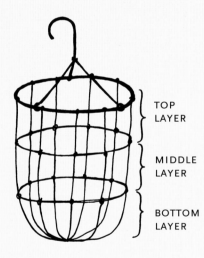

TOP
LAYER

MIDDLE
LAYER

BOTTOM
LAYER

USE 4 LAYERS FOR A 16" BASKET

Growing your own stunning baskets is creative fun, and a worthwhile challenge for both novice and experienced gardeners. The enjoyment of baskets is multiplied when your choice of flowers and plants attract hummingbirds and butterflies.

1. Decide whether you are making a sun basket or a shade basket and purchase plants accordingly (refer to the following lists). Sun baskets require six hours or more of bright sun per day; a basket hanging under the eaves will be fine, as the sun needn't be direct. South, southwest, and southeast exposures are all good. Shade baskets prefer filtered light but will take two hours or so of direct sun per day, preferably early or late in the day when the heat is not so intense. Choose plants according to final location of the basket, as mentioned previously. Success in making moss hanging baskets has a lot to do with experimentation. Variables such as wet or dry years, dappled light, wind, etc. can account for some plants thriving while others do not, even when it seems they should. You can keep a record of which plants you use from year to year to help with future choice of species and varieties.

   - Wear gloves to handle moss during construction phase.
   - Dampen moss in a bucket of water, then wring out.
   - Water all the plants to be used.

2. Line the bottom of the wire frame and 4" up the sides with damp moss—don't skimp on the moss. It keeps the soil in place and helps the basket retain water. Another way to line the basket is to ball up the moss and stuff it in tight around the wire.

3. Some people use a layer of burlap to line their baskets. You can do this after the

moss is in place and before the soil goes in. Plastic plant saucers or pieces of sheet plastic cut to fit are also used in the bottoms of baskets. All are optional.

4. Fill the moss-lined basket with 4" of soil, to the top of the first moss layer.

5. Fit the bedding plants through the wire so they lie sideways on the first layer of soil—you want some stem and all the roots on the inside of the moss, with flowers entirely on the outside of the basket.

6. Sprinkle 1 Tbsp. or so of 14-14-14 fertilizer evenly around the soil.

7. Repeat the first step by adding 4" more moss and soil, and about ten to twelve plants for the second layer. Offset the plants so they are not directly over the layer below (see diagram). Add another tablespoon of 14-14-14 fertilizer.

8. Add moss to the top of the basket frame. Add soil up to the rim, roll moss over the top and into soil like a collar. Use 2" or 3" of moss so it is thick enough to be sturdy. This will guard against the moss ripping away during watering, allowing soil to spill over the sides. Use the top layer of your basket as a focal point. In sun, geraniums are always winners, and for shade baskets, tuberous begonias work well.

9. Around your focal plants use two to four other upright plants such as dianthus or snapdragons, and around the rim use trailing plants that will cascade down—brachycome, nepeta, silver nettle (this plant is extremely invasive, so destroy each year, don't dump out) lotus vine, and trailing lobelia are all good.

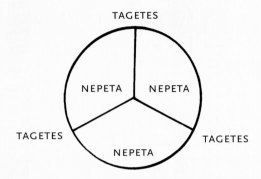

BOTTOM LAYER

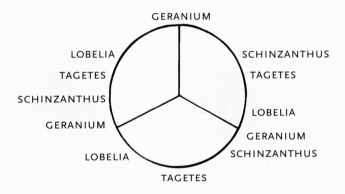

MIDDLE LAYER

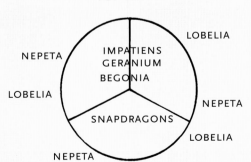

TOP LAYER

SOIL

- Hanging planter mix, with crystals to hold moisture, is fine. Remember, if the summer is very wet, the soil will be too, unless hung under eaves or a porch roof. You can make your own soil mix: one part sterilized soil to two parts peat moss, and approximately half a part of perlite or sand.

FERTILIZER

- Slow release granules such as Nutrocote can be sprinkled into each layer of plants at the time of basket construction.
- Fertilize weekly with 20-20-20 at 1 Tbsp. to 1 gallon of water.
- Around July 1st, switch to 15-30-15 fertilizer to give the flowers an extra boost. Continue with weekly applications of fertilizer until the end of the summer.

PLANTS

- Use a mixture of plants. If you use only one or two types, they will all finish blooming at the same time.
- Use 20 to 25 plants per basket (up to 32 plants for a 16" basket).
- Choose plants for sun or shade locations.
- You can color coordinate plants for a formal appearance (e.g., white, silver, and purple), or you can be adventurous and choose plants for a wild, natural look.

- Herbs such as trailing rosemary, thyme, sage, chives, oregano, and French tarragon can be used in a sunny spot with other plants or on their own.
- Lots of trailers, cascading from your baskets, give them a stunning, professional look (try trailers that grow 5' to 6' feet long)
- Create a hummingbird basket using their favorite flowers, such as single-flowered fuchsias or other pink and red tubular flowers.

WEIGHT

- A 16" moss hanging basket will easily weigh over 25 pounds after watering.

GENERAL CARE

- Remember to water each layer after positioning the plants.
- For spectacular baskets, deadhead (remove spent blooms) every day, and unless the weather is very cool, moss baskets should be watered daily. A watering wand is useful for an all-over, light spray. Remember to water the outside of the basket as well, to keep the moss wet.
- It's advisable to leave newly planted baskets in a bright spot but out of direct sun for a week or two while roots become established, but remember to water.
- Don't be discouraged if your baskets look a little sparse when you're done—it doesn't take long for them to fill out to such a degree that you'll hardly believe you made them yourself. If a few plants die, you can replace them with new ones.
- Many plants such as geraniums, fuchsias, and begonias overwinter well (nursery staff and gardening books can help with

Shade basket.

224

details). If you've lifted trailers from your garden, just stick them back in the same spot for next year, or try leaving them in the basket outside during the winter if you're in a mild climate. The same goes for the moss, as it can usually be reused after a good soaking at planting time, but the soil is generally too full of roots to be of any further use.

PLANTS FOR SUN BASKETS

Alyssum
Artemesia
Bacopa
Brachycome
Creeping Charlie
Dianthus
Dusty Miller
French Marigolds
Geraniums (good for focal plants)
Godetia
Heliotrope
Ivy Geranium
Livingstone Daisy
Lobelia (especially trailing types)
Lotus Vine
Mesembryanthemum
Nasturtium
Nemesia
Nepeta
Nolana
Pansy/Viola
Petunia
Portulaca
Potato Vine
Scaevola
Schizanthus
Snapdragon (trailing types are available)
Tagetes Marigolds
Trailing Verbena

PLANTS FOR SHADE BASKETS

Alyssum
Asparagus Fern
Bacopa
Browallia
Centradenia
Coleus
Creeping Charlie
Fibrous Begonia
Fuchsia
Impatiens
Ivy
Lavatera
Lobelia (especially trailing types)
Lotus Vine
Mimulus
Nemesia
Nepeta
Periwinkle (very invasive: destroy each season)
Schinzanthus
Silver Nettle (very invasive: destroy each season)
Torenia
Tuberous Begonia (good for focal plants)
Verbena
Wandering Jew

Seagull guard and moss baskets.

REMEMBER THE SECRET TO BEAUTIFUL HANGING BASKETS—
WATER, FEED, AND DEADHEAD REGULARLY!

GARDEN ARBOR

TOOLS & MATERIALS

- Table saw or skill saw, band saw or jigsaw
- Router (optional) with a ¾" diameter cutter
- Hammer
- Screwdriver
- Posts (4) – four-by-four red cedar 10' long each
- Arches (2) – two-by-ten × 6'-1" each
- Brackets (4) – two-by-four × 25" each
- Cross-piece (7) – two-by-four × 4'-11" each
- Cap rails (4) – two-by-two × 2'-5" each
- Trellis pieces (4 vertical) – two-by-two × 5'-6" each, (12 horizontal) – 2" × 2" × 28 ½" each
- Gate boards (3) one-by-four × 31" each, (1) – one-by-two × 24" each
- Gate braces (2 horizontal) – 1" × 2 ½" × 20" each, (1 diagonal) – 1" × 2 ½" × 20" each
- Two pairs of heavy duty iron strap hinges
- One set galvanized pivoting bar latch and hooks
- Galvanized nails – 2" and 2 ½" common

The following arbor can straddle a path by itself to define the opening in a stone wall or hedge, or it can be attached to a fence as shown. With or without a single or double gate it can be used for vines and climbing roses. Western red cedar is the most durable wood available and it has the added advantage of weathering to an attractive gray sheen.

1. Make a point on one end of each of four 10' long four-by-four red cedar brackets with a 10 to 12 degree angle at the other end.

2. Cut four 25" long two-by-four red cedar brackets with a 10 to 12 degree angle at the top end and a curved design on one edge like that shown in Figure 1 (front view).

3. Cut two 6"-11" long arches from two-by-ten red cedar with a graceful, full length curve at the top (down to 4" at the ends) and a 5" deep by 33" long curve centered on the underside.

4. Into these notches you will fit seven two-by-four cedar cross-pieces, each 4'-11" long with 4" curves cut on the underside of each end as shown in Figure 2 (sectional view).

FIGURE 1

SECTIONAL VIEW FROM FRONT

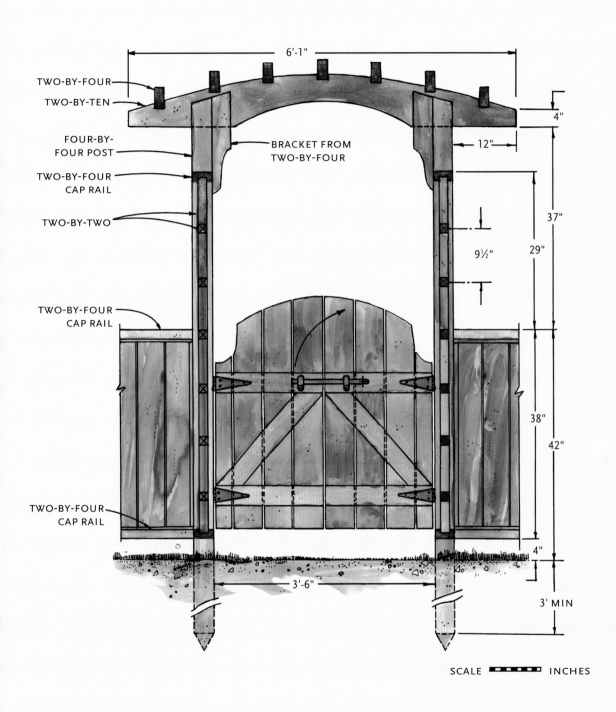

TWO-BY-FOUR

TWO-BY-TEN

FOUR-BY-FOUR POST

TWO-BY-FOUR CAP RAIL

TWO-BY-TWO

TWO-BY-FOUR CAP RAIL

TWO-BY-FOUR CAP RAIL

BRACKET FROM TWO-BY-FOUR

6'-1"

4"

12"

37"

29"

9½"

38"

42"

4"

3'-6"

3' MIN

SCALE ▪▪▪▫▫▪ INCHES

FIGURE 3

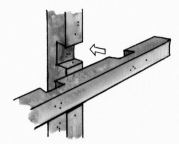

FIGURE 4

CHANNEL

FIGURE 5

NOTCH

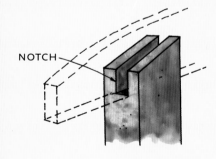

5 Before you assemble the main structural pieces, cut the material for and assemble two red cedar screens. These screens, one on either side of the gate, should be made with two-by-twos (two vertical and six horizontal per screen) at 9½" on center. Cut the two vertical pieces to 5"-6" long and the six horizontal pieces to 28½" long each.

6 Cut the lap joints as shown in Figure 3.

7 Cut ½" deep channels cut in the four-by-four posts (Figures 2 and 4) with a table saw, skill saw, or router. Fit the ends of the horizontal two-by-twos into the channels.

8 Cut similar channels into 2'-5" cap rails, one on top and one on the bottom. Fit the vertical teo-by-twos into those channels.

9 To assemble the arbor, cut a 1½" by 4" deep notch at the angled end of each four-by-four post (Figure 5) to receive the arches.

10 Keeping each pair of posts 3'-6" apart (clear), nail them to each arch as shown in Figure 1. With the two-by-four brackets on the inside face of the arch, nail them to each arch and to the post.

11 Set the pair of post/arch assemblies at least 3' into the ground, preferably in concrete. Nail the two trellis screens between

them with a 4" space between the ground and the underside of the bottom cap rail. When this is done, set the posts firmly by packing gravel and earth around them (or set them in concrete).

12 Nail the seven two-by-four cross-pieces to the arches, leaving a 12" overhang on each side.

13 Make the two gates each from three one-by-four and one one-by-two red cedar boards. These should be held together by three one-by-three red cedar boards. Two of these are set horizontally as shown in Figure 1, 17½" apart (outside dimension). These two are joined by a diagonal. All three should be nailed to the vertical boards.

14 Draw out an attractive scroll design at the top similar to that shown on Figure 1, and cut it out with a jigsaw.

15 Using the first gate as a pattern, draw a mirror image of the top design on the second gate and cut it out.

16 Screw two heavy duty strap hinges to each gate over the one-by three battens.

17 Support each gate 4" or 5" off the ground and screw the hinges into the adjacent four-by-four post.

18 Screw a metal pivoting bar latch and hooks between the gates to complete them.

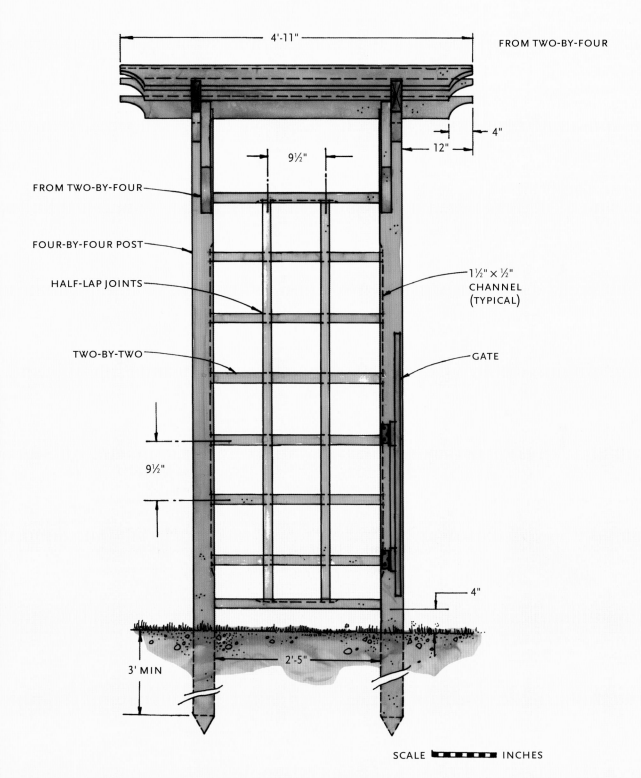

FIGURE 2

SECTIONAL VIEW FROM SIDE

4'-11"

FROM TWO-BY-FOUR

4"

12"

9½"

FROM TWO-BY-FOUR

FOUR-BY-FOUR POST

1½" × ½" CHANNEL (TYPICAL)

HALF-LAP JOINTS

TWO-BY-TWO

GATE

9½"

4"

2'-5"

3' MIN

SCALE ▭▭▭▭ INCHES

— GARDEN TRELLIS AND FENCE —

TOOLS & MATERIALS

- Table saw, skill saw, or hand saw
- Drill with ⅛" diameter bit
- Hammer
- Posts – four-by-four western red cedar 10' to 12' long
- Cross-piece (2 per post) – two-by-four red cedar 2' long
- Horizontal supports (2) – two-by-four red cedar
- Horizontal trellis pieces (4) – two-by-four red cedar
- Cap rails (top and bottom) – two-by-four red cedar
- Battens (4) – ¾" square red cedar
- Panel boards (vertical) – 1" × 6" to 1" × 12" red cedar
- Galvanized common nails – 2½" to 3½" long

One afternoon, while walking along a lane in a residential area of my city that I had not been to before, I came upon a fenced-in yard which was circled by a glorious mass of climbing roses reaching almost ten feet high! This tangled mass was supported by an elegant trellis which had been incorporated into the construction of the high fence.

The following design includes a solid wood fence, but this could be substituted by open lattice-work or the trellis could stand alone over a row of posts. Western red cedar is the ideal wood for the project as it withstands decay longer than other species and weathers to an attractive silver-gray.

The materials list includes only those required for one post. To calculate the total amount of materials, first determine the number of posts required to enclose the area (they should be no more than six feet apart) then multiply that number by the materials on the list.

1. Whether they are open and freestanding or part of a fence, the four-by-four cedar posts must be tied together near the top by horizontal two-by-fours nailed on either side. The top edge of these two-by-fours should be 2" below the top of the post. The trellis must be assembled with the posts in place in the ground. They should be buried at least 3' deep and no further than 6' apart. If the two-by-fours are made perfectly horizontal with a builder's level the top of each post can be trimmed to match by measuring 2" up from the two-by-four.

2. The trellis itself is made up of four pieces of parallel two-by-twos on double cross-pieces (two for each post) from two-by-four red cedar stock. Cut a decorative notch in each end (Figure 3) to give the pieces a lighter appearance.

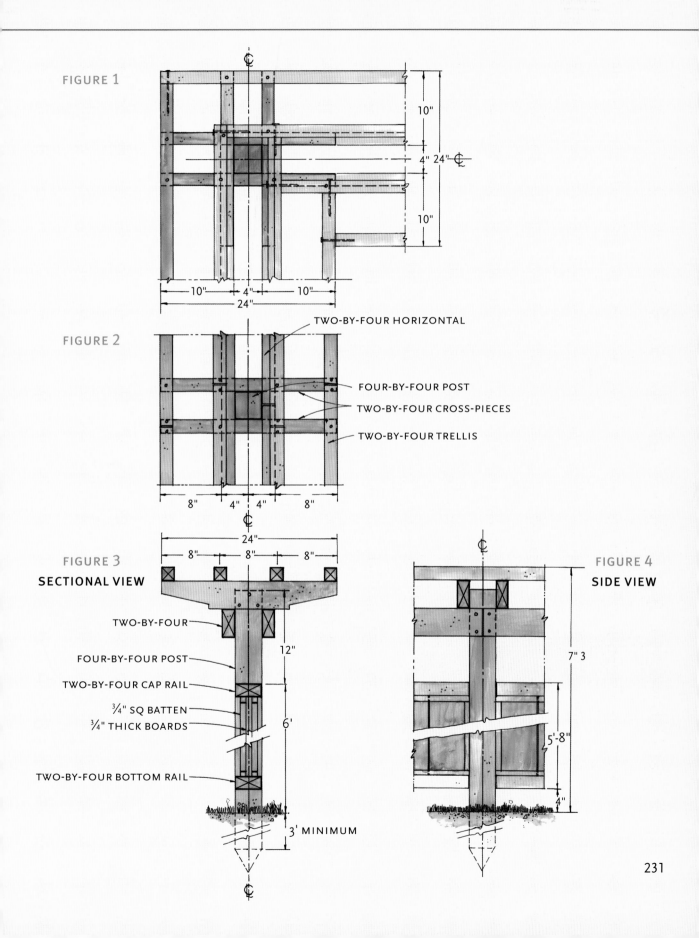

FIGURE 1

10"

4" 24"

10"

10" 4" 10"

24"

TWO-BY-FOUR HORIZONTAL

FIGURE 2

FOUR-BY-FOUR POST

TWO-BY-FOUR CROSS-PIECES

TWO-BY-FOUR TRELLIS

8" 4" 4" 8"

24"

8" 8" 8"

FIGURE 3
SECTIONAL VIEW

FIGURE 4
SIDE VIEW

TWO-BY-FOUR

12"

FOUR-BY-FOUR POST

TWO-BY-FOUR CAP RAIL

¾" SQ BATTEN

¾" THICK BOARDS

6'

7" 3

5'-8"

TWO-BY-FOUR BOTTOM RAIL

4"

3' MINIMUM

3 Nail these pieces to either side of each post on the top of the horizontal two-by-fours.

4 Nail the two-by-twos to the cross-pieces, starting with the one flush to each end.

5 Nail the remaining two-by-twos parallel to the others and 8" apart, as shown in Figure 2. *Note:* It is important to stagger the joints when cutting and nailing the long horizontal two-by-fours and two-by-twos in place. The butt joint where the two ends meet on one post (Figure 4) should not be repeated on the other side of the same post. This would create a potential weak point in the structure. A better option is to sacrifice a long piece. Cut it shorter than necessary in order to stagger the joints. The cut-off length can be used elsewhere on the trellis.

6 The most difficult part of building the trellis comes when it has to turn a corner. The horizontal two-by-fours which tie the posts together must join each other in half-lap joints at the corner on four sides of the four-by-four posts (Figure 1).

7 The two-by-four cross-pieces must do the same (Figure 1).

8 In both cases, the square space between the half-lap joints must be determined by the exact dimensions of the post to ensure a fit around the post that is neither too large nor too small.

9 Study the top view of the corner (Figure 1) to see how the two-by-twos must support each other with a single nail where each end meets its neighbor. Drill a ⅛" diameter pilot hole before nailing, to avoid splitting the

FIGURE 5

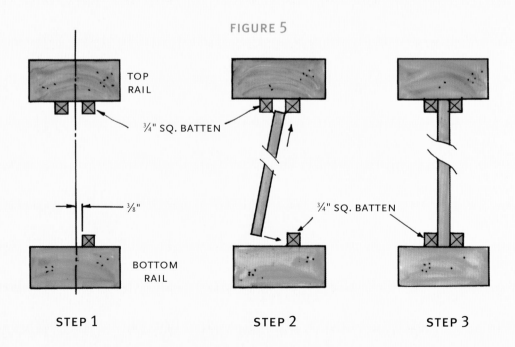

TOP RAIL

¾" SQ. BATTEN

⅜"

BOTTOM RAIL

¾" SQ. BATTEN

STEP 1   STEP 2   STEP 3

wood. When the trellis is complete, the line of posts should be quite rigid and secure, making it easy to fill the space between the posts.

⑩ To build the wood panel fence shown, start by cutting a red cedar two-by-four to fit exactly between the posts and toenail it in place as the bottom cap rail. Leave a 4" space minimum below this rail.

⑪ Make the panels from ¾" thick cedar boards as wide as possible. Their length will be determined by the desired height of the fence. The length of the boards shown is 5'-5". Do not nail the boards in place, so they can expand and contract without splitting. Instead, hold them up with ⅜" square battens as shown in Figure 5.

⑫ Cut a second two-by-four to length to fit between the posts for a top cap rail.

⑬ On both the top and the bottom rails mark the location of the battens (Figure 5, Step 1), allowing the vertical boards to be centered on the two-by-fours.

⑭ Nail two battens to the top rail, but only one to the bottom rail.

⑮ Toenail the top cap rail in place between the posts using two of the vertical boards as a guide and support (Figure 6).

⑯ Push the remaining boards up between the top battens (Figure 5, Step 2) and onto the bottom rail.

⑰ When the space between the posts has been filled with vertical boards, nail the last ¾" square battens to the bottom rail to hold them all in place (Figure 5, step 3).

⑱ Repeat this process between each post until the fence is complete.

FIGURE 6

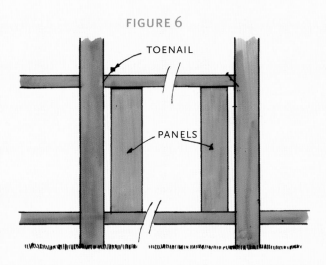

TOENAIL

PANELS

— RUSTIC GARDEN BENCH —

TOOLS & MATERIALS

- Jigsaw
- Bench square
- Measuring tape
- Hammer
- Front legs (2) – four-by-four western red cedar × 2'-3" each
- Back legs (2) – four-by-four cedar × 2'-9" each
- Bottom rails, front and back (2) – two-by-four cedar × 5' each
- Seat rails, front and back (2) – two-by-four cedar × 4'-9" each
- Side rails, bottom (2) – two-by-four cedar × 1'-9" each
- Side rails, seat (2) – two-by-four cedar × 1'-6" each
- Back support rail (1) – two-by-four cedar × 5'
- Back slats bottom sill (1) – two-by-two cedar × 4'-5"
- Back slats:
  - 1 one-by-six × 2'
  - 2 one-by-six × 23" each
  - 2 one-by-six × 21½" each
  - 1 one-by-six × 2'
  - 2 one-by-six × 19" each
- Seat planks (4) – two-by-six cedar × 4'-9" each
- Arms (2) – one-by-six cedar × 18½" each
- Arm support blocks (2) – two-by-four × 3" each
- Common nails (galvanized) – 1½" and 3"

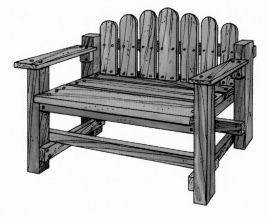

This bench is quite simple to build and, if you can find some boards from an old barn, it will make a doubly charming addition to any garden. I have used materials readily available in any community, and, if western red cedar is used, the wood will soon weather on its own to a nice silver-gray tone. Bird boxes, feeders and trellises can also be added to the bench itself.

1. Cut all of the material to the lengths shown on the materials list.

2. With a 5½" diameter paint can or coffee can as a template, draw a semi-circle at one end of each of the seven back slats. Cut these out with a jigsaw.

3. Nail the side rails to the pair of front and back legs at the dimensions shown in Figure 1. Remember to face the second set of legs in the opposite direction.

4. Nail a two-by-four arm support block to each of the back legs then nail the arms in place (Figure 1). *Note:* Use 3" nails in the two-by-four material and 1½" nails in the one-by-six material throughout the construction.

5. Rest the front and back bottom rails on the bottom side rails against the inside faces of the legs. Nail them to the legs of both sets with their ends flush with the outside edge of the legs.

6 Nail the front and back seat rails into the ends of the seat side rails and butted up against the inside edges of the legs (Figure 2).

7 Nail the back support rail to the back of the back legs with the top edge 1½" below the top of the legs.

8 Nail down the seat planks starting at the back edge of the back legs. Leave at least ⅛" between each plank as a rainwater drain (Figure 3).

9 At the back edge of the back seat plank, nail down the two-by-two bottom sill.

10 Locate the center of the back support rail and the bottom sill then nail the longest back slat to both, centered on this mid point.

11 With a 2" gap between them, nail the remaining slats either side of the center one in descending order of length.

12 Let the bench weather naturally in the sun, wind, snow, and rain.

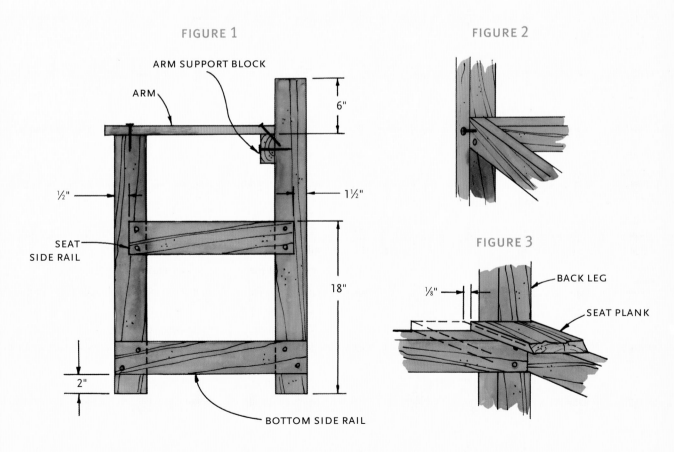

FIGURE 1

ARM SUPPORT BLOCK

ARM

6"

½"

1½"

SEAT SIDE RAIL

18"

2"

BOTTOM SIDE RAIL

FIGURE 2

FIGURE 3

⅛"

BACK LEG

SEAT PLANK

Further Reading

———❖———

Identification guides are one of those items that you can't have too many of, especially as some guides offer photos, while others use illustrations. Both formats have merit, and will help to identify species through use of color, angle, and a variety of text details. When one book doesn't show or tell you what you need, another may. Some of the following reference titles and ID guides are now out of print, but are worth seeking out in secondhand bookstores or public libraries.

Gardening Reference

American Horticultural Society A-Z Encyclopedia of Garden Plants. Christopher Brickell, et al. Mississauga: DK Publishing, 1997

Container Gardening. Sunset Books. Menlo Park: Lane Publishing Co., 1990

Gardening In Containers. Alvin Horton, ed., et al. San Ramon: Ortho Books; revised edition, 1983

Hortus Third: A Concise Dictionary of Plants Cultivated in the United States and Canada. Bailey Hortorium. Etobicoke: John Wiley & Sons, 1976

Index of Garden Plants: The New Royal Horticultural Society Dictionary. Mark Griffiths. Portland: Timber Press, 1994

Identification Series
(check www.amazon.com for comprehensive lists of titles in each series)

Golden Field Guides
National Audubon Society Field Guides
National Geographic Society Field Guides
Peterson Field Guide Series
Sibley Field Guides
Stokes Nature Guides

* Asterisks denote books that are large, expensive volumes, but available in many library reference sections.

Miscellaneous Nature Books

A Field Guide to the Familiar: Learning to Observe the Natural World. Gale Lawrence. New York: Prentice Hall, 1984

Agnes Chase's First Book of Grasses: The Structure of Grasses Explained for Beginnners. Lynn G. Clark, Richard W. Pohl. Washington: Smithsonian Institution Press; 4th edition, 1996

Audubon Life-list Journal. National Audubon Society, ed. Muskogee: Artisan Sales. 1999

Bents Life Histories of American Birds (20 volume series). Arthur Cleveland Bent. New York: Dover Publications Inc., 1964. (Originally published in 1946 as a Smithsonian Institution bulletin.)

Butterflies Through Binoculars—A Field Guide to Butterflies (5 titles by region). Jeffrey Glassberg. Oxford: Oxford University Press, 1999

Circle of the Seasons (and many other titles by the same author). Edwin Way Teale. New York: Dodd, Mead & Company, 1953

Dragonflies Through Binoculars—A Field Guide to Dragonflies of North America. Sidney W. Dunkle. Oxford: Oxford University Press, 2000

The Insect World of J. Henri Fabre. J. Henri Fabre, et al. Boston: Beacon Press, 1991

Grasses: An Identification Guide. Lauren Brown. Boston: Houghton Mifflin Co.; reprint edition, 1979

Handbook for Butterfly Watchers. Sarah Anne Hughes, Robert Michael Pyle. Boston: Houghton Mifflin Co.; reprint edition, 1992

Insects and Gardens: In Pursuit of a Garden Ecology. Eric Grissel, et al. Portland: Timber Press, 2001

Insect Life and Insect Natural History. S.W. Frost. New York: Dover Publications, Inc., 1959

Looking for the Wild. Lyn Hancock. Mississauga: Doubleday of Canada, 1987

National Audubon Society North American Birdfeeder Handbook: The Complete Guide to Feeding and Observing Birds. Robert Burton. DK Publishing, 1995

National Audubon Society Birder's Handbook. Stephen Kress, et al. DK Publishing; 1st edition, 2000

National Audubon Society Master Guide to Birding Series: Vol I Gulls to Dippers, Vol II Loons to Sandpipers, Vol III Warblers to Sparrows. John Farrand, ed., National Audubon Society. New York: Alfred A. Knopf Inc., 1993

Naturescape British Columbia: Caring for Wildlife at Home. Susan Campbell, Sylvia Pincott. British Columbia Ministry of Environment, Land and Parks/Environment Canada, 1995

Noah's Garden: Restoring the Ecology of Our Own Backyards. Sara Stein. New York: Houghton Mifflin Co., 1993

Our Natural World: The Land and Wildlife of America as Seen and Described by Writers Since the Country's Discovery. Hal Borland. New York: JB Lippincott Co., 1969

Songbirds in the City: A Celebration. Valentin Schaefer, Ph.D., R.P. Bio,

237

Leanne Paris, B.A. Van. BC. Douglas College: Center for Environmental Studies and Urban Ecology, 1999

Speaking for Nature: A Century of Conservation. Les Line, ed., National Audubon Society. Beaux Arts Editions, 2001

The Audubon Backyard Birdwatcher: Birdfeeders and Bird Gardens. Robert Burton, et al. Berkley: Thunder Bay Press, 1999

The Beginning Naturalist: Weekly Encounters With the Natural World. Gale Lawrence. Vermont: The New England Press, 1979

The Bird Garden: A Comprehensive Guide to Attracting Birds to Your Backyard Throughout the Year. Stephen W. Kress. DK Publishing, 1995

The Earth Dwellers: Adventure in the Land of Ants. Erich Hoyt. New York: Simon & Schuster, 1996

Web Sites for Wildlife Stewards
American Birding Association
www.americanbirding.org
Bat Conservation International
www.batcon.org

Bird Studies Canada
www.bxc-eoc.org
Canadian Nature Federation
www.cnf.ca
Cornell University Department of Ornithology
www.birds.cornell.edu/pfw
Environment Canada
www.ec.gc.ca
Invasive and Exotic Species of North America
www.invasive.org
National Audubon Society
www.audubon.org
National Wildlife Federation
www.nwf.org
North American Bluebird Society
www.nabluebirdsociety.org
North American Butterfly Association
www.naba.org
Wild Birds Unlimited
www.wbu.com
Wild Ones: Native Plants, Natural Landscapes
www.for-wild.org
World Wildlife Fund
www.panda.org

Photo Credits

Beth Carruthers: 12, 14 (top), 44, 79, 149, 160, 161, 162, 163, 165, 167, 168, 169, 184, 188, 189, 191, 220 (top)

Fred Chapman: 55, 64

Gabor Halasz: 14 (bottom), 19, 21, 54, 71, 72, 115, 122, 125, 129 (bottom)

Greta James: 10, 20 (bottom), 82, 92, 93, 94, 95 (top left), 96 (top), 98 (bottom), 104, 126, 178, 201, 218, 222, 224, 225

Patricia Johnston: 2 (top left, bottom), 3, 7, 11, 20 (top), 185, 186, 190, 214

Bruce Klassen: x, 8 (bottom), 15, 59, 73, 103 (top right), 121 (bottom), 145, 148, 157, 195 (top)

Roy Luckow: 81

Don McPhee: 103 (top left)

Derrick Marven: 4, 95 (top right), 97, 99 (bottom), 101, 102 (top), 109 (top), 114, 120, 123, 129 (top), 130, 156, 158, 174, 176, 209 (bottom), 210, 219, 220 (bottom)

Sylvia Pincott: 8 (top right), 177, 187, 193, 195 (bench, winter), 209 (top), 211

Hank Roos: 124, 127, 212, 213

Glenn Ryder: 65, 78, 182

Edward van Veenendaal: 6, 8 (top left), 13, 16, 17, 76, 80, 83, 96 (bottom), 99 (top), 105, 110 (bottom), 121 (top), 134, 179, 180, 194, 195, 197, 198, 199,

Nancy Vince: 170, 171

Michael Wheatley: 2 (top right), 70, 97, 98 (top), 102 (bottom left, right), 103 (bottom), 109 (bottom), 110 (top), 111, 154, 155, 170, 175, 192, 196, 200, 205

Index

Italicized page references indicate photographs or illustrations